# THE PERSON AND THE HUMAN MIND

# THE PERSON AND THE HUMAN MIND

## Issues in Ancient and Modern Philosophy

Edited by

CHRISTOPHER GILL

CLARENDON PRESS · OXFORD

*This book has been printed digitally and produced in a standard design in order to ensure its continuing availability*

OXFORD
UNIVERSITY PRESS

Great Clarendon Street, Oxford OX2 6DP
Oxford University Press is a department of the University of Oxford.
It furthers the University's objective of excellence in research, scholarship,
and education by publishing worldwide in

Oxford New York

Athens Auckland Bangkok Bogotá Buenos Aires Calcutta
Cape Town Chennai Dar es Salaam Delhi Florence Hong Kong Istanbul
Karachi Kuala Lumpur Madrid Melbourne Mexico City Mumbai
Nairobi Paris São Paulo Singapore Taipei Tokyo Toronto Warsaw

and associated companies in Berlin Ibadan

Oxford is a registered trade mark of Oxford University Press
in the UK and certain other countries

Published in the United States
by Oxford University Press Inc., New York



Reprinted 2000



ISBN 0-19-824460-6

Printed in Great Britain by IBT Global, London

# Preface

This volume of essays originated in a conference held at Aberystwyth in July 1986 on 'Persons and Human Beings: Issues in Ancient and Modern Philosophy'. Seven of the essays are based on papers given at the conference; the remaining essays were either written specifically for this volume, or revised for inclusion in it. With one exception, the essays have not been previously published in any form.[1] The aim of this volume, as of the conference, is to explore analogous issues in classical and modern philosophy relating to the concepts of person and human being. It does not attempt to present a history of the development of these concepts from classical to modern times. The volume is divided into two parts, centred on two related themes: the status and interrelationship of the concepts of person and human being, and the extent to which we should understand ourselves as, essentially, human or rational beings. This division does not reflect the arrangement of papers at the conference; it was adopted in the course of preparing the essays for publication, as a way of underlining certain common concerns in the papers given at the conference and in those subsequently added to the volume.

The planning of the conference and the volume was very much a collaborative process, and I have drawn freely on the advice of my fellow-contributors. I am especially grateful to Adam Morton, Amélie Rorty, and Peter Smith for helping me to explore the modern side of the debate, and to my colleagues in ancient philosophy for their willingness to adopt this particular line of approach to our subject. At the time of the composition of the volume, four of the contributors were members of the Departments of Classics or Philosophy at the University College of Wales, Aberystwyth; I am pleased that the volume can record a period in the life of the College when such cooperation was possible.

Thanks are due to the British Academy and the University of Wales for financial assistance to the conference, and to the University College of Wales, Aberystwyth, for contributing to the cost of typing the volume. David Jackson kindly supplied the

[1] Amélie Rorty's chapter is reprinted, with minor alterations, with the permission of Beacon Press, Boston.

imaginative cover design. I am very grateful to my wife Karen, and June Baxter, for their help in preparing the manuscript. Thanks are due to Oxford University Press for their careful and efficient work in producing the volume, and especially to Angela Blackburn, for her support and advice.

C. G.

# Notes on Contributors

CHRISTOPHER GILL (Editor) is a Senior Lecturer in Classics at the University of Exeter.

GEORGE BOTTERILL is a Lecturer in Philosophy at the University of Sheffield.

STEPHEN R. L. CLARK is Professor of Philosophy at the University of Liverpool.

TROELS ENGBERG-PEDERSEN is a Research Professor at the University of Copenhagen.

ADAM MORTON is Professor of Philosophy at the University of Bristol.

A. W. PRICE is a Lecturer in Philosophy at the University of York.

AMÉLIE OKSENBERG RORTY is a Professor of Philosophy at the University of Rutgers.

CHRISTOPHER ROWE is a Reader in Classics at the University of Bristol.

PETER SMITH is a Lecturer in Philosophy at the University of Sheffield.

P. F. SNOWDON is a Fellow and Tutor in Philosophy at Exeter College, Oxford.

M. R. WRIGHT is a Senior Lecturer in Classics at the University of Reading.

# Contents

*Notes on Contributors* vii

Introduction 1
*Christopher Gill*

PART I: 'PERSON' AND 'HUMAN BEING': THE STATUS AND INTERRELATIONSHIP OF THE CONCEPTS

1. Persons and *Personae* 21
*Amélie Oksenberg Rorty*
2. Why there is no Concept of a Person 39
*Adam Morton*
3. Human Persons 61
*Peter Smith*
4. Persons, Animals, and Ourselves 83
*P. F. Snowdon*
5. Stoic Philosophy and the Concept of the Person 109
*Troels Engberg-Pedersen*
6. The Human Being as an Ethical Norm 137
*Christopher Gill*

PART II: THE HUMAN AND THE RATIONAL MIND: MODELS OF SELF-UNDERSTANDING

7. Human Nature and Folk Psychology 165
*George Botterill*
8. Reason as *Daimōn* 187
*Stephen R. L. Clark*
9. Presocratic Minds 207
*M. R. Wright*
10. Philosophy, Love, and Madness 227
*Christopher Rowe*

11. Plato and Freud 247
A. W. *Price*

*Bibliography* 271

*Index* 281

# Introduction

*Christopher Gill*

A person is an individual substance of a rational nature. (Boethius)

We must consider what person stands for; which, I think, is a thinking intelligent being, that has reason and reflection, and can consider itself as itself, the same thinking thing, in different times and places . . . It is a forensic term, appropriating actions and their merit; and so belongs only to intelligent animals capable of a law, and happiness, and misery. (Locke)

On occasion, almost everyone feels difficulties in holding in a single focus three very different ideas:

(*a*) the idea of the person as object of biological, anatomical, and neurophysiological inquiry;

(*b*) the idea of the person as subject of consciousness; and

(*c*) the idea of the person as locus of all sorts of moral attributes and the source or conceptual origin of all value. (Wiggins)

Who knows whether this 'category' [that of the person], which all of us here believe to be well founded, will always be recognised as such? It is formulated only for us, among us. (Mauss)

It seems to be peculiarly characteristic of humans . . . that they are able to form what I shall call 'second-order desires' . . . Besides wanting and choosing and being moved *to do* this or that, men may also want to have (or not to have) certain desires and motives. They are capable of wanting to be different in their preferences and purposes, from what they are. (Frankfurt)

According to the mixture at any one time of the body as it travels, so is men's thinking constituted. (Parmenides)

I inquire . . . into myself, to see whether I am actually a wild beast more complex than Typhon, or both a tamer and a simpler creature, sharing some divine and un-Typhonic portion by nature. (Plato)

The ethical virtues, those of the composite person [the psychophysical individual] are human; so too is the life and form of happiness that goes with such virtues; but that of the mind [*nous*] is separate. (Aristotle)

Rather we must as far as we can immortalize ourselves, and do everything possible to live in accordance with the best thing in us [mind or *nous*] . . .

I am grateful to Peter Smith for his comment on a previous version of this Introduction.

Indeed, this would seem actually to *be* each man in that it is the authoritative and best part of him. (Aristotle)

Where *id* was, there *ego* shall be. (Freud)[1]

The aim of this volume, as stated in the Preface, is to explore analogous issues in ancient[2] and modern philosophy relating to the concepts of person and human being. The working hypothesis, then, is that there *are* such analogous issues, and that it is worthwhile to discuss them in juxtaposition. Whether or not this hypothesis is justified is something which the volume as a whole will help to bring out. But in this Introduction it may be useful to reflect in general terms on this question, and at the same time to indicate how the shape of the volume is designed to bear on consideration of this question. I will also outline the kind of contribution which (as I see it) each essay makes towards this larger question as well as towards its own specific subject. My discussion will be focused around the two main themes of the volume.

## *'Person' and 'Human Being': The Status and Interrelationship of the Concepts*

The subject of the person is one of the most discussed, and most controversial, in modern philosophy. Faced with the complexity of this debate, it is natural to ask some simple, though fundamental, questions. When philosophers offer definitions of the 'person',

[1] The sources of these quotations are: Boethius, *Liber de persona et duabus naturis*, ch. 3, tr. and cited by T. Engberg-Pedersen, ch. 5 below; J. Locke, *An Essay Concerning Human Understanding*, ed. P. H. Nidditch (Oxford, 1975), II. xxvii. 9, 26; D. Wiggins, 'The Person as Object of Science, as Subject of Experience, and as Locus of Value', in A. Peacocke and G. Gillett (edd.), *Persons and Personality: A Contemporary Inquiry* (Oxford, 1987), 56–74, quotation from p. 56; M. Mauss, 'A Category of the Human Mind: The Notion of Person; The Notion of Self', tr. W. D. Halls, in M. Carrithers, S. Collins, and S. Lukes (edd.), *Category of the Person: Anthropology, Philosophy, History* (Cambridge, 1985), 1–25, quotation from p. 22; H. Frankfurt, 'Freedom of the Will and the Concept of a Person', *Journal of Philosophy*, 68 (1971), 5–20, quotation from pp. 6–7; Parmenides fr. 16, tr. and cited by M. R. Wright, ch. 9 below; Plato, *Phaedrus* (*Phdr.*) 230a, tr. and cited by C. Rowe, ch. 10 below; Aristotle, *Nicomachean Ethics* (*EN*) 10. 8, 1178a20–2, tr. C. Gill; ibid. 10. 7, 1177b33–78a3, tr. and cited by M. R. Wright, ch. 9 below; S. Freud, *Pelican Freud Library*, ed. A. Richards, ii (15 vols.; Harmondsworth, 1973–86), 112.

[2] The 'ancient' philosophy treated here is mostly classical (Graeco-Roman), although S. R. L. Clark also discusses ancient oriental thinking.

what is the basis for these definitions? Are these definitions offered on the assumption that there is a single concept to be defined or a plurality of such concepts? And what is the relationship between the philosophical accounts of 'person' and its meaning in everyday language, which is, I take it, 'individual human being'.[3] These questions are rather obvious ones; but it is not easy to answer them because they raise what are, in themselves, substantive philosophical issues. These are the issues underlying the essays in the first part of the volume. A related question, which is addressed by some of these essays, is whether these issues can arise in anything like the same form in ancient philosophy, where there is no obvious equivalent for the modern notion of 'person', except, perhaps, 'human being', a notion which unlike 'person', is explicitly species-specific.

Amélie Rorty, in the opening essay of the volume, argues that no single formulation can be accepted as being *the* definition of the person. She claims that in recent philosophy the term 'person' has functioned as a place-holder for a plurality of different concepts, and as the focus for a complex of quite different concerns (moral, legal, medical, psycho-metaphysical, etc.); and that it is the concerns themselves that have informed the definition in each case rather than the constraints of an independently determinable concept. She identifies a 'metaphysical longing' for *one* concept which can fulfil in a comprehensive way the unifying role played by the concept of person in each of the different contexts in which it figures. She allows that it may be possible to construct a composite notion out of the various criteria offered for personhood, such as agency, self-consciousness, sociability, and the capacity to shape one's own life. But she argues that these criteria are not inter-entailing, grounded in each other, or even necessarily compatible, and that they cannot, therefore, yield a single coherent notion.

Rorty's stand on this question is more negative, or at least sceptical, than that of most contributors to this volume. However, her essay clearly places on those who posit a single, determinate concept of person the onus of showing the basis for this assumption. Her essay also underlines the importance of defining with some precision the kind of issue we have in view when we discuss the subject of the person (since different issues may involve very different presuppositions). As it turns out, the following three essays do focus on a single question, though one approached from rather different

[3] *Concise Oxford Dictionary* (7th edn., Oxford, 1982), s.v. 'person', sense 1.

directions. This is the question of the relationship between our status as persons and as human beings, and, for Morton and Smith especially, the question whether we can offer a definition of 'person' which is based on anything other than our understanding of what is essential to our existence as human beings.

Adam Morton starts from the assumption that, if there is a single, valid conception of person, it is one which is as applicable, in principle, to intelligent animals and extraterrestrials as to human beings. But he argues that the concept cannot be formulated in a species-neutral way; current formulations capture the combination of characteristics we find in human beings rather than identify a universally valid set of characteristics. Morton takes Harry Frankfurt's well-known characterization of a person as someone who has beliefs and desires about his own beliefs and desires,[4] and constructs imaginary examples (animal and human) in which the components of Frankfurt's definition (first-order and second-order beliefs and desires) are found separately. Such cases are neither clearly persons nor clearly non-persons; and since the components of Frankfurt's definition can be envisaged as existing separately in this way they do not constitute an 'atomic' unity, but rather the kind of unity we encounter in human beings. A species-neutral set of psychological criteria cannot be specified; and, in this sense, there is no *one* concept of person available.

Peter Smith, like Morton, accepts the desirability in principle of a notion of personhood which is not species-specific, and rejects the idea of defining the notion solely by membership of a given biological kind. But he too is sceptical of the idea that we can define the notion in a way that does not depend on our own understanding of what is essential to us as human beings. The concept to work with, he argues, is that of 'human person', defined not in terms of determinate characteristics but rather in terms of the 'right relation', which makes a person 'one of us'. The 'right relation' is elucidated by reference to the interpretability of the human person, and especially by the possibility of explanation by simulation. This type of interpretation involves mutuality ('we' can interpret each other) and presupposes a rich background of shared human life. It is the idea of such a shared life that grounds the notion of a human person rather than the biological specification of a natural kind or

[4] Frankfurt, 'Freedom of the Will'.

the species-neutral specification of psychological criteria of personhood.

P. F. Snowdon takes as his starting-point David Wiggins's insistence that, when discussing personal identity, we should make reference to the fact that we are talking about human beings,[5] or, as Snowdon puts it, about 'ourselves'. His essay centres on the thesis 'I am an animal (of the species Homo sapiens)'; that is to say, I can legitimately identify myself as a human animal as well as a person. In an intricate and dialectical argument, he rehearses the considerations that might count for and against this thesis, centring on the question whether I am to be identified *via* my continued personhood (as identified with some specified psychological capacities) even if this involves interrupting my life as a continuing animal (by 'changing bodies', for instance), or rather with my status as a continuing natural sort. He considers various ways of reconciling the resulting antinomy, including the proposal that I identify myself with my brain, taken both as the central locus of psychological continuity and of my existence as animal. He concludes with a provisional endorsement of the claim that it is legitimate to say both 'I am a person' and 'I am an animal', with the important qualification that the distinctive criteria of my identity depend on my status as animal rather than as person.

It turns out, then, that these three essays not only centre on the same general question (that of the relationship between the concepts of person and human being), but also reach rather similar conclusions on this question. The general type of position they adopt is also present, by implication at least, in Frankfurt's famous article on the person, and is made explicit in Wiggins's most recent treatment of the topic. Frankfurt, while denying that the criteria of personhood are to be regarded primarily as species-specific ones, none the less asserts that 'they are designed to capture those attributes which are the subject of our most humane concerns with ourselves and the source of what we regard as most important and most problematical in our lives.' Again, he describes the problem of the person as being 'that of understanding what we ourselves essentially are', and in his discussion he treats 'persons' as, in effect, a subdivision of human beings.[6] Wiggins focuses on precisely this

[5] He has in mind Wiggins's view in *Sameness and Substance* (Oxford, 1980), ch. 6, esp. pp. 196 ff; a similar view is stated in Wiggins, 'The Person', pp. 56–74.

[6] 'Freedom of the Will', p. 6; cf. the sentences cited at the start of the Intro.

question, and argues, in language which is similar to that of Smith and Snowdon, 'that it is *for us* to make sense of this creature' (the person), and that in this sense there is 'a certain relativity' inevitably built into our conception of personhood. This is so because the criteria we use to determine personhood are not of a kind which we can apply to creatures who are 'alien intelligences'; we cannot 'interpret' such creatures as conscious subjects, moral beings, or even as biological organisms, because we cannot draw on our own experience in these respects to apply the marks of personhood in 'fine grained interpretations'. Hence, in Wiggins's view, personhood is a characteristic we can only ascribe to other human beings, but 'not by an unprincipled transcription of all the marks of being a human being no matter what'. The process is rather that of allowing our experience of human beings to inform our normative ideal of the person and vice versa, so 'letting each of them supply the conceptual lacunae in the other'.[7] That is, I take it, the concept of person is one that (to use an Aristotelian term) 'supervenes' on our understanding of ourselves as human beings, when we give full moral weight to ourselves in this capacity, rather than being one that we can apply to creatures whose existence we cannot understand from the inside.[8]

The convergence of view between these contributors to the volume and some other philosophers is of interest. But it is important to note that other thinkers adopt a very different kind of position on this question. Michael Tooley, for instance, argues in *Abortion and Infanticide*[9] that membership of a biological species is not in itself morally significant; that it is possible to define the concept of person in a non-species-specific way; and that it is possible in this way to reach moral conclusions which do not simply draw on our existing convictions (about the sanctity of human life, for instance) but which enable us to revise these. This alternative approach to the subject of personhood has received its share of criticism, especially as applied to questions of medical

[7] 'The Person', pp. 69, 74; see ch. 6 below, text to n. 71, for fuller quotation of the latter passage.

[8] I have in mind the kind of 'supervening' Aristotle describes in *EN* 10. 4, when pleasure 'supervenes' on a perfect activity (1174b31–3). Smith also uses the notion of supervenience in his (rather more critical) interpretative gloss on Wiggins's conception of the relationship between the two concepts, ch. 3 below, text to nn. 11–12.

[9] (Oxford, 1983).

ethics;[10] but it is important to be aware of the other side in the debate about the relationship between being a person and being human, of which Tooley is only one representative.

When we turn to ancient philosophy, it may seem, at first sight, that this issue cannot present itself in this form because of a simple linguistic fact: there is no term which is the obvious equivalent of 'person', as distinct from 'human being'. It is true, of course, that the term 'person' derives, etymologically, from the Latin term *persona*, and that the latter term, together with its Greek cognate *prosōpon*, has certain interesting connotations in Hellenistic and Roman philosophy.[11] It is also true that medieval conceptions of *persona* (such as Boethius' famous formulation, 'an individual substance of a rational nature'), reflect, and draw on, classical thinking about substance and rationality.[12] None the less, it is clearly not the case that *persona* or *prosōpon* has this kind of role and meaning in classical philosophy; and the closest analogue in that context for the modern notion of 'person', in so far as it exists, is 'human being' (*anthrōpos* in Greek and *homo* in Latin). Given this fact, it might seem that the issue of the relationship between the concepts of person and human being cannot arise in ancient philosophy.

However, the position is rather more complex, and more comparable with the modern position, than at first appears. For one thing, since the notion of 'human' was sometimes used normatively in ancient philosophy to denote *essentially* human characteristics, the question could arise of the relationship between the normative and descriptive uses of this term. This question

[10] See e.g. B. Williams, *Ethics and the Limits of Philosophy* (London, 1985), 114–15, and D. Wikler, 'Concepts of Personhood: A Philosophical Perspective', in M. W. Shaw and A. E. Doudera (edd.), *Defining Human Life: Medical, Legal, and Ethical Implications* (Ann Arbor, Mich., 1983), 12–23.

[11] Cf. M. Nédoncelle, '*Prosōpon* et *Persona* dans l'antiquité classique', *Revue des Sciences Réligieuses,* 22 (1948), 277–99; C. Gill, 'Personhood and Personality: The Four-*Personae* Theory in Cicero, *De Officiis* I', *Oxford Studies in Ancient Philosophy*, 6 (1988), 169–99.

[12] Cf. C. J. de Vogel, 'The Concept of Personality in Greek and Christian Thought', *Studies in Philosophy and the History of Philosophy*, 2 (1963), 20–60; K. Rahner *et al.* (edd.), *Sacramentum Mundi: An Encyclopedia of Theology* (6 vols.: London, 1966), s.v. 'Person', iv. 404 ff.; and C. Stead, *Divine Substance* (Oxford, 1977), s.v. 'person' in index. John FitzGerald, as well as directing my attention to these latter two works, has also suggested to me that we can find both in Stoic theory and in medieval theology the same kind of distinction (between the nature of an entity and its—essential—character or role) which is involved in the distinction between human being and person.

occupies some of the ground occupied in modern philosophy by the question of the relationship between the notions of person and human being. Furthermore, the criteria of normative human status in ancient philosophy were, typically, rationality and sociability; and one of these criteria, rationality, at least in certain forms, was regarded as being characteristically divine as much as, or rather than, human.[13] Hence, one of the essentially human characteristics is not seen as necessarily species-specific but rather as shared by another kind of creature, albeit one of a rather special type. On the other side of the natural order, the possession of rationality was normally taken to *distinguish* men from beasts. Although there is some evidence of philosophical interest in the idea of psychological affinities between men and beasts, there is little evidence of the idea sometimes entertained in modern theory that the higher animals might be regarded as partly rational (or as quasi-persons).[14] On the other hand, there is a good deal of interest in the idea that human rationality (and perhaps human sociability as well) is to be conceived as a form of participation in a larger pattern of rationality which pervades the natural cosmos as a whole.[15] To this extent, the normatively 'human' characteristics of rationality and sociability are not necessarily conceived in such species-specific terms as it might seem; and the question of the relationship between these normative ideals and our existence as human beings can, after all, arise in ancient philosophy.

Indeed, I think it is also possible to isolate two different strands in ancient thinking which are at least partly analogous to the position taken on the question of the relationship between person and human being in modern philosophy (the positions I associated

[13] For these criteria, see e.g. Aristotle, *EN* 1. 7 and Cicero, *De Finibus* (*Fin.*) 3. 5. 16–7. 26, 19. 62–20. 68, discussed by Gill, ch. 6 below; and on rationality as divine as well as human, cf. Gill, app. to ch. 6 below.

[14] e.g. Platonic myths about transmigration of souls between men and beasts, *Republic* (*R.*), 620, *Phdr.* 249b, *Timaeus* 42b–c, 91e–92c); the reading of human physiognomy by a sign-language based on animal characteristics, [Aristotle], *Physiognomics*; the idea that beasts are 'devolved' men, cf. S. R. L. Clark, *Aristotle's Man* (Oxford, 1975), ch. 2. 2. There is also some evidence of interest in the idea that non-human animals may display quasi-rationality, but it is combined with a conviction that they are not rational in the same sense as (adult) human beings: see further G. E. R. Lloyd, *Science, Folklore and Ideology: Studies in the Life Sciences in Ancient Greece* (Cambridge, 1983), 28–9, and J. Annas and J. Barnes, *Modes of Scepticism: Ancient Texts and Modern Interpretations* (Cambridge, 1985), 47–8.

[15] See e.g. Cicero, *Fin.* 3. 19. 62–20. 68, and Gill, ch. 6 below, esp. n. 2. See further discussion below.

earlier with, for instance, Wiggins on the one hand and Tooley on the other). In the first part of the volume, Engberg-Pedersen and I explore aspects of Aristotelian and Stoic theory in which normative ethical ideals are formulated by reflection on what is involved in being human. We also suggest, in different ways, that the formation of the ideal depends, crucially, on reflection on one's own (human) experience and on the moral quality of that experience; and, in this respect, the line of thought we explore has marked similarities to that of Smith in this volume and Wiggins. On the other side, some of the essays in the second half of the volume, especially Clark's, draw on a different strand in ancient thinking. In this strand, one's essence is seen as inhering in a kind of rationality which is divine or daemonic, which comes in 'from outside', and which establishes a form of community with the ordered universe as a whole.[16]

The presence of these different strands in ancient philosophy (if I have identified them correctly) does not, by itself, prove that they were seen by the ancient thinkers themselves as distinct positions in a debate; nor does it prove that the question of whether we understand ourselves as, ultimately, human or divine presented itself to them as an issue in the same way as the question of the relationship between our status as human beings and persons presents itself to us. The fact that we find these two strands coexisting in the same thinker (Aristotle, for instance), indeed, sometimes in the same work (the *Nicomachean Ethics* (hereafter *EN*) for instance) would seem to suggest that ancient thinkers were *not* conscious of this as an issue (especially as modern scholars seem to be more concerned about the contradictions between these two strands in a single theory than do the ancient thinkers themselves). On the other hand Aristotle in *EN* 10. 7–8 (one of the crucial passages for this issue) does seem to present as a distinct issue the question whether one is to regard onself as essentially human or divine, and does seem to be attempting to define a considered position on this (even if it is one that some modern scholars do not much like). Part of this issue (as Aristotle presents it there) is the question whether we should see the individual human being as a psycho-physical unit or as the combination of a 'separable' mind and of other psychological and physical functions; and it seems clear that Aristotle does not overlook the importance and the large

[16] See further below; and also on the rationale for the subdivision of the vol. into two parts.

implications of this issue.[17] Plato too sometimes articulates as an issue the question of who or what we essentially are, and, in particular, how far we should identify ourselves with a 'divine' mind or rationality. The different answers he gives to this question seem to underly, and partly to explain, the variations in the model he posits of the human psyche.[18] Clearly one would need to say much more about this problem to deal with it adequately.[19] But I hope to have indicated how the essays in this volume may be read as providing evidence of these two strands in ancient thought, and also evidence as to whether we are dealing with a recognized issue, and one that is analogous to the modern issue of the relationship between being a person and being human.

These two remaining essays in the first part of the volume are concerned with the use of the notion of the human being as a normative ideal in ancient ethical theory; both essays are also concerned with the relationship between ancient and modern ethical thinking in this respect. Troels Engberg-Pedersen's subject is the Stoic conception of the human being, as this figures in their account of moral development. As he interprets it, this development consists of a certain kind of reflection on oneself, and of progress in one's understanding of oneself; in this sense, the Stoics conceive moral development in 'first-personal' terms. But he emphasizes that this does not entail that they see this process as essentially subjective; rather they see it as a movement from a subjective view (taken as meaning a limited and immature one) of the self and the world to an objective one, in which the subjective character of the earlier view is recognized. However, he also insists that the view so achieved remains the view of a specific individual; it is still

[17] See esp. *EN* 10. 7, 1177b33–78a3, 10. 8, 1178a20–2, both cited at the start of the Intro., and Gill, ch. 6 below, esp. nn. 79 and 82. See also T. Nagel, 'Aristotle on *Eudaimonia*', T. H. Irwin, 'The Metaphysical and Psychological Basis of Aristotle's Ethics', K. V. Wilkes, 'The Good Man and the Good for Man in Aristotle's *Ethics*', and J. McDowell, 'The Role of *Eudaimonia* in Aristotle's *Ethics*', in A. O. Rorty, (ed.), *Essays on Aristotle's Ethics* (Berkeley, 1980), 7–14, 35–53, 341–57, and 359–76, respectively; E. Ostenfeld, *Ancient Greek Philosophy and the Modern Mind–Body debate* (Aarhus, 1987), 37–49; and J. Lear, *Aristotle: The Desire to Understand* (Cambridge, 1988), 116–51, 160–4, 293–320.

[18] Plato seems to fluctuate between regarding the human psyche as essentially tripartite (or bipartite), and as essentially uniform, and rational, with 'accretions' of desire and emotion which result from the (temporary) attachment of the psyche to a body: see e.g. *R.* 611c–612a, *Phdr.* 230a (cited at the start of this Intro.), and Rowe, ch. 10 below.

[19] I propose to pursue the question in another context.

'*somebody's*' view and not a 'centreless' or 'God's eye' view. In insisting on this point, he aims to distinguish the Stoic conception of subjective and objective views from those of Bernard Williams and Thomas Nagel (whose phraseology is cited in the previous sentence). He sees Williams and Nagel as sharing, in spite of other differences, a typically modern conviction of the ineliminability of a *radically* subjective view (that is, one that is distinctive in content as well as in standpoint). He argues that this conviction militates against the classic conception of the person in modern European philosophy (that of Kant, say, or Frankfurt), namely, that of someone who can modify all his beliefs and desires by rational reflection. He believes that this conception is prefigured in the Stoic ideal of the (normative) human being; and that reappraising this ideal can help us to confront the challenge of radical subjectivity and to reinstate the classic conception of the person.

My essay is also concerned with the Stoic account of human moral development, taken in conjunction with Aristotle's famous use of the notion of a 'human function' in *EN* 1. 7; my special concern is with the kind of ethical 'naturalism' involved in these theories. I dispute the view (embraced by Bernard Williams, among others) that the notion of human nature is used in these texts to provide an extra-ethical foundation for ethical conviction ('from an absolute understanding of nature', as Williams puts it).[20] I argue rather that the conception of human nature is envisaged, in these theories, as playing a useful role in ethical enquiry only if it is interpreted by a good moral agent in the light of his own ethical experience and commitment. In other words, the idea of human nature functions as an *ethical* norm in these theories, even if the moral agent draws on his empirical understanding of the world in order to formulate this notion. I also suggest that the ethical-cum-empirical status of such notions is not a conceptual impossibility in modern philosophy; and that Wiggins's conception of the person (as a normative ideal based on our experience of, and moral convictions about, human beings) has marked similarities to the Greek view of the (normative) human being. In making this connection, I seek to underline the analogy I noted earlier between the view of the relationship between personhood and human status represented by Wiggins, among others, and the strand of ancient

[20] *Ethics*, 52.

thinking in which our ethical being is understood as inhering in the realization of a normatively human nature.

## *The Human and the Rational Mind: Models of Self-Understanding*

The second part of the volume should be read as continuing and developing the themes of the first part rather than as broaching a new subject. As Morton's essay especially brings out, the question of the relationship between personhood (or, in Frankfurt's phrase, 'what we ourselves essentially are')[21] and human status can be couched in terms of psychological characteristics or models of mind; and this is the way the issue is predominantly couched in this part of the volume. When we reflect on our own (human) characteristics—or on the subset we regard as 'essential' to us—do we see these as *distinctively* human or as shared (or in principle able to be shared) with other natural and artificial kinds? Is the human mind, one might ask, *essentially* human? One aspect of this question, as Botterill underlines, is the extent to which we actually deploy the notion of human nature as an explanatory category in our interpretation of the behaviour of other human beings. Another aspect, prominent in ancient thinking, is the question of the extent to which we identify ourselves as essentially human, or essentially rational, taking rationality to be a non-species-specific capacity, and one which is as characteristic of some non-human types of being (gods, let us say) as it is of men. The essays by Clark, Rowe, and in a different way, Wright, show how common in ancient philosophy this latter line of thought was; they thus complement the accentuation of the other strand of ancient thought by Engberg-Pedersen and myself. These essays also illustrate the ancient use of the notions of 'human', 'divine', and 'bestial', to characterize, and to grade, the functions (both rational and irrational) of the human psyche. As their discussions show, the question of what counts as one's 'essence' can also be couched in the form of what counts as 'oneself' or 'I', in the full sense; and, to this extent, they take up from a different standpoint the issue of personal identity which figures especially in Snowdon's essay. As Price brings out, in his comparison of Plato and Freud, the question of who 'I' am can be conceived as the question of the aspect of the self with which I

[21] 'Freedom of the Will', p. 6.

identify, and which I allow to be 'I' (*ego*) and not 'it' (*id*). Thus, although the essays in this part of the volume range widely in their specific subjects, they centre on a set of issues which are clearly cognate with the dominant theme of the first part, whether we are to understand ourselves as essentially persons or human beings.

'Is there really such a thing as human nature?' is the question posed by George Botterill; and the context in which he explores this question is that of the psychological explanation of the actions of other human beings. The core of such explanation, as it functions in everyday life, lies, he argues, in the identification of the belief-and-desire combinations that explain a given human action. The fact that we can consistently deploy such a framework of explanation indicates that we have an understanding of a more or less consistent human nature; and the fact that we can give plausible explanations for specific human actions, in spite of the multiplicity of possible explanations, indicates that our understanding has some depth and complexity. But on what does this understanding rest and in what does it consist (over and above the bare capacity to deploy this general type of explanatory framework)? The key to answering these questions, Botterill concludes, lies in recognizing the fact that human beings are self-interpreters, as well as objects of interpretation by others. We interpret others, in the light of their accounts of the belief-and-desire combinations that motivate their actions, and in the light of our understanding of the belief-and-desire combinations that motivate ours. By participating in a community of self-interpreting agents, we build up a stock of interpretative strategies as regards the explanation of human action; and this stock constitutes our understanding of what 'human nature' means.

Botterill's conclusion has points of analogy with that of Smith and myself in stressing the part played by our participation in an interactive social community in informing our conception of person or human nature. Stephen Clark follows a very different line of approach. He draws on a range of classical as well as oriental texts in a challenge to what he presents as a prevalent, and unexamined, contemporary belief that our identity as persons is that of unified psycho-physical organisms which are also unified loci of value.[22]

[22] This belief is presupposed by e.g. Wiggins, 'The Person', p. 56, cited at the start of this Intro., though Wiggins's views are not the specific object of Clark's criticism.

He points out that this belief is already under attack from the kind of 'reductionism' proposed by Derek Parfit, which presents personal identity as no more than the degree of continuity that exists between successive psychological states.[23] But Clark's attack takes the form of reviving the view (held in different ways by Plato, Aristotle, and Plotinus) that our psychic essence consists in a 'separable' reason or *nous*, which enters the psycho-physical organism from outside (as *daimōn*), but none the less constitutes the centre and source of our intellectual and moral being. While constituting our essence, as persons, this entity is also supra-individual, forming a kind of Self or Mind in which different individuals can, at a deep level, participate. And, while participation in this Self involves dissociation from our own particular psychophysical organism, it also involves association with the material and animate universe of which we are a part, and brings a sense of involvement with the cosmos as a whole.[24]

The view of human mind studied by M. R. Wright is, on the face of it, radically opposed to that of Clark. Her synoptic study of the earliest Greek philosophical thinking on this subject emphasizes the fact that their characteristic approach, like that of much modern thinking, is materialist. Thinking and knowing, like perceiving, are analysed in terms of the individual's contact with, and absorption of, objects, and both the thinking subject and the object of thought are taken to be physical entities. However, she also emphasizes that the Presocratics did not go on to make the 'behaviourist' move of treating all human activity as a response to external stimuli, but insisted on man's capacity for independent agency as regards acquiring understanding of himself and his world. To those who exercise this capacity for intellectual autonomy, the Presocratics sometimes ascribed a 'divine' or 'heroic' status, in this respect anticipating Aristotle's advice that we should identify ourselves with the 'divine' *nous* that is the 'most authoritative and best' part of us.[25] This aspect of Presocratic thought comes surprisingly close (given their materialist approach) to the view of mind, as in some sense cosmic and impersonal, given by Clark. This comes out, for instance, in her exegesis of Heraclitus:

[23] D. Parfit, *Reasons and Persons* (Oxford, 1984), pt. III.

[24] Cf. esp. the quotation from Pieper, p. 200, n. 46 below: 'To be possessed of spirit is to be involved with everything that exists, to permeate the whole cosmos.'

[25] *EN* 10. 7, 1177b33–1178a3, cited at the start of the Intro.

The possession of 'dry' soul,—that which is 'wisest and best'—is a state that is achieved by a continuing victory over impulse, and an intellectual dedication that will bring one into that 'super-awakeness' in which awareness of the unseen *harmonia* which governs the functioning of the cosmos is possible. The self-increasing *logos* of the soul makes contact with the 'one wise' which steers all things, and this in turn enlarges the soul's potential for wisdom.[26]

Summarizing the line of thought she analyses, we might say that the Presocratics see human minds either as material objects, or divine entities (or both), rather than as being distinctively *human*.

Christopher Rowe and A. W. Price also treat, from different directions, a thinker—Plato—who is sometimes taken to hold that our essence, as human beings, lies in the divine or cosmic reason in which we have the capacity to participate. Rowe's essay centres on a single text, the myth of the *Phaedrus*, in which Plato seems to address this very question (one signalled earlier in the same dialogue) of the essence of our nature as human beings.[27] Rowe formulates his own interpretation of the myth by means of a critique of a radically novel reading by Martha Nussbaum, according to which Plato, in a revision of his earlier intellectualism, urges us to understand ourselves and each other as unified psycho-physical and psychological wholes, as unique individuals, and as unified loci of value.[28] Rowe argues, in response, that in so far as Plato uses the myth to modify his earlier thinking, he does so in a much more limited way. The imagery of the myth suggests that, while our highest human aspiration is, and should be, to attain 'divine' rationality, we are ineluctably encumbered by 'bestial' psychological elements (especially the recalcitrant black horse) which are not to be seen simply as the product of the (temporary) attachment of the psyche to the body. The moral of the myth, as Rowe sees it, is not that we should value all aspects of the uneasy psychological fusion that makes up the human psyche but rather that we should try to impose divine (rational) order on our bestial aspects. And, while Rowe accepts that (as Nussbaum claims) Plato seems to give more value to interpersonal relationships than before,

[26] See ch. 9 below: for Clark's view on Heraclitus and other Presocratics, see ch. 8 below.

[27] *Phdr.* 230a, cited at the start of this Intro.

[28] *The Fragility of Goodness: Luck and Ethics in Greek Tragedy and Philosophy* (Cambridge, 1986), ch. 7.

he thinks that the relationships so valued are those in which the partners help each other to impose this order on themselves.

In the final essay in the volume, A. W. Price points to some striking parallels between Plato's thinking on intra-psychic conflict and unity and Freud's, despite the obvious differences between the character and aims of their overall theories. The common features he emphasizes include the belief that love is displaceable in its objects, being open to sublimation or debasement, and that the mind forms an arena of conflict between analogously conceived complexes of belief and desire (the 'parts' of the soul). His account brings out the fact that, although Plato insists on the division in the human psyche between 'divine' reason and 'bestial' desire, aspects of his theory, like Freud's, imply underlying connections between the aspects of the human self thus divided. The psychic 'homunculi' generated in both theories can be understood as the products of rather similar patterns of self-identification and self-dissociation, of what one allows to be 'I' rather than 'it'. Since the evidence for the direct influence of Plato on Freud is rather slight, he takes the most plausible explanation for this degree of convergence to be the fact that both thinkers capture, in these theories, 'natural ways in which the Greek and modern mind implicitly appears to itself'.[29]

Price's suggestion that we can find at least some recurrent patterns in the way the human mind pictures itself is partly confirmed and partly qualified by other essays in the volume. As Wright shows, modern materialist models of mind are anticipated in Presocratic thinking; but the Presocratics sometimes allocate a semi-divine role to *nous*, as an independent searcher for cosmic knowledge, that consorts ill with modern materialism. As Clark and Rowe, in different ways, bring out, the disposition to present a 'separable' *nous* as the essential core of the human psyche runs counter to one prevalent modern picture of the person, that of a psychological (and psycho-physical) unit which has value as a unified whole. Of course, as Snowdon reminds us, there are modern thinkers too who would want to identify the 'I' of personhood with my psychological processes (even if this involves my 'changing bodies'). But, as Clark points out, there is a big difference between Parfit's 'reductionism' (which would do away with the idea that one has an 'essential' identity) and the ancient tendency, which he follows, of identifying one's essence with a 'daimonic' *nous*.

[29] Cf. ch. 11 below.

These points of comparison and contrast between specific aspects of ancient and modern philosophy have an inherent interest (although they would obviously need to be pursued further to become fully meaningful); and I hope readers of this volume will find it of value in highlighting such points. However, the volume may perhaps play a more valuable role in helping us to define a larger issue, or complex of issues, to which these specific theories can be seen as contributing. In this Introduction, and in the arrangement of the volume, I have underlined what seems to me to be a central issue in both ancient and modern philosophy. The core of the issue, in both contexts, is whether we are to understand ourselves, essentially, as human beings (with all that this implies, as regards our psycho-physical nature and our specific forms of shared life and self-understanding or whether we are to identify ourselves rather with a certain set of mental capacities, conceived as constituting our 'personhood' or 'divine' essence, which are in principle shared by, and normative for, other forms of life and intelligence. As I emphasized earlier, there is scope for debate about how far this was recognized as a distinct issue in ancient philosophy, and, in so far as it was, how far it is analogous to the modern version of this issue. But there is at least a prima facie case for claiming that there are analogous versions of the issue in both ancient and modern philosophy; and the fact that the volume enables such a claim may go some way towards justifying the kind of project undertaken here.

# PART I

## 'Person' and 'Human Being': The Status and Interrelationship of the Concepts

# I

# Persons and *Personae*

*Amélie Oksenberg Rorty*

There is a philosophical dream, a dream that moral and political ideals are not only grounded in and explained by human nature, but that fundamental moral and political principles can be derived from the narrower conditions that define persons. Though sometimes bold and wild dreamers do go so far, this dream does not usually express a metaphysical wish that could be satisfied by analysing the conditions for reflective subjectivity or the psycholinguistic conditions for the reflexivity of first-person attributions. More commonly, the dream is that normative political and moral principles can be derived from what is essential to the concept of a person.

The strongest version of this dream attempts to use the (initially value-neutral) concept of a person to derive specific rights, principles, and obligations; a somewhat more modest version attempts to use the concept of a person to set constraints on such rights, principles, and obligations; a yet weaker version makes the two notions—the concept of a person and the delineation of moral and political rights—mutually explicative. But all versions of this dream press for a single concept of a person, whose various components form a harmonious structure that could provide adjudication among competing normative claims about what does or does not fall within the domain of the rights and obligations of persons. The press for one well-structured concept that allocates priorities among its various conditions is a demand for a decision procedure to settle disagreements about, and conflicts among, competing values and obligations.

But there is no such thing as 'the' concept of a person. This is so not only for the obvious historical reason that there have been dramatically discontinuous changes in the characterization of persons, though that is true. Nor for the equally obvious anthropological-cultural reason that the moral and legal practices heuristically treated as analogous across cultures differ so dramatically that they capture 'the concept' of personhood only vaguely and incompletely, though that is also true.

The various functions performed by our contemporary concept of person do not hang together: there is some overlap, but also some tension. Indeed, the functions that 'the' notion plays are so related that attempts to structure them in a taxonomic order express quite different norms and ideals. Disagreements about primary values and goods reappear as disagreements about the priorities and relations among the various functions the concept plays, disagreements about what is essential to persons. Not only does each of the functions bear a different relation to the class of persons and human beings, but each also has a different contrast class.

As inheritors of the Judaeo-Christian, Renaissance, Enlightenment, and Romantic traditions, we want the concept of the person to fill a number of functions:

1. The attribution should give us objective grounds for being taken seriously, with respect—and to be taken seriously, with respect, on grounds that can't be lost through illness, poverty, villainy, inanity, or senility. On this view, the idea of person is an insurance policy. Some think of the insurance as guaranteeing us rights. Others think of it as assuring us a certain kind of regard, that we will be treated as ends rather than merely as means, that our activities will be perceived as centrally rational (or at least reasonable) and good-willed (or at least well-intentioned) and interpreted by an extension of the principle of charity. For some, the special status of persons is justified by some set of properties: persons should be respected because they are capable of critical rationality, or because they are free inventors of their lives, or because they have divinely donated souls, or because they can be harmed, frustrated in living out their life plans. For others, specific rights cannot be justified by or derived from the essential properties of the class of persons, because such rights are among the essential properties of persons. For yet others, claims to rights can only be based on the general social and political benefits that such rights might bring.

Among the Hellenes, the contrast class for this notion was the class of slaves and barbarians. Among Christians, the contrast class is that of unsouled beings. For Kantians, the contrast class is that of non-rational beings, incapable of understanding the laws of nature and unable to act freely, from the idea of the laws of morality. This conception of the class of persons intersects, but is not identical with nor subsumed within, the class of human beings: Martians and dolphins might be persons, as might intrapsychic homunculi.

2. Sometimes the respect and rights of persons are assured by law: persons are defined as legal entities. The legal concept of a person is meant to assure, first, liability. This is a retrospective function, defined by the conditions for presumptive agency: bodily continuity, memory, *mens rea*. (The contrast class is made up of those with defective conditions for agency, for example, the insane and the senile.)

Second, the legal concept of persons ensures legally defined responsibility. This is a prospective and regionalized function that defines specific duties and obligations. Such responsibilities are often institutionally defined: sometimes the legal person's duties and responsibilities are contractually fixed, with explicitly articulated sanctions for default or violation; sometimes the obligations are defined informally by commonly accepted practices and sanctions. In such cases, liability is carried by the legal entity, rather than by the individuals—for example, trustees, corporations, guardians, boards of directors, banks—who act as its officers. (The contrast class includes minors and, still in some places, women.)

Third, the legal concept guarantees specifically defined citizen rights and duties. This is a function that empowers a designated class of individuals to act and speak on behalf of the State. They are, as Hobbes put it, its 'artificial persons'. Polities accord specific rights and duties of participation in decision-making, representation, governance. Indeed, this is one way political systems differ: by the different ways they distribute the power and the right to act or speak in the person of the State, as an agent of one of its constitutive institutions. As the frontispiece of Hobbes's *Leviathan* graphically demonstrates, the king of an absolute monarchy is the embodied person of the State. If the State is composed of families or clans, rather than of individuals, those families or clans are the citizen-persons of the State, and their heads or elders speak and act for them. Similarly, representatives of state-defined political institutions (the judiciary, the legislative body, city officials) act in the person of the State: their decisions personify the official acts of the State. When the Pope speaks *ex cathedra*, he speaks as the personification of the Church; the voice of Parliament is the voice of the people; 'We the People'—citizens casting votes on public issues or selecting their representatives—are expressing the views of the person(s) of the State. Even though their rights and welfare are under the legal protection of the state, the disenfranchised—etymologically, the unfree—are the subjects or wards of the State rather than citizen-persons entitled to act or speak as the person of the State. Whether the class of citizen-persons coincides with or is a subset of the class of those who are legally liable is, of course, a political and even an ideological issue. (The composition of the contrast class is usually under contention and may include, for example, aliens, slaves, exiles, and foetuses.)

Neither the Kantian regulative principle of respect nor the Christian idea of the immortal soul have any necessary connection with the legal function of the idea of person. Respect for the person does not entail any particular legal rights; nor does the assurance of legal personhood assure social or moral respect. Furthermore, each of the distinctive legal personae might well select different grounds for the attribution of personhood. For instance, an individual can claim some citizen rights (the right of habeas corpus, for example) without satisfying the conditions for liability. Nor need a legal person be accorded all the rights of citizenship: universities do not, as such, vote or receive social security. The conditions for prospective responsibility are regional and relative: whether an individual or a group is designated a legal person is characteristically a political, and sometimes an ideological, issue.

Some legal theorists argue that no single concept of a person can—or should—be used to derive the wide variety of legislative and judicial policies required to give appropriately differentiated treatment to the varieties of legal personae.[1] They maintain that moral and legal practices contextualize and regionalize the status of a person: a foetus is, for example, accorded the status of a legal person in some contexts and for some issues, but not for others; a corporation has the legal status of a person for some purposes, for others not. We should, they hold, draw our inclusionary and exclusionary classes contextually, following our sense of what is

[1] See C. Baron, 'The Concept of Person in the Law', in M. W. Shaw and A. E. Doudera (edd.), *Defining Human Life: Medical, Legal, and Ethical Implications* (Ann Arbor, Mich., 1983), 121–48; and R. Tur, 'The "Person" in Law', in A. Peacocke and G. Gillett (edd.), *Persons and Personality: A Contemporary Inquiry* (Oxford, 1987), 116–29.

morally and judicially appropriate, rather than attempting to derive our legal practices from a sharply—and, they suggest, arbitrarily—defined class of persons. 'First come the practices of right and wrong, and then come definitions and classifications.' The question of whether there are several distinctive legal concepts of a person, each with its own pragmatically defined domain, or whether there is one concept, with distinctive pragmatic applications is an idle question, since neither legal theory nor legal practice are affected by the answer.

There are, of course, dramatic cultural variations in the criteria for agency, variations in the legal conditions that define persons. The class of liable and responsible persons can, for instance, exclude individuals in favour of groups of individuals (clans or families), or the heads of such groups (the chief patriarch), intrapsychic homunculi, demonic possessors. It can be treated as an all-or-none classification, or as a matter of degree. It is often dificult to determine how to diagnose such cultural variation. Do these differences represent disagreements about the proper analysis of the concept of a person? Do some cultures lack the concept or do they have an analogous construct? Do some cultures lack what we consider a legal system, or do they locate their legal system in a different network of institutions? There may be no fact of the matter: exigencies of theory construction rather than ontology may determine whether we can legitimately project our concept of a legal person on to analogous bearers of liability and responsibility, or whether we should decline the attribution to individuals whose agency is defined within radically different schemes of liability and responsibility.

3. The idea of a person is also the idea of an autonomous agent, capable of self-defined and self-defining choices. There are at least two versions of this idea. The first is primarily negative and defensive, concentrating on the desire to fend off external interference: *Noli me tangere*, or in 'Amerispeak', 'Don't tread on me, buddy'. The second is primarily positive and constructive, concentrating on capacities for self-determination. Both the negative and positive ideas of autonomy emphasize critical rationality and independent evaluation. A person is essentially capable of stepping back from her beliefs and desires to evaluate their rationality and appropriateness; she is also capable (at the very least) of attempting to form and modify her beliefs and desires, her actions, on the basis

of her rational evaluations. (The contrast class would thus comprise the mindless, the non-rational, the dissociated.)

The idea of autonomy, whether negatively or positively defined, also emphasizes imaginative creativity. Because their decisions and actions are intentionally identified, and because they have latitude in transforming, improvising, and inventing their intentions, persons can, in a number of significant ways, form the worlds in which they live. There are two dimensions on which such formations take place: the political and the visionary-poetic.

For the first, since the social and political domain is constructed, it can be reconstructed, if only a piece at a time. To be a person is to participate actively in public life, forming or at least modifying the social and political policies and institutions that significantly and effectively shape life. (The contrast class: the masses, whose opinions and actions can be manipulated.)

For the second, by choosing or constructing systems of values, persons create the categories that structure and interpret their world, that form their ambitions, hopes, and fears. Since they determine what is important and significant, their interpretations structure both what they see and what they do. (The contrast class: the dependent, the fearful, the timid, the unimaginative.)

These aspects of the idea of autonomy mark differences in two faces or moments in Enlightenment political theory. The first stance is defensive: it is designed to protect the person from what is perceived as tyrannical or unjust political or epistemic authority. This concept of a person stresses negative liberty and minimal government. There is some correlation, but no necessary connection, between the defensive boundary conception of the free person and the conception of the person whose critical and rational capacities are primarily exercised in scientific discovery or poetic creativity and only secondarily in defence against error.

Although the Enlightenment concept of a person began with the Christian conception of a person as defined by his free will, his capacity to affirm or deny God's law, autonomy shifted from the freedom of the will to the rational power of independent critical judgements of truth and falsity. When the old order loses its authority, the emphasis on persons as autonomous judges preserving and protecting individual boundaries is replaced by an emphasis on autonomous legislators generating new social structures and practices. Negative liberty gives way to positive liberty; minimal government gives way to a government charged with the formation of citizen values. Protection against error gives way to the power of constructing a systematic science, and eventually to the power of the imagination in constructing a world through poetic language. There is some correlation, but no necessary connection, between the concept of a person as a constructive, self-determining legislator and the concept of a person as primarily a creator. The movement from the earlier defensive to the later constructive conceptions of persons correlates in a very rough way with the movement from early Cartesian Enlightenment conceptions of the independent, inquiring, rational self, free of the claims of dogmatic doctrine, to late Enlightenment Romanticism, with its emphasis on positive liberty, political reform, and poetic creativity.

The conception of persons as deserving respect is sometimes rooted in the conception of a person as capable of self-definition. But of course both the rational and the creative dimensions of the idea of the self-defining person (in its negative and positive forms) leave individual claims to personhood empirically contingent. If claims to respect are based on the capacities for autonomy, we are in deep trouble. Constitutional and socio-political contingencies affect the likelihood of an individual actually (rather than notionally or potentially) developing her capacities for critical rationality; similar contingencies determine whether she is actually (rather than notionally) capable of creative self-determination. Has the individual been well nourished and nurtured, well educated and well formed? Or has she suffered irreparable traumas that make autonomy practically impossible? Logical or notional possibility is not helpful here: aardvarks, baboons, and caterpillars might notionally be capable of autonomy. It might seem as if this concept of a person provides grounds for normative political claims. Precisely because certain kinds of political structures are required to actualize otherwise only notional claims to personhood, there is a prima facie obligation to structure political systems in such a way as to allow the best development of the capacities for critical self-determination. Unfortunately, many extra premisses are required to substantiate this claim, premisses about the primary and the proper functions of the obligations of political systems. The obligation cannot follow solely from the requirements for personhood. (This conception of the class of persons intersects, but is not identical with or subsumed within, the class of biologically defined human beings. The contrast class is composed of all those incapable of self-correcting and self-legislating critical reflexivity.)

Christianity is, for once, surprisingly open and generous. If part of the point of the concept of a person is to assure respect, it is wiser not to rest one's hopes on such fragile and vulnerable capacities as those for autonomy or creativity. Maybe a divinely assured immortal soul—or even just a divinely assured soul, immortal or not—would provide more secure grounds for respect. To be sure, conditions for rationality and autonomy are standardly regulative rather than empirical: we might take comfort in the principle that every rational being *ought* to be treated with respect. But it takes unusually good luck to get that regulative principle realized under harsh circumstances, just when it is most needed. Respect may be well grounded without being well assured. What recourse do the unrespected have when they most require respect? Moral indignation? Righteousness in the eyes of history—itself a politically variable matter—is not reliably effective in assuring entitlements.

More recently, the Christian conception of persons as endowed with a free will capable of affirming or denying God's law has been redefined: the rights of persons are accorded to all those capable of suffering, those whose naturally formed life histories can be harmed, shortened, frustrated. Whether the sentient are self-consciously aware of the natural shapes of their lives, whether they form plans and expectations (the transformation of the idea of the will as legislator), matters less than the fact that their lives can be painful or unfulfilled. It is the sheer fact of sentience that qualifies an individual to the rights of persons.[2]

4. Social persons are identified by their mutual interactions, by the roles they enact in the dynamic dramas of their shared lives. There are several varieties of this conception.

The idea of a dramatis persona as the bearer of roles in a dramatic unfolding of action has its source in the theatre. A persona is the mask of an actor cast to play a part in developing a narrative or a plot. Essentially meshed with others, the social person's scope and directions are defined by her role in a complex course of events, involving the interactions of agents whose varied intentions modify the outcomes—and indeed sometimes the directions—of one another's projects. While the dramatic conception of a person is

[2] See K. Capek, *War with the Newts* (London, 1985); and P. Singer, *Animal Liberation* (New York, 1977).

only indirectly linked to the concept of a person as entitled to respect, or with that of a self-defining individual, it bears some kinship to the idea of a person as an agent, as the source of liable and responsible action. When *dramatis personae* are in principle able to predict their effects on one another's lives, their intentions can carry moral or legal weight. (The contrast class includes whatever is inert, without the power of intentional action. Since inanimate objects and events—volcanoes, wars, famines—can forward or redirect dramatic action, they are sometimes personified; but they are accounted persons only if intentional action is attributed to them.)

Some psychologists introduce a normative notion of a person as capable of taking others seriously, capable of entering into mutually affective and effective relations. To be a person is to acknowledge the reality of others, living in a commonly constructed world, actively and cooperatively sharing practices. Some psychologists attempt to connect the social with the respect-based definitions of persons, treating them as mutually supportive conditions.[3] But there is not necessarily a link between the two conditions. On the one hand, respect might be grounded in the idea of a (divinely donated) soul, whose sociability is contingent on the identity and roles assigned to it; on the other, some conceptions of sociability might valorize a type of intimacy that minimizes respect across individual boundaries. Such a manifestly culture-bound concept of personhood can easily come into conflict with the (equally culture-bound) concept of the ideal person as capable of radical autonomy. (The contrast class in this instance is made up of dissociated personalities and psychopaths.)

There is a presumptively ontological, pre-psychological version of the concept of persons as essentially formed by their relations to others. It perceives the person as constituted, formed by 'the look of the other'. According to this theory, consciousness is initially unreflective, without a sense of self; it acquires an image of itself—an image that comes to form the person's somatic sense of self—by seeing itself mirrored in the eyes of others. We form one another's identities by the act of mutual mirroring, mutual regard. A person's life is constructed from, and constituted by, such interactive formative relations. Though there may be normative claims about how we *ought* to regard one another, the conception of a person as

[3] See H. Kohut, *The Restoration of the Self* (New York, 1977).

interactively emergent neither entails nor is entailed by the conception of a person as entitled to respect or to specific legal rights. (The contrast class: non-conscious beings, beings incapable of self-conscious reflection.)

Associated but not identical with the psychological condition is the honorific attribution of personhood. Some individuals are accounted *real* persons: 'She's a real mensch!' But although the capacities for autonomy (rationality or creativity) might be ingredients in the qualifications for being a *real* person, in contrast to the usual humanoid, they are not sufficient. Indeed, a partisan of the concept of a person as an autonomous creator might well be disqualified as a real mensch-person. On this view—to be sure a view not widely shared as definitive of the concept of a person—*real* persons are generally distinguished by fortitude and reliability, by their presence, their style and individuality, often combined with compassion and a humorous sense of proportion, an ironic recognition of human frailty and finitude. (The contrast class: the psychopath, the creep, the jerk, the whine, the brute, the Neanderthal.)

5. The concept of personhood is also used to sketch the norms for the appropriate shape and structure of a life. Those who identify persons by a characteristic life history or life plan require an account of a standard—or maybe not so standard—shaping of a life, one that goes beyond biologically determined patterns of maturation and ageing. This view originally derives from the Christian conception of the soul, whose life and choices move it toward salvation or damnation; it is a descendant of the definition of persons as constructors of their fates. The emphasis shifts: the person is first identified as the author of the story, then by the activity of story construction, and then simply by the emergent content of the narrative.[4]

There are two versions of this focus. The first, which postulates a fact of the matter, can give an account of how a culture can malform and misdirect lives, as well as misunderstand the processes by which it shapes typical life stories. The second might be characterized as the 'It's all up to us' version, with the 'us' referring either to individual free spirits or to the members of a self-defining community.

[4] See J. Bruner, *Actual Minds, Possible Worlds* (Cambridge, Mass., 1986).

While the narrative conception of personhood is compatible with the definition of persons as autonomous, it neither entails nor is entailed by that conception. A person's life story need not be autonomously constructed; nor need it provide grounds for respect. Even more dramatically, the conditions for autonomy need have no bearing on the shape and events of life histories, which are, after all, contingent and heteronomous. In a Kantian framework, for example, the conditions for autonomy are purely intellectual: they neither affect nor can be affected by the contingent narrative of a life. Nor is the possibility of reflective subjectivity essential to the construction of a life story: a life can have the shape of a well-formed narrative without its subject experiencing anything like first-person inner subjectivity. It is the convenience of theory construction rather than brute ontology that determines whether the narrative condition for personhood requires further qualification. As it stands, the view that a person is one who possesses a life story seems to allow any subject of a narrative history to qualify even if that subject is not conscious of itself as a subjective centre of experience. An individual might have a life story without being subjectively aware of it, and certainly without being self-consciously reflective about her shaping of it. Yet if the unadorned narrative condition of personhood allows mice and mountains to qualify as persons, the additional requirement of active subjective reflection seems too strong: it appears to disqualify individuals who might, on moral or political grounds, qualify as persons. The capacities for active subjective reflection—for constructing life plans—might turn out to be consequences of, rather than presuppositions for, an individual's qualifying as a social and political person.

The contrast class for the conception of persons as characterized by life stories is difficult to define. Everything temporal can be construed as having a life story, even a life story with a normative form. This criterion allows squirrels, a particular patch of pachysandra, and the Mediterranean basin to qualify as persons because they have life stories with a beginning, middle, and end. If we attach the further condition that persons must be capable of reflecting on, if not actively forming, a life story or a life plan, the contrast class is no easier to define. Who has the capacity for the autonomous construction of a life plan? Should the class include individuals who in principle might acquire the capacities for reflective agency, for constructing and following a life plan, if they could be accorded the status of persons? How are such counter-factual claims evaluated in holistic systems?

6. The biological conception of an individual is sometimes taken to provide the foundation or basic structure of the concept of a person. Biologists want a concept that will provide (*a*) the unit of genetic individuation and (*b*) *conatus*: the determination of growth and immunology, the energy and direction of action, reaction, and defence.

Persons are, among other things, self-sustainers and self-starters. The biological account of organic independence provides the practical origin of the more far-reaching notion of autonomy. But the concept of an organic individual does not necessarily provide a sharp distinction between human beings and other species, let alone between persons and other sorts of organic entities. Whether there is a subclass, a variety of human beings who can be designated as persons by virtue of a special set of standardly inheritable properties is a matter for empirical determination. If rationality marks the class of persons, are the various properties and capacities that constitute rationality biologically fixed, genetically coded? How do the conditions for reflective critical rationality described by Kant and Frankfurt function in the organism's system of action and reaction, expansion and defence? If self-determination marks the class of persons, are those properties and traits that constitute an individual's capacity for self-determination biologically fixed, genetically coded? How do the various capacities for creative self-definition affect a person's constitution? We are a long way from having a reasonable speculative theory, let alone a sound research programme, connecting the moral, political, and legal notions of persons with the biological notion of a reproductive, self-sustaining, defensively structured organism.

It has been argued that just as women and blacks were once excluded from the class of persons on presumptively biological grounds, so too we are now misled by superficial speciesism to exclude dolphins and mammals. But we are a long way from an account of the criteria for appropriate classification: what formally identical or analogous constitutional structures qualify non-humans as persons? Why should baboons but not robots qualify? Or Martians but not crustaceans? While empirical considerations are relevant (do dolphins have central nervous systems?), they cannot settle the questions of whether corporations and robots only qualify as persons by metaphorical courtesy, while dolphins and chimpanzees qualify as full members by an appropriate corrective extension of the class. When is a batch of wires a central nervous system and when is it only an analogue? When is an analogue good enough? When is it all too good? When does behavioural similarity qualify for literal attribution? What are the criteria for identifying biologically based behavioural similarity? Both the arguments for excluding corporations and the left hemisphere of the brain and the arguments for including robots and Martians depend on normatively charged conceptual analyses. Since similarities and differences can be found wholesale, other, further considerations are required to select the features that demarcate the class of persons. What considerations select the capacity to feel pain, rather than for rational thought, as the criterion for the class? Indeed, because the classification has significant political and social consequences, we should not be surprised to discover that conceptual analyses of biological functions—particularly those presumed to affect intentional agency—are strongly, though often only implicitly and unself-consciously, guided by moral intuitions, ideology, and taste. Controversies among sociobiologists about drawing relevant analogies between humans and other animals—their hierarchy or altruistic behaviour, their protection of property—should make us suspicious about attempts to support policies concerning the rights of persons on what are allegedly purely empirical, biological considerations. (The contrast class comprises inanimate objects.)

7. Psycho-metaphysicians have a notion of the elusive, ultimate subject of experience, the 'I' that cannot be reduced to an object, even though it can treat itself objectively, as the focus of introspection and investigation.[5] But this 'I' can be diachronically discontinuous: the subject of 'sequential' experiences need not be strictly identical. And even synchronic subjects of experiences need not be united: every aspect of a complex act of awareness could, in principle, have its own subject. The subject who is aware of the acute pain of loss need not be identical with the subject who is at the same time aware of the shifting pattern of light on the leaves of a tree. Or at any rate, the transcendental unity of apperception (if there is such a thing) does not necessarily provide specific closure to what is, and what is not, included within the bounds of such a presumptive unity. The limits of the domain of experience cannot

[5] See T. Nagel, *The View from Nowhere* (New York, 1986).

be set by the subject of a transcendental unity of apperception without circularity.

In any case, there are a number of distinctive construals of subjectivity as the condition for personhood, and while each has quite different consequences for the concept, none has any necessary consequences for morality, or for political or legal theory. The 'I' that is the subject of experience serves as the contrastive notion, but the various contrasts are not isomorphic. The person as the 'I', the subject of experience, has been identified with the interior or internal perspective in contrast to the external; with the subjective in contrast to the objective; with the subject-of-experiences in contrast to its experiences; with rationality and the will in contrast to causality and desire; with spontaneity and creativity in contrast to the conditioned; with the decision-maker and agent in contrast to the predictor and observer; with the knower or interpreter in contrast to the known or interpreted; with reflective consciousness in contrast to the content of reflection; with mind in contrast to body.

Although each of these juxtapositions marks a quite different contrast, each is guided by the intuition that persons are capable of bearing a unique reflexive, reflective relation to themselves, a relation that somehow shapes them. Persons are sometimes characterized as capable of having a distinctive set of experiences—ego-oriented attitudes of anxiety, remorse, pride, guilt—that originally give rise to the idea of self. But the reflective 'I' can reject or identify with these ego-oriented attitudes as easily as it can with its body or its habits. It is no more identical with any set of 'existential attitudes' than it is with any of its more externally defined attributes. The *act* of reflecting on an attribute or attitude, asking 'Is that *me*?' ('putting the self in question'), is always different from the attitude or attribute itself, even if the attitude reveals—as anxiety is said to do—the precarious position of the 'I' as the act of self-constituting reflection. Being anxious is one thing; being the act that identifies with anxiety is another. Both are different from a something, perhaps a nothing I know not what, or a simple soul beyond experience, or a pure act of reflection that constitutes itself. All these—different as they are from one another—are far from the original starting-point of the 'I' as a being whose experience, and especially its experience of itself, is *sui generis*. None of these reflexive attitudes carries specific political, legal, or moral consequences. In *Notes from the Underground*, Dostoevsky's dramatic explorations of the subterranean destructiveness of the endlessly ironic, self-mirroring self-consciousness demonstrate that even rational, self-critical reflexivity can assure neither sociability nor morality; and it can destroy self-respect. (The contrast class: objects; those incapable of self-conscious reflection.)

The variety of functions that 'the' concept of a person plays—the variety of conceptions of personhood we have—cannot be plausibly combined in a single concept. At most, one might settle for a heterogeneous class, defined by a disjunction of heterogeneous conditions. Even if some rough construction of a denominator common to all these notions and functions were proposed, that conception would be so general that it could not fulfil—nor could it generate—the various functions performed by the various regional and substantively rich conceptions.

But this stark conclusion seems premature. Perhaps we can characterize persons by attempting some sort of synthesis of our various conditions: *A person is a unit of agency, a unit that is* (1) *capable of being directed by its conception of its own identity, and by what is important to that identity, and* (2) *capable of acting with others, in a common world. A person is an interactive member of a community, reflexively sensitive to the contexts of her activity, a critically reflective inventor of the story line of her life.* Surely this is a parody of a characterization. The conditions only cohere if one does not look too closely. It is not clear whether these conditions are conjunctive or whether they are nested. After all, the conditions for strong autonomy might well on occasion conflict with those for strong sociability. The conditions of critical rationality might well on occasion conflict with those of poetic creativity. The conditions for personhood—and indeed the class of those qualifying as persons—are quite different if critical rationality dominates over sociability, rather than sociability over the capacities for critical rationality. Societies that weight these capacities differently differ dramatically; and sometimes ideological or political issues determine the weighting and priority of the various conditions.

Might the metaphysical notion of a person be primary, in a way that would settle these questions of priority? Primary to what? A universalistic metaphysical notion can constrain, but it cannot select or determine the priorities among competing politically and ideologically defined persons. The notion of a human being is a notion of a biologically defined entity; the notion of a person is, however, normatively and sometimes ideologically charged. It expresses a view about what is important, valuable about being creatures like us, in having this or that set of significant traits and properties. Such creatures need not belong to our biological species. Martians or Super-Robots could be persons; organically organized families and clans might qualify, as could intrapsychic demons, homunculi, or consciences. For some, this notion designates a natural kind, there is a fact of the matter about what ought to be important and significant to us. For others, we are that natural kind whose primary attributes are plastic: within limits, we are self-legislatively self-defining, even self-constructing, creatures.

But even those who think of persons as self-defining creators of their identities do not agree about the extension of this class. For some, self-determination is a matter of individual volition; for others, only historical communities with self-perpetuating practices can be considered self-determining. For some, *all* individuals, no matter how pathetically malformed, however constitutionally or socially deprived or deformed, are equally the creators of the stories that are their lives. No matter what story one tells about one's life, that story *is* one's life as a person. For others, only Nietzschean self-creating and free individual spirits, the solitary ones who transcend the herd and the conventions of the herd, are capable of self-definition. For others, only cultural and political communities can define or create themselves: individual persons are self-legislating only as members of a community defined by shared interactive practices, which define the boundaries and the essential traits of persons. On this view, the definition of persons is implicit in the practices that express and reproduce the community's cultural forms, especially the practices of parenting and education and the distribution of legal and political power.

These reflections on 'the' concept of a person seem unsatisfactory: all we have is a complaint inspired by vulgar forms of Wittgensteinianism, that shifts the burden of analysis. Instead of dispatching yet another vexed philosophic issue, counselling Quixotic philosophers to stop looking for a non-existent essential definition of persons, we should perhaps more modestly end with an account of the many different reasons we have wanted, and perhaps needed, the notion of a person. These are, after all, honourable desires, as philosophic desires go. We have, in a sketchy way, explored some of the reasons that philosophers and legal-political theorists want the concept: those reasons are given by the heterogeneous list of functions—some of them rhetorical—that the concept has played. The Procrustean tactic of cutting limbs to fit an arbitrary, if elegantly designed, form neither illuminates nor gains anything: it limits rather than enhances an understanding of the various functions of 'the' concept.

It is of course possible to legislate one central notion of a person, and to fend off strong contending candidates for definition. Such legislation might express a moral or an ideologial victory; if it is widely accepted, it might even succeed in being a culturally self-fulfilling prophecy. But it would not on that account alone constitute an insightful illumination into the nature of persons. Such legislation about the essential character of persons expresses rather than grounds or legitimates our moral and legal principles. But, significantly, the deep fissures and conflicts that are central to moral experience, and that make their way into the complexities of legal practice, are reintroduced among, and even sometimes within, the various functions of the concepts of persons. We do not even have the luxury of assuring ourselves that at least the concept of the person is co-ordinate with the concepts of moral and legal practices. At best we can say that the tensions and conflicts at the heart of moral and legal practices are reflected in, and sometimes clarified by, tensions and conflicts in conceptions of persons.

Why, then, is there such a metaphysical longing for one concept? (Or is it a longing for one metaphysical concept?) Perhaps the explanation is that the various functions the concept plays are each unifying functions: 'the' locus of liability; 'the' subject of experience; 'the' autonomous critical reflector or creator. Since these various functions are unifying functions, there might be a strong temptation to look for their unified source. But this is an elementary error, on a par with illicitly extracting and then detaching an existential quantifier from its proper nested location. A desire for unity cannot by itself perform the conjuring trick of pulling one rabbit out of several hats: a transcendental unity of the concept of person, unifying the variety of distinct, independently unifying functions that each regional concept plays.

Our reflections leave our conclusions open: we might conclude that there is no such thing as the concept of personhood, that there are only highly regionalized functions that seemed, erroneously, to be subsumable in a structured concept. Or we might conclude that the various functions of the concept are sometimes at odds, that the concept of a person cannot function to provide decision procedures for resolving conflicts among competing claims for rights and obligations because it embeds and expresses just those conflicts. Nothing hangs on the choice between these conclusions because neither political practice nor philosophic theory is affected by the outcome. For all practical and theoretical purposes it doesn't matter whether the concept of a person has multiple and sometimes conflicting functions, or whether there is no single foundational concept that can be characterized as *the* concept of a person. As long as we recognize that such appeals are, in the classical and unpejorative sense of that term, rhetorical, we can continue to appeal to conceptions of persons in arguing for extending political rights, or limiting the exercise of political power. The success of such rhetorical appeals depends on whether the proposed concept expresses some of the active values and practices of the audience.

Another metaphysical longing remains unsatisfied. But of course that does not mean that we shall be freed of metaphysical longing, nor even of this particular metaphysical longing.[6]

[6] This chapter is based on a paper given at the Aberystwyth conference on 'Persons and Human Beings'. An earlier version of this chapter appeared as 'Persons as Rhetorical Categories', *Social Research*, 54 (1987), 55–72; and the present version appears in 'Persons and *Personae*', in A. O. Rorty, *Mind in Action* (Boston, 1988), 27–46; it forms part of 'Relativism, Persons and Practices' in M. Krausz (edd.), *Relativism: Interpretation and Confrontation* (Notre Dame, Ind., 1989).

# 2

# Why there is no Concept of a Person

*Adam Morton*

## *The Aim*

It is easy to imagine thinking creatures that are not biologically human. Every human culture has imagined them: gods and demons, ogres and sprites, benevolent and malicious spirits, angels, centaurs and houyhnhnms, trolls. They are particularly familiar from Greek and Roman mythology. And it is very natural to use the ease with which we can imagine such creatures as a way of making plausible two conclusions, which are attractive in their own right: (1) that our concept of a thinking and acting being (of a mind that is an agent) potentially covers far more than just biological human beings—if in fact our species is the only species in the universe with the relevant characteristics then this is a sort of a cosmic accident; (2) that the bundle of characteristics that make up a thinking agent defines a single characteristic that is of basic moral importance—so that whatever value attaches to human beings and human life could potentially attach to creatures that were not biologically human. To accept these two conclusions is to accept that there is a concept of a person.

I accept many consequences of these two conclusions. I do not think it at all impossible that we will eventually meet intelligent extraterrestrials whose lives we will think of as morally on a par with our own. And I think that 'species chauvinism', the view that human life is valuable just because it is human, is a moral mistake. But I have come to doubt some of the usual grounds for them. What I doubt is that there is a single set of characteristics which would

---

Drafts of this paper were read at Aberystwyth, Oxford, and Bristol. Audiences at all three gave very constructive abuse. I am particularly grateful to Steven Blackstock, Troels Engberg-Pedersen, Christopher Gill, Peter Smith, Willie Watts Miller and Christopher Williams.

qualify a creature for intellectual and moral personhood. I think that we overestimate the simplicity and unity of the criteria we would apply in judging a creature's application for personhood, and I think that there are many more unclassifiable cases, in which there is no fact of the matter about whether or to what extent the creature in question is a person. (To put it differently: in the wake of a close encounter with extraterrestials it is likely that rather than being able to say that they are persons or non-persons or somewhere manageably on the boundary between, we may find ourselves at a loss for words, unable to describe in anything like the person/non-person distinction what we have discovered.) It is not just that I think the notion is vague, with wide fuzzy areas around many different edges. Its defenders would admit that. Rather, I suspect that there is no single concept there at all.

(I think that something similar holds for all of a family of related words, in particular 'sentient' and 'alive'. In each case the full wide range of what the world does and can contain may have some shocks for those who think that they have a simple grasp of what the word involves.)

The reason why we can easily give the concept of a person a definiteness that it does not really have is simple. We import into it more biologically parochial characteristics of human beings than we realize. The purpose of this paper is to show how one class of human characteristics, those centring on our possession of a conception of self, can invisibly infiltrate what purports to be a more general conception of a person. I shall first outline what has come to be the standard picture of personhood among modern philosophers, which is in some ways very different from the way the concept emerges in ancient philosophy.[1] Then I shall give two very different examples, each turning on a different aspect of the way in which thinkers conceive of themselves, which are meant to undercut the standard picture.

Will I then have shown that there is just no concept of a person? I certainly will not have shown that the term 'person', when used, say, to raise doubts about the moral status of new-born human

[1] Before the Aberystwyth conference I thought that the situation was simple but paradoxical: classical culture has more, and more serious, examples of non-human persons, than ours, but classical philosophy strangely fails to separate 'person' from 'human'. At the conference I came to realize that this is too simple. See the papers of Troels Engberg-Pedersen and Stephen Clark in this vol.

babies or to argue for the moral importance of adult elephants, is unintelligible. What I will have shown is that our use of the word is based on a set of rather indefinite family resemblances more than on simple and definite criteria, and that the resemblances focus on parochial features of the human organism. It is this parochiality that seems to me the most important point, for one of the main purposes of speaking of personhood, from Kant to Frankfurt and the recent debates about the status of new-born babies and higher animals, has been to separate our conception of what is valuable about ourselves from the details of our biology. If what I am arguing is right, the idea of personhood can only take us a small way into this project.

## *The Standard Picture*

One very natural and plausible approach to describing a concept of a person-in-general is worked out by Harry Frankfurt in a famous paper.[2] Frankfurt's theory can be seen as exploiting the insight that two very natural aspects of personhood can easily be developed together. One is the idea that persons can have more complicated thoughts than non-persons (cf. Wittgenstein's observation that a dog can think that his master is behind the door, but not that his master will return next Thursday). The other is the idea that a person has a reflexive capacity: a person cannot be completely ignorant about his own thoughts and motivation. Frankfurt's strategy is to use the first idea, in its modern appearance as the doctrine that belief and desire are propositional attitudes, to incorporate some of the consequences of the inevitably more obscure second idea. I shall give a very brief exposition of Frankfurt along these lines.

A belief or a desire always has a content, which we may take to be given by a proposition: John believes that *the earth is round*, Mary wants John to ignore her (i.e. Mary wants that *John ignores Mary*), Sam wants an apple (i.e. Sam wants that *Sam eats an apple*). This content proposition can be complicated, and a natural index

[2] See 'Freedom of the Will and the Concept of a Person', *Journal of Philosophy*, 68 (1971), 5–20, repr. in G. Wilson (ed.), *Free Will* (Oxford, 1982), 81–110; D. C. Dennett, 'Conditions of Personhood', in A. O. Rorty (ed.), *The Identities of Persons* (Berkeley, 1976), 175–96, repr. in Dennett, *Brainstorms: Philosophical Essays on Mind and Psychology* (Hassocks, Sussex, 1979), 267–85.

of the intellectual capacity of a creature is the complexity of the propositions that can intelligibly be attributed to it. (So that although cats and infants can have desires, it makes no sense to suppose that a cat or two-year-old is wanting that her mother go away in two days time and return three days after that. The concepts of mother and of a day, and of going and returning, may be available to her, but the complexity of the proposition that combines them is beyond her resources.) One very important source of complexity lies in the possibility that the content proposition have another proposition imbedded in it. Thus in 'Mary believes that Sam wants to steal her Volkswagen' the proposition giving the object of Mary's belief is 'Sam wants to steal Mary's Volkswagen', but that proposition itself has a proposition embedded in it, as content of Sam's desire, namely 'Sam steals Mary's Volkswagen'. Any belief or desire whose content refers in this way to another belief and desire is in the wide sense second order. Sometimes the belief or desire that is the object of the 'outside' belief or desire is a belief or desire of the same person, and these are second-order beliefs or desires in the narrow sense. Examples are: Sam believes that he wants Mary's Volkswagen (i.e. Sam believes that Sam wants that Sam has Mary's Volkswagen), Mary wants to believe that Sam is telling the truth (i.e. Mary wants that Mary believes that Sam is telling the truth).

For Frankfurt, in order to be a person a creature must have second-order beliefs and desires in the narrow sense. Particularly important are desires about one's own desires, for, as Frankfurt argues, the possibility of conflict between what one wants and what one wants to want makes possible some of the characteristic motivation of the moral agent. And it is clear in a general way that beliefs about one's beliefs and desires are rather like consciousness and that desires about one's beliefs are part of such things as self-deception. So a creature with second-order states of mind is likely to have a lot of mental structure, and to be capable of living the kind of complicated reflective life that a person lives.

Moreover the capacity to form a conception of oneself based on one's past experience and guiding one's future actions is crucial to the distinction between living a life and merely being alive, and can thus be seen to be necessary if a creature is to be of value as an individual. And to treat an individual as having this capacity to make its own life is to apply to it the value of autonomy, central to many moral theories.[3] When you add to this the fact that, given the intrinsic connections between the concepts of belief and desire, it is hard in principle to conceive of a creature with second-order beliefs not having some capacity for second-order desires, and vice versa, the result is that a good deal of what we would intuitively include in personhood can be made to follow from the possession of desires about one's own desires. Frankfurt takes persons to be just those creatures which have second-order desires about their own desires and which have desires about which of their desires should result in action.

I shall not develop Frankfurt's picture beyond this point, since his own writings are very readable and there are a number of good papers commenting on them. For my purposes, the important feature of Frankfurt's analysis is the way in which the question of personhood comes down simply to the propositional content of the agent's beliefs and desires. Nothing more is required for personhood than the capacity to have desires with a propositional content complex enough to represent the agent's own desires and their connection with action.

## *Argument One: A Concept of Oneself*

I shall present examples, in this section and the next, which are meant to show that the capacity to have desires with the right propositional contents cannot establish uncontroversial personhood. *No* definite condition we could set on the contents of desires—or, for that matter, of beliefs—could give all that would be needed. Neither Frankfurt's second-order volitions nor any variant idea will do the job.

The strategy for constructing the first example is to begin with a sentient non-person and to add capacities to it in such a way that Frankfurt's definition comes to be satisfied, although the resulting creature is not intuitively recognizable as a full or uncontroversial person. The strategy requires that one be able to conceive of a creature of a certain degree of mental complexity, but falling short

[3] See M. Tooley, *Abortion and Infanticide* (Oxford, 1983); R. Wollheim, *The Thread of Life* (Cambridge, 1984); I. Kant, *Groundwork of the Metaphysics of Morals* (Berlin, 1785), tr. H. J. Paton (London, 1964), pt. II; K. Graham, *The Battle of Democracy* (Brighton, 1986), ch. 5; R. Lindley, *Autonomy* (London, 1986).

of personhood. I shall assure that many higher mammals qualify: they have beliefs and desires and can think thoughts of some complexity, but are not persons.

Imagine a super-intelligent rabbit, that is, a creature biologically like a rabbit in physical and sensory organization but with vastly increased capacities of memory and inductive reasoning. I shall call this creature the hyperrabbit. Imagine further that the hyperrabbit is capable of using human language, either by the application of enormous inductive powers to her observations of human speech or thanks to the presence of an innate disposition to structure observed speech according to the 'right' syntactical forms. None of these capacities are beyond the biological potentialities of non-human mammals. (For all that, creatures like the hyperrabbit clearly do not exist on this planet, as becomes more evident below. But I argue later in the paper that the example is nearer the condition of actual creatures than one might at first think.) Such a creature would be capable of playing a role in human life, and I imagine her working in an office. The department of education, say, processing reports on the political opinions and statements of intellectuals.

Since the hyperrabbit can use language, she can use proper names correctly to refer to particular people, places, things, and animals. Animals include hyperrabbits, and she understands and uses the public name for herself. ('Hype', say.) And indeed documents about her pass across her desk occasionally, and her reports mention herself as well as others. She thus has beliefs about herself, and indeed beliefs about her own beliefs and desires, since her job is to report on intellectuals' opinions. And since her reports contain recommendations, she has desires about her own desires, which she wants to see translated into action. Her reports will contain recommendations such as: Morton and Hype are thoroughly reliable and their work is to be encouraged, but it would be desirable if their interest in pursuing their own work were more thoroughly subordinated to their civic duty.

She seems thus to have second-order desires, and to qualify for personhood. Her claim seems less strong, though, when we consider some features that I have deliberately omitted from her constitution.

First, although she can have beliefs and desires about herself, all that 'about herself' amounts to is that she understands her own name. She understands it in the way in which she understands the names of others, by having various beliefs which for the most part truly describe her, involving terms whose use traces back causally to her, and which are sufficiently similar to those of others that communication does not get snarled up. But that is not the way in which *we* have concepts of ourselves. The difference can be brought out by considering how a person normally answers a question such as 'where are you?' Imagine that Hype is on the telephone with a colleague who should bring her some data. The colleague asks where she is. To answer it Hype reasons as follows: ' "you" in this context is coextensive with "Hype" [*linguistic competence*]; Hype is an employee of the education ministry [*belief about self*] and in fact looking up under H in the ministry directory 'Hype' is listed as room 999 of the Joseph building; and during working hours Hype is found in that room [*belief about self*]; and so the report to give is that room 999 is Hype's location.' Now a human person might on occasion deduce their location in roughly that way, but normally a quite different class of considerations would apply. One would first think: *this* body is at this location in space, and so this is where I am. And then one would go on to find a useful description of this location in space. Hype cannot do it that way, for her conception of herself—the meaning she attaches to 'Hype', and to 'I' in suitable contexts, and which fills out her beliefs and desires about herself—is not essentially linked to any indexical: it is tied neither to 'the person associated with *this* body', nor 'the person at *this* location', nor even 'the person thinking *this* thought', in any way in which the indexical *this* requires a demonstrative awareness of one's immediate situation.

The other gap in Hype's constitution is closely related to this. Being basically a rabbit (in much the way in which a human person is basically a lemur) she has a rabbit's conception of self, alongside her sophisticated edifice of second order beliefs and desires. That shows itself in several ways. She has typical rabbit emotions such as fear and lust and parental concern. And these have primitively conceptualized contents: to fear something is to be apprehensive lest it harm *me*, where *me* is tied not to the sophisticated sense of 'Hype' but to a rabbit's bodily awareness. It governs impulses to get her body away from 'here'. And, similarly, she has desires whose content involves the primitive self-concept. If she wants a carrot then she wants that *she* have that carrot. But none of this is conceptualized, and we can simply take all these self-references as denoting 'here', 'this body', and so on, as the case demands. And so although she has emotions and desires which we might naturally elaborate using an 'I' on her behalf, that 'I' is misleading: it does not represent a concept which enters her thoughts or, in particular, her second-order beliefs and desires.

One result of this is that her second-order desires are not exactly those of ordinary persons. If an ordinary human person wants not to want a carrot the proposition which expresses the content of the second-order want would be

> I do not want that I eat a carrot,

where the 'I' represents that indexical description-free reference to self. But if Hype wants not to want a carrot the content of the second order want is

> Hype does not want that Hype eats a carrot,

which does not involve the primitive 'I'. As a result when Hype wants not to eat a carrot her second order desire cannot conflict with a first order desire to eat a carrot, whose content proposition would be

> I eat a carrot

or

> This rabbit eats a carrot

in the direct way in which the human person's second-order desire conflicts with the same first-order desire.

(This point can be put in a slightly different way using a device due to Castaneda. Castaneda would write 'Peter wants to eat a carrot', where the implicit subject of 'eat' is the indexical 'I', as

> Peter wants that he* eat a carrot.

Then the logical form of 'Peter wants not to want a carrot' would be expressed as

Peter wants that he* not want that he* eat a carrot.

But the most that can be truly asserted by saying that Hype wants not to want a carrot is the proposition which would be expressed by

Hype wants that Hype does not want that Hype eats a carrot

And the conflict between this and Hype's simple desire for a carrot, expressed in Castaneda style by

Hype wants that she* eat a carrot,

is pretty indirect, since the ultimately embedded propositions in the two cases are not negations of one another.)[4]

The essence of the situation is a certain dissociation in Hype's self-concept. There is the descriptive grasp of self involved in her higher-order beliefs and desires, and there is the indexical element involved in the more primitive parts of her psychology, but there is no conception which unifies the two. The result is in some ways rather machine-like and in others rather like a sage or a god: Hype sees herself impersonally as just one individual among others; her idea of herself is made of exactly the same materials as her ideas of others.[5]

One might think that Hype could construct a primitive 'I' for herself. She could answer 'where are you?', for example, by construing the indexical 'you' as 'the individual to whom these words are addressed' and 'I' as 'the individual who is speaking these words', so that she could take the question as asking for an utterance which identified the location of its utterer, and then think out loud 'these words are uttered in room 999, and words that Hype utters after them will have the same location, so an utterance

[4] See J. Perry, 'The Problem of the Essential Indexical', *Noûs*, 13 (1979), 3–21; id., 'Frege on Demonstratives', *Philosophical Review*, 86 (1977), 474–97; D. Lewis, 'Attitudes *De Dicto* and *De Re*', *Philosophical Review*, 87 (1980), 513–43; H. N. Castaneda, ' "He": A Study in the Logic of Self-Consciousness', *Ratio*, 8 (1966), 130–57.

[5] More God-like than sage-like, actually, since a Stoic sage, at any rate, has a thoroughly human sense of self, but does not attach much importance to it. See Engberg-Pedersen in this vol., ch. 5. Still, this disregard of something intrinsically human is a more delicate form of Hype's disassociation.

of "I am in room 999" will say, truly, what is asked for'.[6] And it is true that by mastering some standard demonstratives—here, now, this—some of the force of the indexical 'I' can be captured.

But not all of it. There seem to be two sources of trouble. The first is just the imprecision of the demonstratives. For example, agents normally know what they are doing, and Hype too has normal motor control which involves some representation of where her body is and what it is up to (and so, in this sense she does have a primitive representation of self, an 'I') as well as knowing by observation and other means what Hype's current actions are. But she cannot replace 'what I am doing' with 'this action', since there may be too many actions happening in the near vicinity. ('These actions.' Which actions? 'Well,' we would have to respond, 'these that *I*'m doing.') Similarly 'the individual uttering these words' is not really enough to capture 'me the speaker', since others may be speaking at the same time. (Which words? 'Mine, of course.')

There are unanswered questions here about how Hype can keep her first- and second-order states so separate. They are as much questions about human psychology as about Hype. How do ordinary human persons' second-order desires influence their first-order desires? How do desires with a descriptive content influence the largely indexical content of the intentions which shape action? How do our capacities to perceive qualities of things connect with conscious or verbal thought, to become part of the indexical component of conceptualized beliefs and desires? These questions are just as hard and confusing when asked about human beings as when asked about Hype. The last of them is particularly important here. We have more perceptual capacities than we are conscious of, or can put into words, and some of these capacities give content to some of our emotions and inarticulate desires. So we are not so different from Hype in this respect.

The second reason why 'I' cannot be synthesized out of easier demonstratives lies in our capacity for self-knowledge. Human persons know when they are unhappy, in pain, having indigestion, or imagining a holiday in Vienna. The result is that they have propositional beliefs about themselves—'I am unhappy', 'I am imagining a holiday in Vienna'—which need some conceptual grasp of the self, but which link it not to public descriptions but to a

[6] This is essentially Reichenbach's theory of indexical terms. See H. Reichenbach, *Elements of Symbolic Logic* (New York, 1948).

network of innate and acquired capacities of self-attribution. To believe that one is unhappy is to believe that '*this* individual is unhappy' where the *this* is, as in the examples above, really a pretty complex business and no improvement on an unexplained 'I'. A human person's self-attributions are often perspectival in this sense—perhaps illusory but a fairly basic part of what it is like to be human. They present themselves as if they were reports on an object, the self, on which the person has a privileged perspective.[7]

Human persons have the status of persons in part because they possess the characteristic grasp of self of human persons. Frankfurt is right to that extent, and it is surely one of the reasons that human persons are both moral agents, having capacities for self-evaluation and normative reflection, and objects of value to other agents. One fact basic to both is that we live lives that develop as unities in accordance with our developing conception of ourselves. But this human grasp of self is no single thing. It is certainly not the same as simply having a name one can apply to the individual who one happens to be. Nor is there any small and natural list of demonstrative capacities in terms of which it can be characterized. What then should we think of an agent who has *a* grasp of self, but not that characteristically human grasp of self? Hype, for example: is she a person? Two contrasting facts pull us in opposite directions. On the one hand what it is like to be Hype is extremely different from what it is like to be a human person. But on the other hand the life that she leads, the complex of things she can accomplish alone or with others, is not very different from ours. She could be a party to a social contract, and she could be a valued member of a community. I hope that it is clear by now what we should say. *If* there is no simple unity to the collection of skills that go into using and understanding 'I' and which are presupposed by the normal form of our second-order desires, and beliefs, then such individuals are neither clear persons nor clear non-persons, nor in any useful way in between. They are moral agents in some ways, and in others not, and they are objects of value in some ways and in others not. For moral agency and moral value are not themselves unsplittable conceptual atoms.

[7] If you need convincing that the indexical grasp of self in introspection is not the same as the indexical awareness of one's body and action, read D. C. Dennett's very entertaining 'Where am I?' in *Brainstorms*, pp. 310–23.

### *Argument Two: Personal Identity*

The example I built the first argument around is meant to undermine the synchronic aspect of the concept of a person, that is, it is meant to make you doubt that there is always an objective fact of the matter whether a particular individual at a particular time is a person or not. A number of writers, of whom Derek Parfit is the most successful, have tried to undermine the diachronic aspect of the concept. They have produced examples which are meant to lead you to doubt that it is always an objective matter whether a person at one time is the same as a person at a later time. These examples have a certain fantasy-like or science fictional quality to them. They involve brain transplants, matter transmitters, memory extracting machines, and the like. One might well grant them their intended point and still conclude that the identity-through-time of no *real* person will ever be indeterminate. The aim of this section is to produce an example of a situation which can and does happen to actual human beings, in which their identity is—or so I shall argue—indeterminate.

My cases are inspired by real cases found in neurological literature: people whose memory only extends back a few hours. I shall modify the details in the direction of a neatness which is medically extremely unlikely but not impossible: what I am describing could happen to human beings.[8]

I shall call my person Fred. Fred, as a result of alcoholism and bad luck, is struck by a peculiar form of Korsakoff's psychosis on the first of September 1980. For the rest of his life, his days follow the same general pattern: he wakes in the morning, thinking it must be the second of September 1980. The discovery that it is not is extremely distressing to him, but he is a person of emotional resilience as well as of formidable intellect, and during the day he comes to terms with his situation, to the extent of grasping roughly what it is, and even, on some days, gathering the outline of 'his'

[8] See H. Gardner, *The Shattered Mind* (New York, 1975), ch. 5; O. Sacks, *The Man Who Mistook his Wife for a Hat* (London, 1985), ch. 2; and, though it presents a rather different case, A. Luria, *The Man with a Shattered World* (London, 1973). On personal identity in general see D. Parfit, *Reasons and Persons* (Oxford, 1984), pt III. Parfit's purpose is ultimately not to make one doubt the intelligibility of personal identity as much as its importance. S. Shoemaker and R. Swinburne, *Personal Identity* (Oxford, 1984), brings out clearly the centrality of the sense of self-identity in our intuitions about the identities of persons.

history since September 1980. And then in the evening he sleeps, and the memories of that day are swept into oblivion.

Fred's case differs from actual periodic amnesias in the tidy coincidence of the time through which memory is preserved with the sleeping/waking cycle. This coincidence is also found in some fictional variations on the same idea.[9] It does not affect the issues involved. But it does make the situation much more easily imagined, partly because many of us who habitually wake in a state of disorientation which can take hours to dissipate often find ourselves in a mildly analogous condition. Parfit refers to cases much like these as 'branch line' cases, not dwelling on the fact that they are much more easily realized than many of his other cases.

There are two ways of reacting to cases like Fred's. One of them is implicit in the way I have told the story and obviously comes very naturally. Call it the linear version: there is a person and *he* is terribly damaged and then later *he* spends each day without any memories of the day before. According to the linear version Fred is one person throughout, and Fred at any one time has a radical lack of memories of immediately earlier times. The other way of telling the story comes less easily as a narrative, but makes sense as a description or an analysis. Call it the branching version: there is a person Fred-0 who is terribly damaged, and thereafter there is a succession of persons associated with Fred-0's ageing body. Call them Fred-1, Fred-2, Fred-3, . . . Each Fred-*n* is a continuation of Fred-0, but each Fred-*n* and Fred-*m* are distinct (when *n* and *m* are distinct). According to the branching version Fred is not so much damaged as fragmented into a series of people.

The linear version is the natural way to tell the story. (But then stories are linear things.) It also fits a lot of what would be said. Fred's children going to visit him say 'I'm going to see Fred again. I hope he has got over the cold he had yesterday.' But the branching version also fits a lot of what we would say and do. If Fred on one day makes a promise to do something the next day and then does not, we would not berate him or even remind him of it. The promise is as if made by someone else. In fact, one would avoid receiving promises from Fred, just as one would rather avoid receiving promises from someone who one knows will die before he

[9] See A. Budrys, 'The End of Summer', in B. Aldis (ed.), *Penguin Science Fiction* (Harmondsworth, 1961); P. J. Farmer, 'Sketches among the Ruins of my Mind', in H. Harrison (ed.), *Nova 3* (London, 1973), 150–92.

can fulfil them. And if one made a promise to Fred and then found that one could not keep it, one would not apologize to the next day's Fred or feel that one owed *him* some recompense, although one might well feel a guilty debt to the Fred of the day before. Similarly, one would not hold successive Freds responsible for the misdeeds of previous Freds, or in fact assume that any of the moral connections between earlier and later stages of a person's life hold of the succession of Freds.

And to balance the narrative naturalness of the linear version there is the emotional appositeness of the branching version. To a friend or relative grieving over the difficulty of maintaining a relationship with someone who does not remember one day what he has done or said the day before one could, and surely at some stage would, argue that the relationship is misdirected: it would be gentler on all concerned to think of the enterprise as a series of encounters with the person one loved and loves, each presenting one with another day's continuation of that person but each disconnected from the others.

Both linear and branching versions can seem right, and there are both physical facts and social intuitions to support each. And each one can to some extent accommodate the intuitions that support the other. The linear version can accommodate the pro-branching intuitions I described just above by appealing to a distinction between what is emotionally convenient to think and what is actually true. And the branching version has two ways of accommodating some of the force of the impulse to say, e.g., that one visited Fred yesterday and will visit him again tomorrow. One way is to construe the pronoun here as one would the 'he' in 'I talked to the Dean of Arts last year, and when the same problem arose this year I went to him again', when it is a different Dean from the one year to the next. And the other is to distinguish between 'same person' and 'same human being': one visited Fred yesterday and will visit the same human being tomorrow, but unfortunately the same human being will not be the same person.

Which one is really right? It should be clear by now, that in the absence of facts or arguments of some completely new kind, the only reasonable course is to accept that both are legitimate ways of seeing the situation. Is Fred-36 the same person as Fred-37? Or, to put the same question in a less natural form, is Fred-37-plus-Fred-

38 a (temporal part of) a continuing person? The concept of a person is not up to answering the question. 'Yes', 'No', and 'To some extent', are equally wrong answers; the only right answers begin with 'it depends what you mean by . . .'.

### *Second Case into First Case*

The case of fragmented Fred can be made to approach that of heterogeneous Hype, though only by giving it a little of the science fictional quality of the earlier example. Suppose that each morning Fred is first given an understanding of his condition and then a summary of his life since his amnesia. (Imagine that Fred is valued for his unique skills as a government decision-maker and negotiator. Each day there is a new problem that only Fred can handle, but in order to handle it he has to be briefed, and the briefing must include a fair amount of his past history.) Enough information about his past, absorbed thoroughly enough, will give an approximation to the continuity his broken memory-links cannot supply. Extra-ordinary intellectual power would be needed to manage a good approximation. Postulate the required intellectual power, which would certainly be beyond the ordinary human scale. Is the result—Hyperfred—then a single continuing human person?

Again the answer seems to be 'it depends what you mean by . . .'. A person is something that lives a life, and a life is something that is knitted together over time in part by the agent's organization of it, her capacity to turn her past into her future.[10] Human persons do this largely by virtue of their ability to remember their pasts. This ability makes a person relatively independent of others for her knowledge of who, historically, she is. And it presents the relevant information in an agent-centred way: a person does not have to sift through all her beliefs about elephants in order to tell whether she rode an elephant last week; she can just remember what she was doing then. Memory information is filed as a special subset of one's information about the world, accessible by different means and presented in a form suitable for making a unity of one's actions. As a result, Hyperfred in the modified example will differ from human persons both in his dependence on others (or possibly on

[10] See Wollheim, *Thread of Life*.

mechanical devices) to connect him to 'his' past and in his lack of a distinction between his beliefs about the world-in-general and his beliefs about himself.

Hyperfred and Hype are thus very similar. In fact, since Fred's situation is biologically possible for human beings and since Hyperfred results from Fred simply by the addition of intellectual power, we now have a way of imagining what it is like to be a creature like Hype. First imagine that you lose your memory in the way that Fred has. (I do not think that is very hard to imagine. Terrifying, but not difficult.) And then imagine that each morning you are given and absorb your biography for the time between the onset of your amnesia and the present. (That too is not hard to imagine in principle, just because what one's imagination grasps is the absorbing of vastly less information than would actually be necessary.) Then, after both steps, what one is imagining is the condition of a creature very similar to Hype: all one's second-order beliefs and desires, except those about this day's acts and states, are non-indexical and non-perspectival.

Hyperfred's claims to personhood seem much the same as Hype's. And so if either of them is a person Fred is a potential or quasi-person. And in all three cases it is really the same aspect of human personhood which is lacking: the human capacity to have a concept of self which is linked to a complex of very specific ways of obtaining information about oneself. But one's intuitive willingness to accept Hyperfred and Hype as persons can be rather different. Many people find they want to classify Fred and Hyperfred as persons and exclude Hype. Yet there is not much difference between Hype and Hyperfred when both are described abstractly. The details that make them different leave a lot of room for human sympathy for Fred and Hyperfred, though. Should this be relevant to their moral status? It depends what you are going to use the status for.

### *Biology versus Imagination?*

It may well seem that my arguments so far—and they are the main arguments of the paper—amount to just a quibble about something pretty marginal to our conception of a person. I think that this is not so. Let me try to develop the worry into an objection, so that in dealing with the objection we can see how fundamental the problems I am raising are.[11]

To begin, it may seem that the gap I have pointed out in the Frankfurtian concept of a person is easily filled: to the possession of second-order beliefs and desires (and volitions) one needs just to add a requirement that persons have indexical thoughts about their present and past states.

But this cannot be right. Hype has indexical thoughts about her present and past states, inasmuch as she can think about 'this body' and the mental and physical states it supports, and she is not at all obviously a person. And Hyperfred lacks the capacity to have some important indexical thoughts about his past, but it is not at all clear that he is not a person. So just having some indexical thoughts about oneself cannot be enough. They have to be the *right* ones. And how can this be specified except in such question-begging terms as 'the indexical thoughts that normal humans have'?

What is needed is a general specification of the kind of *combination* of indexical capacities that is characteristic of a person's grasp of self. The capacities that normal human beings have keep them in touch with a self which has an immediate spatial location, a past history, a present flow of thought and activity, and a future of projected actions. The capacity for this combination of indexical thoughts is not a luxury for a creature that is going to act in the physical world and carry out tasks that take a long time to finish. And so—one might argue—evolutionary pressures are likely to result in creatures with capacities to co-ordinate direct awareness of such things as their locations, the actions of their bodies, and their planned future actions. Thus even though it may be very hard to say in a sufficiently general way what the right combination of capacities is, it is biologically necessary—according to this line of thought—that there must *be* a constrained set of right combinations of capacities.

I think there is something right about this form of the objection. It focuses on what a person does rather than on what a person is. It makes the Wollheimian point that some of our primary intuitions concern the kind of life that a person can live, which involves action governed by reasoning, desires governable by reflection, and

[11] This objection was put to me at the Aberystwyth conference by Peter Smith and Troels Engberg-Pedersen.

intentions governed by memory, in order to fill out a constantly changing plan. A person is something that can have such a life.

To accept this is not, however, to accept that there is any right combination of capacities which underlies a person's grasp of themself. (Or even any right set of combinations.) For one thing, it is not at all clear that the life of a person requires a particular kind of psychological organization. I do not myself think it impossible for us to discover (or be discovered by) a species clearly living as persons—communicating with each other with something like speech, forming social institutions, creating works of art—but who seem to have a psychology resisting the concepts of belief and desire, let alone of second-order desire and of human-like self-conception. I will not try to argue for such a dramatic conclusion now. In the special case of a person's grasp of self, however, something of the kind is not hard to make plausible.

Hype and Hyperfred are unnatural creations. The argument at hand suggests that creatures like them can only exist in imagination. That is far from obvious. Consider Hyperfred. His characteristic difference from a normal human being is that his contact with his past passes through the assimilation of facts rather than first-person 'from the inside' experiential memory. He never relives his past, but just knows that various things were true in it. Could no natural animal be like this? That is, could a creature not have all its knowledge of its past in terms of factual knowledge rather than first-person memory? Just to ask the question is to wonder what counts as memory. And it does not take philosophical or psychological sophistication to doubt that there is much biological unity to all the things that are commonsensically classified as memory. Human persons typically remember their past in (at least) three distinct ways. They can re-experience events, having replicas or representations of the original experiences. They have a great deal of knowledge of vital identifying and signposting facts about themselves. (Presumably experiential memory would be a confusing jumble without the presence of this knowledge.) And they have an accumulation of skills, learned in the past and reusable to varying degrees. Any great discontinuity in any of these would count as amnesia. In human psychology they are distinct, and no one of them need be a neurological unity.[12] And the grasp that different

[12] See K. V. Wilkes, 'More Brain Lesions', *Philosophy*, 55 (1980), 455–70.

humans have of their pasts may well vary in its dependence on these various different capacities.

The same is true of any of the capacities I mentioned as being employed in a person's life: reasoning, reflection, intention, memory. None of them are inevitable biological unities. And the presence in a creature of the behavioural capacities that they represent in us need not rest on anything like the same complex of psychological functions which give their contribution to what it is like to be a human person.

That is my main defence against the threatening argument, and I derive my final conclusion from it below. Before stating that, though, I think it may help strengthen the intuitive case to consider an example, again of a possible creature, of a quite different sort. This one has *more* indexical capacities intrinsic to its concept of itself than we do. Imagine, adapting a suggestion of Lewis Thomas's,[13] a dog-like creature with a capacity to tell non-inferentially the degree of genetic relatedness to itself of any member of its species. A creature of this species can locate itself non-inferentially in genetic space and consequently thinks of itself as, among other things 'the individual with *this* genetic constitution', thus relating itself to parents, siblings, and possible descendants. (There would be an obvious biological advantage to this.)

Such a creature might think conceptually, have second-order desires, and live the life of a person together with others of its kind. The capacity I have mentioned could be basic to some part of this life, making it richer than ours, and it might allow the creature to live the life of a person without the use of some capacities which for us are essential. (Perhaps some kinds of human memory might be lacking.) From this creature's point of view creatures like us would lack a very basic element of personhood. A human does not know who he is, in a very basic way. Humans lack a fundamental component of 'I', the capacity to know of a certain node in a genealogy that that is *me*, and as a result the best that human beings can have is a bloodless over-abstract conception of themselves, not tied to any capacity to know which biological individuals they are. Or so my creatures would say.

To end, let me return to the claim with which I began this paper, that we import biologically parochial features into our picture of

[13] *The Youngest Science* (Oxford, 1985), ch. 19.

personhood. We can now see two ways in which this happens. One is, of course, the assumption that there is a simple unity to our indexical self-grasping skills. The other is the assumption that a creature capable of living a life structured like ours must have a psychology like ours. In fact there are indefinitely many ways both in which a creature can gain the capacity for a richly structured life and in which it can organize its capacity to have thoughts about itself. And if the way in which it does either is sufficiently different to the way in which we do it we find ourselves unable to classify them as persons.

The concept of a person can therefore be developed in either of two directions, and its problems come from the way it is caught between them. They are (1) the capacity to lead the life of a person and (2) the quality of having experience like that of a human person. (The capacity to have human-like indexical thoughts is part of (2): if a creature has the right combination of indexical thoughts, then what it is like to be it will in this respect be like what it is like to be a human person.) Both (1) and (2) capture some important features of personhood. We may think of (1)-type persons (for example Hype) as potential members of social contracts and potential formulators of the categorical imperative. And we may think of (2)-type persons as having a special if mysterious intrinsic value our reverence for which underlies our reluctance to harm or destroy small children or the various Freds, whether or not they are capable of living a planned, extended, contract-making life.

We cannot centre personhood on the (2) aspect, for very few of the creatures whose lives we may come to value and balance against our own will have just our combination of capacities. What it is like to be most of them is just beyond our imaginations. And we cannot centre personhood on the (1) aspect for several reasons. First, this would leave out cases like the Freds which seem intuitively to have a lot of the importance of personhood. Then there is the enormous variety of ways in which an individual in a community may be capable of leading a structured person-like life. Then also there is the indefiniteness of this conception of a person-like life: is it lived by hermits or by the insane or the amoral, let alone by the participants in the more remote social arrangements possible elsewhere in space and time? For all these reasons there really is not a very managable concept centred on (2) for all that (1)-type considerations would often lead us to treat creatures *as* persons.

So there is nothing we can analyse and define and present as '*the* concept of a person'. Nothing whose sense will settle in advance the status of all the beings we might value for the reasons we value human persons. For these values are not any single thing. And possible creation is too varied. Not to see this is to think that all advanced creatures must be humans in disguise. To think this is not only to reveal a limited imagination, but also to miss some of the richness of what it is like to be, and how it is good to be, human.

# 3

# Human Persons

*Peter Smith*

## I

We can imagine that, not so many years ago, we were astounded to discover that we do not all belong to the same biological kind. It was found, let us suppose, that we comprise two superficially very similar but distinct species whose genetic materials code for significantly different neural fine structures (perhaps two evolutionary pathways have converged to produce different realizations of the same main structures of mental organization). These two species are indeed quite separate, incapable of interbreeding; this had escaped detection over the ages because the selection of mates is sufficiently well guided by subconscious cues to make infertile couples relatively uncommon. Successful breeding apart, however, we have all lived a common life together, sharing the familiar human world.

This fantasy is an extremely modest one by science fiction standards and is surely entirely coherent. It is enough to remind us that it is an empirical, not a conceptual, issue whether we do indeed all belong to the same species. In other words, to be one of us is not, as a matter of a priori analysis, to be a member of a particular biologically defined kind. But neither is it to be a member of some very abstractly characterized category, such as the category of intelligent thinking beings capable of reason and reflection. Of course, it is plain that the pronoun 'we' does not have the same content as any non-indexical general term, whether from biological science or elsewhere: but this truism is not what I am driving at. The idea is rather that someone counts as one of us partly because he or she is of a certain general kind, and it is this general

---

My thanks to audiences at the universities of Aberdeen, Dundee, Edinburgh, Keele, and Stirling for very helpful reactions to an earlier version of this paper, and to George Botterill, O. R. Jones, Gregory McCulloch, and Adam Morton for generous written comments. Particular thanks are due to Christopher Gill for encouraging me to write the paper in the first place.

(non-indexical) kind introduced by the (indexical) 'we' which—I claim—is neither scientific nor highly abstract. I explain.

To think of a being as one of us, as included within the scope of 'we', is to think of that being as standing in the Right Relation (whatever precisely that is) to you and me. Later, I will be saying something about the character of the Right Relation: but it is clear at the outset that it is not a relation that can sensibly be supposed to obtain between things of just any sort. Contrast the relation that holds between two things if the first is mentioned in the Aristotelian corpus before the second: the individual Anaxagoras, the element water, the virtue of courage, and the number one are all relata of this promiscuous relation. On any sane view, however, the Right Relation is a lot more choosy: an element, a virtue, a number are not even candidates for being one of us. There are a priori limits on the sort of relata which can stand in the Right Relation; in other words, there is some reasonably circumscribed kind—though not necessarily a 'natural kind' in the standard sense—membership of which is an a priori condition for being one of us. Membership of this kind may not be a sufficient condition, however: for it seems that we must allow the possibility that there may be other beings which are of the Right Kind but which do not in fact stand in the Right Relation to you and me.

The schematic picture, therefore, is this: a being counts as one of us—in the intended sense—if it stands in the Right Relation to you and me, and this requires it to be something of the Right Kind. And the thesis I am aiming for is equally schematic: the Right Kind is neither, as matter of a priori analysis, a biological kind nor a highly abstract kind capable of being instantiated by radically non-human creatures (angels or Alpha Centaurians). As we have already seen, the first half of this thesis is quickly secured. By hypothesis, you and I are of the Right Kind; but the evident coherence of the fiction with which I began shows that it is not a priori that you and I both belong to the same biological species. The second half of the thesis may initially seem less certain. It might be suggested, for example, that to be of the Right Kind is just a matter of belonging to the abstract type *thinking being*; and a thinking being such as an angel or Alpha Centaurian fails to count as one of us, not because it is of the wrong general kind, but because it doesn't stand in the Right Relation to you and me. On reflection, however, this suggestion is problematic. Suppose that kind *K* is such that it is possible for there to be something of this sort which evidently couldn't stand in the Right Relation to us: then a specification of kind *K* cannot include all the a priori requirements for being a relatum of the Right Relation. In other words, kind *K* is not yet the Right Kind. Hence it should at least make sense to suppose, of anything which *is* of the Right Kind, that it *could* have stood in the Right Relation to us. But now consider: does it really make sense to suppose of any alien intelligence whatever that, although it isn't one of us, it could have been? Suppose that Alpha Centaurians have the size and something of the superficial structure of large forests: could such a being become fully 'one of us' in an unqualified sense? Surely not. Likewise, does it make sense to suppose of an angel that, although it isn't one of us, it could have been? Again it seems not. The best we can do is imagine an angel animating a human form, and this composite being dwelling among us undetected; but that would still not make the angel really one of us. Simulating an embodied life of our kind is not living such a life. Hence the Right Kind cannot be so wide as to include angels or Alpha Centaurians.[1]

## II

The Right Kind, I therefore claim, is neither narrowly biological nor very broadly abstract. I have no doubt arrived at this conclusion far too quickly, not least because there are obvious problems about the way in which the notions of the Right Relation and the Right Kind have been introduced. But let me postpone tackling these problems for a moment, and assume that the argument so far can be made cogent. Then the obvious next question is: just what *is* the Right Kind?

It is already plain that neither of the two obvious candidates will do. We might say: someone counts as one of us if he shares the human world of interpersonal relationships with you and me—and the Right Kind of being to share the human world is, of course, a human being. But the notion of a human being is nowadays tied tightly to biology (Amélie Rorty: 'The notion of a human being is a notion of a biologically defined entity'[2]). And it makes sense, as we

[1] The claims made in this paragraph need, however, to be qualified in the light of n. 16 below.

[2] 'Persons and *Personae*', p. 36 above. This purely biological understanding of the notion of a human being is stipulative: but it is a stipulation which has become

noted at the outset, to imagine our living a human life together with creatures of a significantly different biological make-up; such creatures would be of the Right Kind but, in virtue of their biology, they would not count as humans. Alternatively, we might say: someone counts as one of us if he shares the human world of interpersonal relationships with you and me—and the Right Kind of being to enter into interpersonal relationships is, of course, a person. And there must surely be something right about this: it seems compelling to say that what someone shares with you and me *qua* being 'one of us' is—in some sense—personhood. However, conceptions of personhood as they have featured in much philosophical discussion seem too wide. I have already alluded to Locke's familiar definition of a person as a thinking being capable of reason and reflection: on this definition, even supernatural beings such as angels would count as persons although they are plainly not (I have argued) of the Right Kind. Or, to move to our own times, consider P. F. Strawson's classic discussion, where the concept of a person is understood to be 'the concept of a type of entity such that *both* predicates ascribing states of consciousness and predicates ascribing corporeal characteristics, a physical situation etc. are equally applicable to an individual entity of that type'.[3] This understanding at least debars essentially immaterial beings from counting as persons, but it is still far too inclusive for our purposes. The most alien of beings imagined by science fiction writers (e.g. the dendritic Alpha Centaurians) can, it seems, count as Strawsonian persons although they are by very deliberate invention not of the Right Kind to be capable of being or becoming one of us. Consider thirdly the Frankfurtian concept of a person as the subject of second-order mental states: this too can apparently encompass radically alien beings, and so is again too wide a concept.[4]

The Right Kind, then, is neither so narrow as the biological kind *human being*, nor so broad as *person* (at least as that has typically been understood by philosophers): but if both these candidates are

fairly standard and which I will follow. But I agree with those who would argue that we have a concept of a human being which isn't tied to biology: this is just the concept of a *human person* which I am about to explore.

[3] *Individuals* (London, 1959), 101–2.

[4] H. Frankfurt, 'Freedom of the Will and the Concept of a Person', *Journal of Philosophy*, 68 (1971), 5–20, repr. in G. Watson (ed.), *Free Will* (Oxford, 1982), 81–110. But again, cf. n. 16 below.

ruled out, we might seem to be left with nothing familiar to play the role of being the Right Kind. What to do?

I shall be arguing that what we need here is some less biological notion of the human, some less abstract notion of a person—the idea (shall we say) of a *human person*, understood neither very abstractly, nor scientifically, but in terms of its typical *bios*, its manner of living. The thought that we have need of such a notion is hardly original and is surely attractive, yet it remains underplayed. Much later, in section VII, I will briefly discuss whether there also remains a role for a more sweepingly inclusive notion of a person; but my main concern in this paper is with the credentials of the restricted notion.

## III

But first, we must backtrack. For the question 'What is the Right Kind?'—that is, the question 'What is the Right Kind of being to be a relatum of the Right Relation'—is only worth pursuing if the notion of the Right Relation is in good order, and that may very well be doubted. So we need to think rather more (and indeed, much more than is usual) about uses of the pronoun 'we' and the correlative phrase 'one of us'.[5]

Plainly, uses of the pronoun are many and various. For a start, the intended scope of 'we' can vary very widely from context to context—sometimes the pronoun covers the most limited and ephemeral gathering (those around my dinner table tonight, those at today's faculty meeting), sometimes much broader and less transient groupings (philosophers, English speakers). And 'we' can embrace more than just people: we all went to the beach yesterday, including the dog, and some of us went swimming, again including the dog. More inclusively still, we may speak for wider groups of creatures: 'We mammals are threatened by the continued depletion of atmospheric ozone'. Now, these very trite reminders already raise a problem for what has gone before: for they suggest that the use of 'we' that I made earlier (very broadly inclusive but barring

[5] As noted above, it is compelling to say that persons are what we are: so my strategy is, in effect, to try to extract some conclusions about our core notion of personhood from reflections about our conception of what it is to be 'one of us'. It might be supposed that this conception is not substantial enough to bear any philosophical weight. But I hope to show otherwise.

the dog) is just one among indefinitely many, and it needs argument that my particular use deserves to be given special philosophical weight.

A much more interesting distinction can—on the face of it—be drawn between what I will call relation-based and property-based uses of 'we'. I took it earlier that, in thinking of a being as 'one of us', we are thinking of that being as standing in the Right Relation (whatever that might be) to you and me: so in this case I was assuming that the domain of the associated 'we' is fixed as being the class of those who stand in a certain relation to the speaker, and maybe to the audience as well. Such cases are common enough. For example, the context may make it clear that a particular use of 'we' covers just the speaker's immediate family, i.e. just those who are closely related to him. But there are other kinds of case: suppose someone says 'We are all at risk from high-sided lorries' where the context makes it clear that 'we' covers the speaker's fellow cyclists (or perhaps he explicitly says 'We cyclists . . .'). Here, the domain of the 'we' is fixed as those who share the property of being a cyclist, and relations to the speaker apparently don't enter into it.

But doesn't this flatten the distinction between 'We cyclists are *F*' and the non-indexical 'Cyclists are *F*'? Not so. The former says much the same as 'Cyclists—and as I speak as one—are *F*', and this is naturally regimented as 'I am a cyclist and cyclists are *F*': thus understood, the composite proposition is indeed indexical, in virtue of its first conjunct—but the domain of the generality in the second conjunct is fixed non-indexically. This contrasts with a relation-based claim of the form 'We are all *G*', which is naturally regimented into the form 'I am *G* and all who are *R* to me are *G*', where the domain of the generality itself is fixed indexically.

It might be objected that, in the supposedly relation-based case where 'we' covers the speaker's family, we could as well suppose that the scope of the pronoun is fixed as those who share the property of being (say) one of the Smiths. But if someone has the property of being one of the Smiths this is in virtue of standing in the right familial relations with some others (though we needn't suppose the latter reference group is rigidly fixed): so the domain of the original pronoun is still ultimately determined relationally. Again, it might be objected that, in the supposedly property-based case where 'we' covers cyclists in general, we could as well suppose that the domain of the pronoun is fixed as those who stand in the relation of being a fellow cyclist to the speaker (indeed, isn't that how I initially put it?) But this relation can apparently be decomposed: *X* is a fellow cyclist of *Y* just in virtue of *X* being a cyclist and *Y* being a cyclist. So the domain of 'we (cyclists)' is still ultimately fixed by a shared property. The distinction between the relation-based and property-based cases doesn't collapse *that* easily.

With this distinction to hand, we can now pose another problem about the earlier discussion. I there took a certain sweeping use of 'we' to invoke what I called the Right Relation, and so construed the generality in a proposition like 'We all belong to the same species' as relation-based. But now that we have noted the existence of 'we' generalizations whose domain is understood as determined by a shared property, then surely—it will be said—it is at least as natural to construe the sweeping use of 'we' on this second model: and then we will no longer need to invoke the Right Relation.

We therefore have two questions to consider. First, isn't my earlier generic use of 'we' just one among many, with no special status? Second, is there any need to give a relation-invoking treatment of that use? I will take these issues in the reverse order.

## IV

Suppose that the distinction between relation-based and property-based uses of 'we' is well founded: it might be suggested, however, that the distinction is in the end of little interest in the present context. After all, suppose I was wrong to treat the relevant use of 'we' as invoking the Right Relation, and thus wrong to introduce the schematic notion of the Right Kind in the way I did. The alternative is to take the coverage of 'we' as fixed by a shared property; and won't this immediately reintroduce the idea of something's being of the appropriate kind to be 'one of us'? Either way of construing the pronoun introduces some property shared by the individuals in question; either way, we get to the centrally important question of what the relevant property of personhood precisely amounts to. So does it really matter which route we take, which way we construe the pronoun?

It does. For remember that, on the relation-based construal, we are members of the Right Kind but perhaps not (as far as any a priori considerations determine) the only members of the Right

Kind. The inhabitants of an actual Twin Earth, although not included in the domain of the use of 'we' which concerns us,[6] may yet share with us enough intrinsic characteristics to be fellow members of the Right Kind. By contrast, on the shared-property construal, just those within the domain of 'we' will be members of the relevant kind: Twin Earthers are excluded. Hence the first construal but not the second implies that what we qualitatively share *qua* being 'one of us' may, for all we know, also be shared by non-terrestrials, an implication which accords with a very familiar pair of thoughts, namely (1) that what we share is (in some sense) personhood, and (2) that there may, for all we know, be non-terrestrial persons.

The property-based construal requires the shared property to be such that we all possess it and Twin Earthers don't: and how can that be guaranteed? Consider three ways of trying to pull off the trick: first, an obviously indexical property like being-Right-Related-to-you-and-me will certainly serve to rule out the Twin Earthers. But the idea that we are grouped together by such a property immediately takes us back to the relation-based reading of 'we'. Second, on the assumption that we and the Twin Earthers have different evolutionary histories, it follows from a plausible view about the identity of biological natural kinds that we and the Twin Earthers belong to different natural kinds: so can such *origin-defined kinds* provide a better model for the sort of property needed? Hardly so, given that there is no a priori guarantee that we earthlings in fact share the same origins.[7] As a third shot at finding some property which could sustain the property-based reading, we could try taking the relevant property to be that of being a *terrestrial F*, for some suitable (non-biological) *F*. But although this bars the Twin Earthers, it could in principle still include too many—e.g. terrestrial quasi-humans such as hobbits. And in any

[6] For instance, the supposition that we *do* all belong to the same species is not vulnerable to refutation by the existence of Twin Earthers.

[7] If we suppose that we are members of some origin-defined kind, we also run up against the plausible general point that we shouldn't ultimately base moral discriminations upon membership of such kinds. If others have the same mode of life, have just the same capacities and dispositions, and behave in just the same way, then shouldn't it be irrelevant whether they ultimately share the same origins? And this latter point generalizes: in other words, there seems to be no obvious way of developing the property-based construal which readily squares with the familiar thought that what we share *qua* being 'one of us' is of fundamental moral significance.

case, 'terrestrial' here must be construed indexically, as specifying *this* planet rather than its twin: hence the suggestion is that we are constituted as a group by being appropriately related to this planet. But then why should this be thought any improvement on the idea behind the original relation-based proposal, namely that we are grouped together in virtue of being appropriately related to each other?

Such considerations strongly suggest that we should adopt the relation-based reading of the generic 'we' which concerns us. It would perhaps be unwise to insist that these considerations are absolutely decisive or that our pre-philosophical usage suffices completely to fix the proper construal; the exercise here must frankly be one of theoretical regimentation rather than analysis of an antecedently fully determinate practice. Take my claim, therefore, to be that the relation-based regimentation is significantly the more attractive and plausible.

Yet maybe this claim *can* be pushed further. For it can be argued that on reflection the alternative property-based construal of certain 'we' propositions is revealed as merely superficial. Consider again the schematic 'We cyclists are *F*': that sort of assertion is presumably not intended to cover (say) Twin Earth riders of pedal bicycles—so why not analyse it along the lines of 'Those among us who ride bicycles [and I am one] are *F*'? Here the relative clause serves to select a subclass from among us, where the coverage of the generic 'us' is arguably to be determined as those standing in the Right Relation to you and me. And once we suspect that some restricted uses of 'we' can be regimented by using a relative clause to cut out part of the domain of a generic use, we might try imposing this sort of regimentation more generally. For example, why not read 'We [those here at the faculty meeting] should deplore the staffing losses' as roughly 'Those of us [very broadly construed] who are here—and I speak as one—should deplore the losses'? This tactic would impose a tidy discipline on a variety of uses of 'we', treating them uniformly as involving a generic, wide-ranging use plus explicit or implicit restrictions. That leaves over the dog-including case to be dismissed as mildly deviant exaggeration, and the cases of (as it were) 'speaking for the biosphere' can perhaps be regarded just as rhetorical variants on a plain universal quantifications over mammals or whatever.

Be all that as it may. For however we handle the cases that

initially invite a property-based treatment, the considerations in favour of a relation-based construal at least of the sweeping use of 'we' can stand: and even if the suggested regimentation of the narrower uses is too procrustean for one's taste, the underlying idea that some generic use has a non-arbitrarily privileged status seems defensible (and here I touch on the other of the two problems raised in the last section). Consider the cyclists again: when we talk about 'us cyclists'—or indeed about plain 'cyclists'—the question of non-terrestrial riders of bicycles (if such there be) normally just doesn't arise; nor, come to that, are we concerned with trained chimpanzees, cycling robots, or any other oddities. Pressed, then, to specify who we *are* talking about, what should we say? To reply that we are talking about those riders who are persons (philosophers' broad sense) won't do, for that could let in the Twin Earthers. To reply that we are talking about those riders who are human beings is better; indeed it is no doubt true that the cyclists in question are biologically speaking members of the human species (and an indexical treatment of natural kinds could rule out Twin Earthers from belonging to the very same species). Still, it is not in virtue of belonging to a particular species that a given bicycle-riding creature counts within the intended coverage of our talk about cyclists—recall our initial fantasy that those with whom we share our life (including outings on our bicycles!) may not all be members of the same species. It is surely being one of us, sharing our human life, that actually matters here: the domain of 'we cyclists', or equally of most uses of 'all cyclists', is thus naturally understood as carved out from the domain of a generic 'we'. Whatever the problems raised by this generic use, it seems central and indispensable.

## V

Let's take it, then, that the use of 'we' that concerns us is to be given a relation-based treatment: a being counts as one of us if he or she stands in the Right Relation to you and me. But what is the Right Relation?

The obvious answer, as I have already implied, is something along the following—rather limply Wittgensteinian—lines: someone stands in the Right Relation to count as one of us if he shares with us enough of the human world constituted by interpersonal relationships. But this answer will need to be understood correctly if we are to eliminate the appearance of blankly unhelpful circularity ('a *person* is someone who can have inter*personal* relations'). So take talk of interpersonal relations to be a place holder for some set of independently specifiable relationships: Jack and Jill talk to each other, habitually read each other's face and gestures, go out together for meals, lend each other books, laugh together at the same silent movies, occasionally play tennis, and so on and so forth—these and many more are the sorts of ties which go to make up the web of our shared human life.

It is evident that such human ties are themselves interrelated by complex links of interdependency. To take just one case, playing tennis together is obviously not just a matter of banging balls about. Jack and Jill must each have some understanding of the point of such activities, and enough understanding of the basic rules of this particular game. If they are to get along adequately, they must also share a grasp of the acceptable modes of on-court conduct—which presupposes a grasp of the acceptable modes of conduct more generally. And this point that the shared experience of playing tennis requires a wider context of mutual understanding can be extended in less obvious ways. For example, Jack and Jill will need to find sense in each other's gestures and posture and facial expression. For imagine trying to play opposite a figure whose movements seem utterly robotic and alien, whose face never expresses any recognizable reaction or emotion, whose very posture seems not just inhuman but unlike any animal we know: we could not feel at ease with such a being—and while it may efficiently return the balls across the net, we would have the sense of banging balls *at* it, rather than of participating *with* it in a shared experience. (We need not worry whether we should still describe what is being done by the Martian across the net as 'playing tennis'; the point is that the experience of playing tennis is for us embedded in a shared understanding of face and gesture—along with very much more—and the game's role in human life would be quite different were it otherwise.)

The rather trite observation that the particular activity of playing tennis is inseparable from a rich context of mutual understanding invites generalization: it is plausible to claim that the ties that constitute our shared human world all engage with our intentional understanding of each other. It doesn't follow, of course, that this mutual understanding is—so to speak—the underlying real essence of the surface phenomena of the human world (as if the talking, the cinema going, the tennis playing are all dispensable vehicles for the *real* business of life). And it would be wrong to think of the understanding involved in human relationships as a simply structured, homogeneous affair. The first mistake is, I trust, not very enticing: the second one is rather more tempting—and I shall return to say more about it in section VII below.

Jack and Jill, then, are tied by a manifold of understanding-involving relations. Now, your dealings with (say) the neighbour across the road, with the shopkeeper who sells you your bread, or with your favourite author in the daily newspaper, are very much more limited than Jack's dealings with Jill: but even these more transitory encounters still involve pretty complex sets of understanding-involving relations. But of course, we are not all *directly* interrelated even by these thinner ties. Our human world is, however, constituted by a network of such direct links, which ultimately connect each of us, perhaps at very many removes, to everyone else. (Objection: this exaggerates the interrelatedness of terrestrial persons—can it really be supposed that you and I stand in the ancestral of immediate human relations to (say) a Saharan nomad? Reply: but surely we *do* conceive of this man as one of a social group which is not utterly cut off from the rest of human kind—indeed, how else is it that we know of the existence and something of the manner of life of such people? Objection: still, why couldn't there be an isolated group entirely cut off from you and me? Reply: there could indeed be Twin Earthers, or their terrestrial equivalent in some as yet undiscovered corner of the world; but someone in such a group would not count as currently one of us in the sense that I am regimenting—he might be of the Right Kind, but he wouldn't as yet be Right Related. Objection: isn't it morally disreputable to treat someone in an isolated group as beyond the pale in this way by refusing to acknowledge him as 'one of us'? Reply: it would indeed be objectionable to refuse to acknowledge the moral status of those who contingently are not Right Related to us; but I am not committed to taking this line—moral status, say I, mostly goes with being of the Right Kind, not with happening to be Right Related.)

The suggestion, therefore, is that the rather bloodless and abstract Right Relation is supervenient upon more familiar direct interpersonal relations: two individuals stand in the Right Relation if they occupy nodes of a network constituted by direct understanding-involving relations. This leaves it unsettled how tightly linked into the network individuals must be in order to count as members, and consequently it can be somewhat indeterminate whether two individuals are indeed Right Related. Perhaps there are some individuals whose direct relations are too abnormal (e.g. the sufficiently insane) or as yet too few (the recently conceived child) for them to count as one of us: but there will certainly be no sharp demarcation between the wildly abnormal and the normal, or between the tenuously linked and the fully related. Still, this sort of vagueness in the Right Relation is ineliminable, and trying to impose sharp distinctions on the graduated facts here can only lead to metaphysical and moral errors.

## VI

Given this initial rough characterization of the Right Relation, what can we say concerning the Right Kind? What is the Right Kind of being to be a relatum of the Right Relation, to occupy a node somewhere in a web constituted by 'thick' ties of the sorts I have mentioned?

The answer is plain enough (at least in programmatic outline): the Right Kind comprises those beings—call them 'human persons'—which have rich enough aptitudes for the understanding-involving activities characteristic of human life.[8] Now, we can 'fine tune' that answer in a number of ways: for example, one obvious variation would be to allow a being to count as a human person so long as it will, in the normal course of its development, have rich enough aptitudes for the understanding-involving activities characteristic of human life (that allows very small babies to count as human persons although not yet full participants in characteristic human relationships). But I'm not here going to be concerned with the fine tuning,[9] but with two basic features of any concept of a human

[8] In terms of A. O. Rorty's taxonomy in 'Persons and *Personae*', the concept of a human person belongs, if anywhere, in her class 4, second para., text to ch. 1 n. 3. I would, however, prefer a more structured taxonomy; and it is then open to argument that the concept of a human person will play a pivotal role in the structure.

[9] Such fine tuning will typically, though not exclusively, be governed by moral considerations. And it is worth remarking that, as introduced, the notion of a human person carries no independent moral weight of its own: rather, such moral significance that it has derives from the values that we already put on the various capacities for engaging in human life upon which personhood supervenes.

person introduced in something like the way that I am suggesting. First, as introduced, the Right Kind is in a very broad sense of the term a *functional* kind: in other words, something belongs to the Right Kind if it can occupy a node in a certain web of relationships—and what matters for that is not the intrinsic constitution of a being, nor the natural kind which it belongs to, but its functional capacities. And secondly, given our current rough specification of the Right Relation, the Right Kind is—for want of a better label—a *fortuitous* kind: being a human person means having a variety of capacities which (it seems) are in no sense necessarily co-present. I want to consider these two points in turn.

The suggestion that human persons form a functional kind conflicts with the idea—familiar from the work of Strawson and Wiggins—that 'person' locates a basic or fundamental sort of Aristotelian substance. Of course, this conflict would be side-stepped if we could say that our functional concept of a human person regiments some of the content of the pre-theoretic notion of a person, while Strawson and Wiggins are concerned to explore other elements of that notion. But this anodyne resolution is problematic because it is very difficult to see how there can in fact be room on the conceptual map for a basic substantival concept of a person as well as some corresponding functional notion. For presumably these two concepts would have to fit tightly together, and any being which is functionally a person, i.e. functionally of the Right Kind to count as one of us, would also necessarily belong to the fundamental substantival sort *person*. But the trouble is that we already seem to have a perfectly good candidate for the fundamental substantival sort to which we at least belong, namely *human being*. And two candidates for the basic sort is one too many.

There is a number of ways in which one might respond to this difficulty, and try to sustain the idea that *person* is a fundamental sort, though to my mind none is satisfactory.[10] I can here consider just one response, which is at the same time both modest and radical. David Wiggins has suggested that *person* and *human being* can each be a fundamental category because they are in fact the same category: he claims, more or less, that while the two terms have different senses, they both refer to one and the same sort of

[10] See P. F. Snowdon, 'Persons, Animals, and Ourselves', ch. 4 below, for some congenial arguments.

creature.[11] This position is modest in neither requiring us to deny that *human being* is a fundamental sort, nor on the other hand requiring us to recognize an embarrassing multiplicity of fundamental sorts: but it is radical in its apparent rejection of the firm intuition with which we started out—namely it might have been the case that we are not all of the same biological species.

Wiggins's argument to the radical conclusion that to be a person is to be a human being involves a good deal which is consonant with the drift of the present paper. In particular, he makes much of the open-ended character of our understanding of the sense of 'person': to grasp this sense involves knowing that persons are beings who perceive and feel, who talk to each other, who are susceptible to concern for other people, who engage in projects together, *and so on and so forth*. What disciplines the way in which we fill out the place-holder here? As Wiggins puts it,

> No doubt we grasp some stereotype. But what makes up this stereotype? Are the constituents of the stereotype organized by anything substantially different from the reference that holds together the stereotype for 'human being'?[12]

The answer to the latter question seems plainly negative. But to show that our notion of a person is held together and organized by our grasp of facts about human beings surely falls well short of demonstrating the conclusion that our notion of a person and our notion of a human being must locate one and the same sort of creature. Consider again the functional notion of a human person, introduced as the idea of a being which exhibits capacities for the

[11] 'The Person as Object of Science, as Subject of Experience, and as Locus of Value' in A. Peacocke and G. Gillett (edd.), *Persons and Personality* (Oxford, 1987), 56–74. I am distorting Wiggins in two ways: first, his claim is actually *W*, that the terms 'person' and 'human being' have the same Fregean concept as reference. Now, *that* assertion may well be true, given that (the analogue of) identity for Fregean concepts is coextensiveness. But this concession falls far short of giving Wiggins what he wants, if his aim is to sustain the idea that *person* is a basic or fundamental sort. For however exactly we gloss the notion of the basic deployed here, it is a thoroughly modal notion—as a first shot, *S* is a fundamental sort if it is *impossible* for a particular which is *S* to continue to exist while ceasing to be *S*—and consequentially, even if the sorts $S_1$ and $S_2$ are coextensive, one may be fundamental and the other not. To make his case, then, Wiggins needs to establish something stronger than *W*, and I will assume that he is aiming to do so. Second, Wiggins in fact sometimes qualifies his identity claim, saying that 'the relation of the [Fregean] concepts *person* and *human being* is one of either dependency or identity' (p. 60): my argument is that the weaker claim is all he is entitled to.

[12] 'The Person', p. 69.

sorts of human relations which we can readily recognize each other to share in. Obviously enough, grasp of this notion will presuppose a grasp of the human stereotype. But a functional notion such as this locates a second-order property, i.e. a property had in virtue of having some first-level property or other which enables such-and-such behaviour to ensue in such-and-such circumstances. Thus understood, a second-order property is not identical to any first-order property, but rather supervenes upon the first-order base plus the operative causal laws: and in particular, the second-order property of being such as to exhibit typically human capacities is distinct from the first order property of being human. In short, then, there seems to be no inconsistency in holding, with respect to the notion of a human person, that it locates a kind other than the first-order kind *human being* although it can only be grasped via the human stereotype.

But is the difference between Wiggins's thesis (as I have supposed it to be) and the position I have been presenting really worth fussing about? After all, we will both line up on the same side against overly generalized conceptions of the person; we both think that we need to take seriously the fact that human beings provide our only paradigm of personhood; does the residual difference between saying with Wiggins that 'person' and 'human being' locate the same property, and alternatively regimenting 'person' to locate a functional kind modelled on human beings, actually matter? Well, in the real world, where we presently encounter neither Twin Earthers nor hobbits, not a great deal hangs on it. Still, it is worth preserving conceptual room (if we can) for the thought that there could be persons who are not biologically human—a thought which seems near enough constitutive of the received idea of a person. And aiming to preserve this thought is not simply conceptual conservatism: the underlying point is that the notion of a person belongs to the lived world conceptualized by folk psychology, and our folk psychological notions generally are (for familiar reasons) plausibly regarded as locating types of state, event or whatever, which could at least in principle be materially realized in different ways. If the spectrum of mental states and capacities constitutive of our human mental life could be realized by something with—at some level—a different biology, then the notion of the sort of being which can exemplify such states is the notion of a sort which can, at least in principle, be multiply realized. Such general considerations[13] in the philosophy of mind naturally underwrite a functional regimentation of the concept of a person.

## VII

To return, however, to the point on which I agree with Wiggins, namely that a grasp of our respective favoured concepts of a person depends on a prior understanding of the human stereotype. Combine this with the point that there seems to be little inevitability about the way that the human stereotype happens to be organized, and we arrive at the conclusion that the *human person* is, as we might put it, a fortuitously structured kind. I explain.

The notion of a human person was introduced as the idea of the sort of the being that can occupy a node in a network of relationships of the kind that we humans go in for. At first blush, the actual set of relationships that link us is a very motley collection, whose current shape is no doubt the arbitrary product of a variety of historical accidents. However, as I suggested before, there seems to be something of an underlying unity here, given the common way that the various relationships engage with our intentional understanding of each other. But we mustn't exaggerate this underlying unity, for our intentional understanding is itself a many-stranded affair, and it seems that we can easily conceive of the various strands becoming unravelled. To take an obvious example, consider our broadly shared sense of what is funny and what is not; many of our shared activities evidently depend on our understanding each other as finding humour in situations. But as far as anyone can tell, the requisite sense of humour is external to the rest of human psychology. In other words, we must at least allow for the possibility of a creature which has the rest of our capacities but lacks the human propensity to be amused by various kinds of situation. Such a creature would no doubt strike us as cold and alien, a profoundly creepy and uncomfortable companion: small touches of humour play such a part in oiling the wheels of

[13] Note, however, that these considerations fall short of committing us to 'functionalism' as a general philosophy of mind, so it would be a misunderstanding to suppose that what I have called a functionalist construal of the concept of a human person entails a more general functionalism.

social intercourse that the quite irredeemably humourless could not long pass for one of us (even ordinary human dourness, a resolute determination not to give way to frivolity, requires a recognition of what it is to find things amusing, if only to deprecate it—and we are conceiving of a creature who lacks any such understanding). In the terms of the previous discussion—where I was working with what might be called an 'all in' conception of the direct relationships on which the Right Relation supervenes—some sense of humour is going to be needed by any creature which is of the Right Kind fully to occupy a node in a network of normal interpersonal relationships. In other words, a humourless creature would not count as a full human person in the sense we have introduced, although it could be (so to speak) next door to being human.

Consider another example: one element of many human relationships is a shared awareness of the other's sexual attractiveness. So occupancy of a node in a network of relationships which includes such elements is going to require an understanding of the possibilities of erotic attraction. But again, it seems that we can conceive of creatures who lack such an understanding, perhaps because they ultimately arrange their reproductive affairs differently, but who otherwise have the same capacities as we have. Such a creature would again not be of the Right Kind to be fully one of us, although it would share a great deal with us.

We can plainly multiply such examples. The human propensities and modes of understanding which sustain our personal relationships are only loosely unified, and we can readily conceive of creatures having various proper subsets of them. If we tie our regimentation of the notion of a person to the idea of a being capable of taking a full place in a normal network of human relationships, then we are assuredly fixing on a fortuitous kind with no claim to any more than parochial standing.

This is a conclusion which I am happy to live with. The notion of a person has its home in the parochial enterprise of folk psychology and is none the worse for that. But this conclusion plainly runs counter to the long tradition which supposes that we have a much grander, non-local notion of a person, and maintains that in this wider sense there could be persons who are not only not biologically human, but who are *very* different from us (like angels or Alpha Centaurians). The idea, in other words, is that human persons (in our usage of the phrase) are only a subclass of a wider and—in some good sense—much more 'natural' functional category *person*. It would be foolish to deny the initial attractions of this idea: but if we acknowledge, as I think we should, that much of our pre-philosophical thinking about persons is adequately regimented by the narrow notion of a human person, it is not easy to find a clear remaining role for the supposed wider notion.[14] Anyway, I want to press the obvious question: the traditional suggestion is, in effect, that a certain selection of human aptitudes and modes of understanding qualify us for membership of the grand-kind *person*—but on what criteria are we to make the selection, and why are they relevant to personhood? It is easy to suppose that a sense of humour and a susceptibility to erotic attraction, though pervasive, are peripheral to core personhood; but as we start peeling off one after another of the characteristics which make us what we are, what determines where are we to stop and why?

It is not enough simply to appeal to common-sense notions like 'self-consciousness': in other words, it won't take us very far to say that what is essential to core personhood is whatever is required for self-consciousness. For as Adam Morton in effect shows, human self-consciousness is not a simple unified state, but rests on a congeries of contingently related capacities, which can come in various combinations and degrees. So the question just becomes: which of the variety of capacities underlying human self-consciousness is essential to core personhood?

The only reasonably plausible and disciplined way forward that I know invokes some variation on the following line of thought. What matters for personhood in the wide sense is having a core belief-desire psychology which includes second-order beliefs and desires, i.e. states with contents which concern others of our own beliefs and desires; this enables us to be Frankfurtian persons with some elements of self-consciousness. And having such a psychology—the answer continues—is a matter of instantiating a certain very general functional design; and by ringing changes on a creature's basic modes of belief formation (its modes of perception and its available forms of memory) and the settings of its primitive desires, we can conceive of beings who are *very* different to us in their

[14] It is this supposed grander notion that A. Morton is arguing against in his 'Why there is no Concept of a Person', ch. 2 above: where I differ from Morton—though this is largely a matter of emphasis—is in finding a significant residual role for the more restricted concept of a human person.

actual ways of life, although still sharing the same (person constituting) essential design. Hence, in paring away the happenstances of our own mental life in order to arrive at what is essential to our personhood (in the wide sense), we can dispense with whatever is extrinsic to our instantiation of the fundamental architecture, and no more.

The attractions of the conception of the mind assumed here are familiar enough: but so too are the difficulties which this conception meets once it stops trading in airy generalities and tries to articulate the supposedly basic design of the mind in more detail. Philosophical attempts to recover the principles governing the fundamental causal interactions of beliefs, desires, and actions just don't seem to deliver anything significantly more impressive than the likes of 'people tend to do what they expect, in the light of their beliefs, will satisfy their desires'—and there remains a big gap between such extremely general and vague principles and the detailed predictions and explanations of action we routinely manage to deliver in practice. But if we don't arrive at our practical predictions and explanations by employing our grasp of suitably detailed (and presumably recoverable) principles that articulate the architecture of the mind, how do we do the trick? Well, by my lights, there is no mystery here: we use simulation strategies. If I want to work out what you are going to do, then I put myself imaginatively in your shoes, feign that my informational state is suitably adjusted (for example, to take account of what is available to someone in your perceptual position), feign appropriate adjustments in my desires, and then run through the practical reasoning that I would then engage in. To use this predictive strategy, I need some folk knowledge about how beliefs are affected by perspectival position, for example, and about the ways that desires can vary: but I can then use myself as a predictive device, without having a grip on any theory about the detailed design of the mind. Now, it isn't clear what the relation is between various forms of functionalism and the simulation theorist's account of our folk psychological strategies of prediction and explanation;[15] but the latter certainly does nothing much to sustain the particular idea that we exemplify an abstract belief-desire architecture of a kind that may be shared

[15] See J. Heal, 'Replication and Functionalism', in J. Butterfield (ed.), *Language, Mind and Logic* (Cambridge, 1986), 135–50. Cf. A. Morton, *Frames of Mind* (Oxford, 1980).

by radically different creatures. For on the simulation theorist's view, the workings of our folk psychological strategies, which give content to the very ideas of belief and desire, are irredeemably anthropocentric, and we are left with no handle by which we might seek to pull the putative core structure of the mind apart from the supposedly dispensable human contingencies.[16]

Theorists have frequently sought for a concept of a person which has more descriptive content than the purely formal Kantian notion of an equal citizen of the Kingdom of Ends, yet is not narrowly anthropocentric. But the desired generalized notion of the person needs to be supported by suitably general model of the mind, and—to put it bluntly—such models are hard to come by. As far as I can see, there is a serious challenge here for anyone who wants to work with a substantive concept of the person much more general than the idea of a human person.

[16] To note the anthropocentricity of folk psychology is not to prejudge the question whether, in a future golden age of cognitive science, we might not develop concepts which enable us to describe interestingly abstract cognitive architectures which we can share with the radically non-human. The claim is only that the folk concepts of belief and desire are ill-fitted to serve the purpose. Note that if our folk concepts are indeed anthropocentric, then traditional formulations aimed at locating a wide notion of personhood, such as 'a person is a self-conscious, rational thinking being', may after all cover no more than the narrower class of human persons. So my earlier claim in section II that 'conceptions of personhood as they have featured in much philosophical discussion seem too wide' must be understood against the background of the common presumption—here rejected—that properties like self-consciousness or rationality can be unproblematically predicated of the radically non-human.

# 4

# ’ersons, Animals, and Ourselves

*P. F. Snowdon*

### *List of Discussed Theses*

is chapter certain propositions are regularly referred to by
ɔers or abbreviated names. For ease of reference, a list of the
important ones is set out straight away.

(1) I am a person.
1E) I am essentially a person.
(2) The notion of a person involves distinctive criteria of identity.
(3) I am an animal (of the species Homo sapiens).
3E) I am essentially such an animal.
(4) The notion of such an animal involves distinctive criteria of identity.
(5) If an object is an animal then it is not possible for that object to carry on existing without remaining an animal.
(6) There are possible circumstances in which I carry on existing without being an animal.
AT (short for Animal Attribute Theory of Personhood): X is a person if and only if X is an animal . . . of a kind whose typical members perceive, feel, remember, etc. . . . , conceive of themselves as perceiving, feeling, etc. . . .
PA (short for Psychological Animalism): any psychologically endowed thing must be an animal.

## I

regrettable that, for a long time, the notions of ‘human being’
‘animal’ were neglected in discussions of, what is called,

---

to thank Drs Martha Klein, Grant Gillett, Galen Strawson, and Christopher
r helpful comments on an earlier version.

'personal identity'.[1] The neglect is regrettable for two reasons. First, it meant that certain *problems* were not recognized. Second, it meant that certain *truths* were not recognized. At least, that is what I shall claim. As a piece of rather rough and ready history we can say this neglect has been ended, as far as recent discussion goes, by the writings of David Wiggins, some of whose arguments I shall discuss.[2] However, I want to begin by specifying some propositions with which the discussion will be concerned.

When philosophers ask what the criteria of personal identity are, it is clear that they do not distinguish the question they are considering from the question as to what the criteria of identity are for *themselves*. This is manifest from the practice of testing a suggested criterion by asking; must I fulfil that condition to remain in existence? If they recognize no distinction between these questions it is, I think, because they are making two assumptions. The first is about themselves, and would be expressed by each of them thus:

(1E) I am essentially a person.

(Obviously, if they accept (1E) they will also accept:

(1) I am a person.

I introduce (1) because I shall refer to it later.) The second assumption I shall express, perhaps infelicitously, as follows;

(2) The notion of a person involves certain distinctive criteria of identity.

I am going to assume that it is clear without much amplification,

[1] It is quite possible to study the discussion of personal identity from the 1950s and 1960s in the works of e.g. Williams and Shoemaker, and hardly encounter the concepts of animal and human being. Fashions have, of course, changed. However, one purpose of this paper is to indicate that the right to think of ourselves as animals has to be earned.

[2] See 'Locke, Butler and the Stream of Consciousness: And Men as a Natural Kind', in A. O. Rorty (ed.), *The Identities of Persons* (Berkeley, 1976), 139–73, and also, and principally, *Sameness and Substance* (Oxford, 1980), esp. ch. 6. Although I discuss (in sects. IX and X) some claims made by Wiggins I do not regard what is written here as anything like a complete assessment of his complex arguments or of the motivations which underly the development of his theory.

what the attitude is which the words in (2) are intended to express. It should be made explicit that when it is said (as in (2) ) that a certain kind has distinctive criteria, it is meant, not that they are unique to that kind, but that they are the ones to which the kind is tied.

Let me introduce three other claims, related as the above are, but containing a different concept from that of person. They are:

(3) I am an animal (of the species Homo sapiens).
(3E) I am essentially such an animal.
(4) The notion of such an animal involves distinctive criteria of identity.

Assuming that the identified claims are sufficiently clear to consider, the question arises as to which of them are true. There are, I believe, two approaches which have been elaborated in the literature. The first accepts (1E), (2), and (4), but denies (3E) and (3). This I shall call the Lockean theory, for this combination corresponds to a natural way of stating (some of) Locke's conclusions in his chapter on identity.[3] Amongst current writers we can cite Shoemaker as someone who accepts the Lockean view.[4] The second approach accepts, in effect, all the claims (1)–(4). I take Wiggins, in chapter 6 of *Sameness and Substance*, to be propounding this. In this account the crucial thought is that to be a person just is to be an animal of a certain kind.

It would be incorrect to assume that we are limited to choosing between these two approaches, but the disagreement between them highlights a crucial question; is (3) true? I want, in this paper, to consider (some of) the arguments for and against it. In Section II, I shall give what I consider to be the main argument against (3). In Section III, a group of what seem to be very strong considerations in favour of (3) will be propounded. We shall then have something

[3] Locke expresses his views in *An Essay Concerning Human Understanding*, ed. P. H. Nidditch (Oxford, 1975), II. xxvii. In other parts of the *Essay*, of course, Locke made claims that would count against supposing that he would acceept (1E). In calling this first combination the 'Lockean theory' I am, therefore, thinking only of his ch. on identity. Also, in calling it Lockean I am not giving expression to a conviction that acceptance of this combination commits one to acceptance of the actual analysis of personal identity which Locke himself advocated.

[4] See S. Shoemaker, 'Personal Identity: A Materialist's Account', in S. Shoemaker and R. Swinburne, *Personal Identity* (Oxford, 1984), 67–132.

like an antinomy, with (3) and its negation strongly supported. Subsequent sections will mainly be concerned to pursue (but certainly not to suggest how to conclude) the debate about resolving this antinomy, a debate which will touch on some of the other numbered propositions.

In the discussion I shall take some things for granted. Given the first-person content of (3), I shall state these assumptions as assumptions about myself, but it should be obvious that these are merely applications to myself of quite general assumptions. First, there certainly is an animal where I am now. This animal is as natural a member of the Order of Primates as are, for example, particular monkeys and apes. This particular animal, which I shall call H, is, clearly, the animal I am if I am an animal. Second, if I am not H, it is not because I am an entity currently existing separately from H or from what is going on in H. That is, the discussion will be conducted in a materialist framework. Third, despite the difficulties that arise, I shall not consider the option of relativizing identity as a possible escape route.[5]

## II

The argument against (3) draws on familiar resources so I shall expound it in a brief way. Expressed in a very general form, it infers that (3) is false from two premisses. They are:

(5) If an object is an animal then it is not possible for that object to carry on existing without remaining an animal.

(6) There are possible circumstances in which I carry on existing without being an animal.

The inference (to the falsity of (3)) from (5) and (6) is, I hope, beyond criticism on logical grounds. How plausible, though, are the premisses?[6]

[5] For an explanation and criticism of the thesis that identity statements are relative see Wiggins, *Sameness and Substance*, ch. 2. This thesis is not the only one which might be suggested in response to the difficulties raised by our questions and which I ignore. Another such response is that the difficulties show that our concepts of person and self are inadequate and should be regarded as lacking application. In ignoring them here, I am not implying that these suggestions are not worth discussing.

[6] It is, to some degree, a matter of choice how to formulate the sort of argument against (3) which I am interested in setting down. It would have been possible to use

About (5) I shall, at this stage, say little. It is standard to distinguish between two sorts of sorts. The first sort are those to which a thing can belong at a given time and then cease to belong, despite remaining in existence. A clear example is that of being pretty. The second sort are those which have the following property: if an entity belongs to one of them at a given time, then that entity must belong to it as long as that entity remains in being. Call these *abiding sorts*. Different kinds of properties, of course, possess this property, but it would be widely agreed, and it is surely plausible to say, that 'being an animal' is an abiding sort.

What of (6), the second premiss? This is supported by describing circumstances which it is taken are possible (in the relevant sense of possible) and about which it is claimed to be true (*a*) that I survive, but (*b*) that there is no animal that I am. If we grant both (*a*) and (*b*) of the imagined possible circumstances then it seems that (6) is correct. The examples which, it might be supposed, reveal this have been used in recent discussion, not in arguments explicitly directed against (3), but rather in ones against the claim that (fairly full) bodily continuity is a necessary condition for survival of the person.

the following, slightly different, premisses. (5′) If an object is a certain animal then it is not possible for that object to carry on existing without remaining that animal. (6′) There are possible circumstances in which I carry on existing without being this animal H. This is as valid a ground for the denial of (4) as the argument in the main text, and has the advantage that to sustain (6′) we need not envisage the supposed possibility of vat-sustained consciousness; we need only envisage brain transplants into other human bodies. There are, therefore, possible grounds for objection to (6), which are not grounds for objecting to (6′), and which, if relied on to block the argument involving (6), would not amount to full solutions of the problems raised by this sort of case. However, in the present discussion, there is, I hope, no reliance on objections with that character. The reason for using (5) and (6), rather than (5′) and (6′), is that a defence of (5) is slightly more straightforward than one for (5′). (A remark by Colin McGinn prompted this clarification.) A far more important contrast is between the sort of grounds developed in the text for (6), (and which could have been developed for (6′) ), which are grounds to do with brain transplants, and another sort of ground which has sometimes been influential. When (6) is supported in this second way something along the following lines is said. 'Surely it is just possible for you to switch from this body to another one; surely you can envisage simply waking up, after a night's sleep, in a new body, and, perhaps, looking across the room and seeing your old body.' Crucially, when argued this way, the basic description is simply in terms of the person or self transferring from his initial body to something else. In contrast, the account on which the argument in the text relies is in terms of a switch of a real substantial item (namely the brain) which is assumed (and not simply fantastically) to have certain functions. This latter basis evidently has a link to reality which is missing in the other one, which can, therefore, be dismissed as a fantasy which our account of the actual nature and identity of the things involved need not countenance as any sort of real possibility.

So (*b*) has not normally been emphasized in the presentation of such cases.

Viewed in an abstract way, one source of the plausibility of agreeing that there are possible circumstances where (*a*) and (*b*) hold are the fundamental and apparently plausible intuitions Locke had about personal identity. These intuitions are, first, that the survival of a person is crucially linked to the persistence of, in some sense, his consciousness or capacity for consciousness; and second, that, in principle (although maybe not in fact) the persistence of a stream of consciousness (the direction in which it might go) is not clearly linked to any particular substance.[7] Locke developed his theory of personal identity to make these ideas coherent and explicit, a task in which, it is generally agreed, he failed. What is important for us though, is not the theory he developed, but the appeal of the ideas behind it.

Locke expresses one of his intuitions this way:

> Thus everyone finds, that whilst comprehended under that consciousness, the little finger is as much part of itself, as what is most so. Upon separation of this little finger, should this consciousness go along with the little finger and leave the rest of the body, 'tis evident the little finger would be the Person, the same Person . . . (*Essay*, II. xxvii. 17).

Locke's talk of the finger is fanciful, but Locke's story updated is, of course, the brain-removal story, the development of which is due to Shoemaker.[8] Imagine a surgeon removing from your head the whole of your brain. He needs to preserve during the operation its long-run capacity to function. He then relocates it in a stable environment so that it can resume its normal function. The brain is, we think, the seat or organ of consciousness and of attendant psychological functions—such as memory, calculation, and thought. So, given that the organ for these is refunctioning, those operations are resumed. Sequences of events of this sort have seemed possible, in the relevant sense, to many people, and have also seemed to be the circumstances about which we should hold

[7] It would be wrong to think that a belief in the possibility of circumstances where (*a*) and (*b*) obtain has to reflect a commitment to the plausibility of both these fundamental Lockean intuitions. The belief can be generated by a combination of what I have called Locke's first intuition (which is an almost universal one) and the rather less extreme intuition that the particular substance, if any, to which a particular stream of consciousness is essentially linked need not be on the scale of the whole animal.

[8] See *Self-Knowledge and Self-Identity* (New York, 1963), 22–5.

(*a*) that I survive the operation but (*b*) there is no animal I am after it. Now, we can vary the precise details of the story to reinforce our sense that these judgements are appropriate. In particular we can tell different stories about what happens during the operation and what happens after it. Such stories have been told repeatedly and well in recent discussions. I do not, therefore, want to elaborate the familiar transplant stories in order to elicit agreement to (*a*) but I do take it that (*a*) can be made to seem very plausible; and that (*b*) can be rendered plausible by envisaging the new stable environment as consisting in a totally artificial support system which both meets the brain's energy requirements and gives it suitable input and output channels, a piece of equipment commonly known as a Vat. Prima facie, this support system could resemble ones which are quite familiar in the study of other important organs—for example, hearts or kidneys. The crucial point is that no one has the slightest inclination to think these systems sustain an animal—rather they provide temporary support for an organ from an animal. That, I suggest, is the natural way to think of such an experiment even if it involves the brain.

Since both (5) and (6) are plausible, we have a strong case against (3). I shall call someone who accepts that (3) is false a 'non-animalist'.

## III

At this point some will accept that (3) is false. But the denial of (3) itself faces serious problems. I want to advance three reasons which seem to strongly favour (3).

The first reason basically consists in pointing out that any denier of (3) must meet the challenge of providing a better explanation of how (3) can be false than was managed by Locke. Locke's explanation would be this; just as we need to distinguish the lump of matter here and the animal here, to recognize, that is, that they are two different sorts of thing, so we must also recognize a third sort—the person here. (3) can be false because I am something of that third sort—a person. But Locke also, and not surprisingly, says what sort of thing a person is: 'a person is a thinking intelligent being that has reason and reflection and can consider itself as itself, the same thinking thing in different times and places'.[9] That is to

[9] *Essay*, II. xxvii. 9.

say: Locke thinks that that captures the kind of thing *I* am, so that, being that kind of thing, I can be contrasted with the animal here (another kind of thing) and the lump of stuff here (still another kind of thing).

Now, it is not at all hard to sympathize with this definition of the concept of a person; in effect, it makes 'person' a functional predicate, applicable to entities capable of a certain sort of higher cognition. Crucially, it allows 'person' to apply across animal species and, for all that it says, to non-animals. However, there are two comments I want to make. (i) It is hard to believe that 'person' as explained by Locke is an abiding sort; if it is not, then it does not mark out a basic sort of thing, the distinctive persistence conditions of which we can trace. One reason this is hard to believe is that, as defined, it appears very similar to lots of across-species functional classifications which do not mark out abiding sorts, e.g. 'is a teacher', 'can play chess at a grandmaster level', 'is a prodigious calculator'. The point can be put this way: if you concentrate on the functions alluded to in the definition, then there seems no difficulty in supposing that a creature at one time capable of carrying them out should itself lose that capacity. (ii) Surely if we ask to what entities the functional predicate (person), as elucidated by Locke, does apply, the answer we all want to give is—a certain kind of animal, namely human beings. They are animals which reason, reflect, and talk of themselves! So, rather amusingly, Locke defines a notion which he thinks picks out a sort of thing to be contrasted with the animal sort, but which actually applies to certain animals. In this sense of 'person', some animals are persons: they are fundamentally animals, which function so as to be persons. So Locke does not provide a coherent framework underpinning the person and animal contrast. I have not at this point been concerned with difficulties in what Locke says about personal identity; rather the objection has been that Locke's account of the conditions for falling under the person-concept does not leave room for contrasting the person I am with this animal which I am calling H.

What is the force of this difficulty in Locke's theory for us? My aim at the moment is to set up a powerful case *for* (3), so that, given the intuitively plausible argument of the previous section, we generate an antinomy (in a loose sense). The question, therefore, is how far does the Lockean difficulty support (3)? It is not, I think, a very direct argument for (3). It gives support, however, on certain assumptions. If we are inclined to agree that, if I am not an animal, then there is some other sort of thing I must be; that that sort of thing is a person; and that Locke characterizes more or less adequately what it is to be a person, then there seems to be no room for the denial of (3). In fact, these assumptions are not uncommon, so we have an argument with some bite.

The second argument for (3) points out a related problem in denying (3), but this time not to do with the concept of a person. If someone says (3) is false he is saying that when *I* say on this occasion (call it O) 'I am an animal' that remark is false. But we have to ask such a person this question: cannot animals ever think about themselves? cannot animals use the first-person pronoun? The answer has surely to be that they can; surely some animals could and have evolved with that capacity. Now, if it is agreed that animals can, then, surely, H (this animal) is one such. But if H can talk of itself using 'I', then it seems that the remarks made at O through the mouth of H are such remarks. Clearly there could not be any better candidate for such a case. (What must the animal H do to speak about itself which it did not do then?) If, however, that remark was a case where an animal spoke of itself, and what it said was 'I am an animal', then that must rank as a truth. That seems to settle the question we begin with. (I call that the reductio argument).

I have, so far, presented two lines of thought, pointing out these problems with the conclusion of our first argument: (i) that Locke's elucidation of 'person' quite fails to sustain it, (ii) that it is an animal talking here, so when it says 'I am an animal' that must be true. I want to mention a third point (or type of point)—namely, that to think of yourself as a animal (to acknowledge that) coheres with, and acts as, a potential explanation of the way we do think of ourselves. Here are three examples. It has always been a serious embarrassment to Lockean, or Lockean inspired, accounts of our identity, that we think of those accidents and illnesses which disturb the normal flow of our mental life as things we live through and hence undergo. If we are the animals, then this would be, of course, the correct way to think. More controversially, it seems to me that many of us are inclined to side with Bernard Williams's (tentative) judgement as to what the mental-characteristic switching machine of 'The Self and the Future' achieves; he prefers to think that he stays with his body.[10] Again, this opinion is validated if we think of the subjects involved as animals. Finally, in all actual circumstances that we are acquainted with, the principle 'some person, some human being' holds. To deny (3) is, then, to deny the most obvious ground for all our convictions about actual cases, and many of our convictions about supposedly possible cases.

## IV

I have now set up an antimony concerning the proposition 'I am an animal'. In the face of it, there are two things we might do. We might provide a full resolution of, that is, a full adjudication of, all the arguments involved. There are three options available: first, accept the argument against (3) and defuse the arguments for it; second, accept the arguments (or some of them) for (3) and defuse the argument against it; third, defuse both sets of arguments. Alternatively, we might be less ambitious; we might aim to strengthen one conclusion, giving us confidence that the alternative side is wrong, without, however, pin-pointing any error in the considerations apparently supporting it. I want to do the less ambitious sort of thing: I want, first of all, to strengthen the case for (3), by considering replies that non-animalists might make to the arguments for (3).

Before I do that, I wish to set aside a suggestion of Shoemaker's which, it might be thought, could solve our problem.[11] In discussing personal identity, Shoemaker becomes worried about the status of (3). He points out, though, that even if we wish to assert a non-identity between myself and H, we can interpret (3) in a way which makes it come out true. It will be true if we interpret 'am' as meaning 'am composed of the same stuff as . . .'. Even if I am not identical with H, I am now composed of the same stuff as H. Does this suggestion contribute anything to a solution of our antinomy? Shoemaker's suggestion arises from his belief that the argument I presented in Section II (or, at least, something like it) is correct, and that the fundamental problem over (3) is that we have a strong intuition that, despite the correctness of the argument, (3) expresses a truth. Viewing the problem this way, his response is, naturally enough, to search for an interpretation of the words in (3) which,

[10] See 'The Self and the Future' in *Problems of the Self* (Cambridge 1973), p. 63.
[11] Shoemaker, in Shoemaker and Swinburne, *Personal Identity*, sec. XI.

despite the soundness of the argument, allows it to be true. The problem which I have tried to establish is that (3), when interpreted in a way which makes the earlier argument count against it, that is, when it is interpreted as involving an identity, also has powerful arguments in favour of it. This problem is not, therefore, alleviated in the slightest by making (3) come out true *on some interpretation or other*. Shoemaker's suggestion is irrelevant to the achievement of a resolution of our problem.

## V

The third sort of argument for (3) attempted to display it as something acceptance of which can explain and ground the basic ways we think when considering ourselves in normal, abnormal, and unrealistic circumstances. The rejoinder to this will be that there may be ways of accounting for our attitudes which equally fit the cases and which do not involve (3). It seems to me that the most likely possible alternative position here is that supported, in different ways, by Mackie and Nagel which treats a person as tied to that object which crucially sustains the mental operations the occurrence of which are required for a person, namely, his brain.[12] It can be argued that this view accounts for everything cited in support of (3) in the third argument. Indeed, this approach is overall in a very good position because it also accepts the intuitions about brain transplants we are inclined to have. That is, it accepts something like (6). One of its strengths is that it can accommodate the first argument. Now such a view need not deny (3), but it might do so. Therefore, unless something is said to block this suggestion, the third argument must be acknowledged to be inconclusive.

The first argument attempted to show that Locke's definition of what a person is provides no coherent ground for sustaining the assertion of (1) along with a denial of (3). In fact, what was argued is that, according to Locke's definition of 'person' and in light of the facts, this animal here (H) is a person. This confronts a non-animalist with a choice. Since he, evidently, does not wish to abandon (1), he has either to say: (A) let's stick with Locke's

[12] See J. L. Mackie, *Problems From Locke* (Oxford, 1976), ch. 6, esp. p. 200, and Thomas Nagel, *The View From Nowhere* (New York, 1986), ch. 3, esp. p. 40. This view was earlier endorsed by Wiggins; see *Identity and Spatio-Temporal Continuity* (Oxford, 1967), 51.

definition (or something like it) and say: 'I am a person, H is a person, and so there are two persons here'; or (B) modify our account of person so that H is not counted a person; there may, therefore, be only one person here.

But both of these options are very unappealing. The reason that (B) is unacceptable is that there is nothing about H which can ground the denial to him of the status of a person. After all, H can think, is self-conscious, can deliberate, hold moral opinions, etc. No one should withhold from such a creature the title of 'person'. (A) is equally unappealing. In the first place, the suggestion that there are two persons in this chair is not one that anyone would accept.[13] In the second place, if H is a person, then persons cannot be things which, in their natures, are distinct from animals. The confidence of the non-animalist must be shaken by this.

I am suggesting, therefore, that the difficulties which were developed for Locke's approach, turn out on investigation to be (or, perhaps better, turn into) general ones; any non-animalist seems to have problems about counting persons, which I have not found any way of resolving satisfactorily.

What is also troublesome, it seems to me, is the reductio argument. There is, as far as I can see, though, one desperate option available to the non-animalist.[14] If they grant the asumptions, they

[13] It will occur to some that my claim that no one would agree that there are two persons here is false. David Lewis and John Perry, in contributions to the personal identity debate (stimulated by Parfit's discussion of the split-brain transplant case), suggested views which would not rule this out in principle. That is true, and my remark is a little too strong. However, their approach will not allow the quite general consequence that there are, come what may, two persons here. They hold that, just as we can say with roads, where e.g. the road from Oxford to London and the road from Oxford to Aylesbury take the same route out of Oxford and, thereafter, diverge, that there are two roads which overlap at certain places, so we can say about a body whose brain was about to be split, that the pre-splitting stage involved two, at that point, overlapping persons. However, even theorists taking this view would not suppose that if there is no split then there are still two completely overlapping persons. Hence, neither they nor anyone else would be prepared to accept the consequence which grounds the objection to (A).

[14] Another reply that can be made is that from (i) the animal is speaking and it says 'I am an animal', we should no more infer that what was said is true, than we should infer from (ii) the mouth is speaking and it says 'I am a mouth', that what is said is true. This comparison, however, is very difficult to sustain. Thus, to the mouth we ascribe no intentions, plans, action-capacities, beliefs, awareness and so on. If those are ascribed to the animal, then how can it be denied that it can speak? If it can speak, then it can refer to itself. So, to hold out against the 'reductio-argument' on the basis of this reply, it must be claimed that the animal lacks these psychological characteristics. That, however, is not a serious option.

must agree that 'I am an animal', (3), as uttered by me now, is true. However, that does not exclude regarding it as false, so long as an ambiguity is postulated. Now, the ambiguity to be postulated must concern the reference of 'I': that is, it must be supposed to have a dual reference. They will have to say, there is not just one thing talking of itself, there are two. One is an animal; interpreted as referring to it, (3) is true. Another, however, is an entity of the person variety, an entity with that distinctive sort of life history; interpreted as referring to it, (3) as false.

In this way they can absorb the argument and maintain their own view. That is to say, the reductio argument is not a reductio strictly speaking; it does not reduce to absurdity the supposition that (3) expresses a falsehood. Rather, it reduces to absurdity the supposition that (3) does not express a truth. However, there is, surely, a strong inclination to regard what is involved in thus avoiding the objection as absurd. In the first place it concedes that the animal H can talk and think of itself, and is presumably therefore a person. So this reply is committed to the thesis that there are two persons. In the second place, the effort, while thinking first-person thoughts, of trying to keep the present suggestion alive induces extreme intellectual vertigo. Thus, how would one handle such a practical question as 'what ought I to do now?' while allowing that there is both the animal-person and the non-animal-person simultaneously thinking? Should we allow, and how should we cope with, the possibility of the animal-I concluding that he ought to do F and the non-animal-I concluding that he ought to do G? It is, surely, very hard not to think that 'I', unlike 'you' and 'there', is an indexical expression for which in normal conversational circumstances no supplement to its mere use can be needed in order to determine its reference. I think, therefore, that the present reply to the reductio argument is very hard to defend.

## VI

Having set up a dilemma over (3), I have considered what might be said in reply to the arguments for (3). The conclusion has been that, with two of the arguments at least, the replies only sink the opponent of (3) into further problems. At the moment, therefore, I do not see any room to manœuvre for the opponent of (3), the non-animalist. It is reasonable therefore to conclude that (3) is true.[15] This means that I need to answer the Lockean argument which attacked (3). What options are there?

I want to distinguish three options. First, we can question (5); given the trouble the argument causes, maybe the thought that an object can be an animal and then cease to be should be revalued; maybe it is true.[16] Second, we can deny premiss (6), by saying this: we agree that the envisaged circumstances are, in the relevant sense, possible, but we deny that I and this animal ever, as it were, come apart in them. This requires us to identify which of the possible outcomes in the original case would be the outcome, given that we are not prepared to assent to both (*a*) and (*b*). The available alternatives are, roughly, that, after the operation, there is still an animal, or there is no longer me, or it is a borderline case to the same degree for both myself and the animal. There is, though, a third option: premiss (6) can be denied by claiming that the circumstances envisaged as possible, and about which we are invited to make judgements, are not actually possible at all in the relevant sense. This is a response available to someone who accepts recent ideas about genuine (metaphysical) possibility being determined empirically.

Now, it is not my intention to say what is wrong with the argument against (3). I do not know what, if anything, is to be rejected about it. I want, however, to consider the options, beginning with the suggestion that (5) ought to be abandoned.

[15] I think that my acceptance of (3) on the grounds that have been presented might be challenged in at least two separate ways. First, it might be said that there is something spurious about the difficulties now alleged to be involved in denying (3). It is impossible to dismiss this suggestion outright, but unless something more specific is said, consideration of it cannot be taken any further. Second, it might be suggested that it is methodologically improper to regard (3) as more strongly supported than its denial simply because difficulties have been found in direct replies to the arguments for (3). After all, maybe the same will happen to direct replies to the argument against (3), and which arguments were discussed first should not affect the view we take. I do not have the space or enough understanding of the issues raised by this objection to discuss it properly. However, my inclination is to say (i) that given a prior expectation that an acceptable view about the truth-value of (3) can be found without commitment to grossly counterintuitive claims, it is reasonable at this point to regard (3) as true, given the difficulties of denying (3), but also (ii) that we should be prepared to revise our attitude to (3) if the difficulties pile up for an acceptance of it.

[16] I had this option in mind when, in sec. v, I remarked that someone who believes that a person is tied, essentially, to his brain, need not deny (3).

## VII

Should we reject (5)? To discuss this I shall take (5) to say: if something is an animal, then it (that thing) cannot cease to be animal. There is, it must be agreed, some attraction to resolving things by abandoning (5). People are often strongly wedded to the intuitions about brain transplants, and so, if the arguments for animalism are as strong as I claimed, premiss (5) has the least strong attachment, and can go.

I think, however, that we should be reluctant to abandon (5). In part, the attractions of making (5) the casualty in the conflict derive from its having received least attention so far; what can be said in its favour has not yet been said. I want, therefore, to sketch such a case. What we are trying to show is that if, at $t$, there is an animal, and at $t + n$ there is something which at that time is not an animal, then the thing which, at $t + n$, is not an animal is not the same thing as the thing which, at $t$, was an animal. We have, fundamentally, two notions in play. The first is that of an animal, the idea of what is to count as an animal. The second is that of a single persisting thing, the idea of an individual which exists over time. To make a case for (5) we need to bring these notions together—to show that being an animal is being a persisting thing, hence to lose an animal is to lose a thing (an individual).

The claim which I want to endorse (or, given how unambitious these remarks are, perhaps, better, *remind* you of) about persisting material things, that is to say, about what we recognize as such, is that we regard the persistence in a certain materially continuous form of a fundamental explanatory unity as the persistence of a thing. The details of what amounts to the persistence of such an explanatory unity I shall not attempt to fill in. However, I shall assume that the idea is a sound one. On the other side, it is plausible, surely, to think that an animal is, precisely, a materially continuous locus of fundamental explanation.[17] So, in our example, the move from the pre-operational animal to the post-operational functioning brain, marks a significant explanatory change; the powers and explanations are fundamentally different. If both these

[17] The viewpoint I have expressed in these simple, not to say over-simple, claims has received further, more cautious and, I think, convincing expression in recent writings. See Wiggins, *Sameness and Substance*, esp ch. 3 sec. III, and R. G. Millikan, *Language, Thought and Other Biological Categories* (Cambridge, Mass., 1984), ch. 17.

claims are correct, then premiss (5) is vindicated. Animals are kinds of things.

Thinking of identity in this way provides the major ground for retaining (5), but it is, perhaps, worthwhile to add three things. The first two are that thesis (5) is, surely, intuitively plausible, and has received assent by most people who seriously study identity. The third is that (6) (or something like it) receives a sort of confirmation in reactions to a famous Monty Python sketch, in which it is said that something is an 'ex-parrot'. Why is that so funny? The explanation, which involves (5), is that the predicate-modifier 'ex-', forms a new predicate, when concatenated to a predicate F (. . .), which counts as true of an item *i*, at a time just in case *i* was F but is no longer F at that time. Abiding predicates cannot sensibly be modified in this way; nothing ever is an ex-F, where F is an abiding predicate. According to (5), plus certain assumptions, '—is a parrot' is an abiding predicate. The humour of the remark, I want to suggest, lies in this logical incongruity.

I have not, in these remarks, properly argued for (5), the rejection of which may be the correct way to destroy the case against (3). I have tried to show, however, that (5) is anchored in a popular and persuasive way of thinking about identity, and is not easily rejectable.

## VIII

If (5) is accepted, premiss (6) is all that is left to reject. I want to consider the first way of rejecting it, that of accepting that we are dealing with possibilities, but disputing the inclination to affirm both (*a*) and (*b*). One line here is to deny (*b*). But this suggestion I have, in effect, rejected in the previous discussion (that concerned with (5)). It seems that the kind of object an animal is, the kinds of explanations definitive of it, are simply not preserved in the thing remaining after the operation. It is, surely, a mistake to see the animal as preserved and much more plausible to regard the functioning brain as a preserved *organ*.

This leaves it open to argue directly for the rejection of (*a*). I shall consider one remark made by Bernard Williams in support of this. The argument invokes (or expresses) a supposed tie between a person and his body. Since the brain transplant leaves the body behind, grounds for linking a person to his body undermine the idea that he is transplanted with the brain. Here is how Williams tries to ground this idea, considering the possibility of a switch of persons between an emperor's and a peasant's body.

> The requirement is . . . that the emperor's body, with the peasant's personality, should be on the throne, and the peasant's body, with the emperor's personality in the corner. What does this mean? In particular, what has happened to the voices? The voice ought to count as a bodily function, yet how would the peasant's gruff blasphemies be uttered in the emperor's cultivated tones, or the emperor's witticisms in the peasant's growls?[18]

In fairness to Williams it should be said that he was not dealing with brain transplants, nor did he generalize strongly from the quoted remarks. However, it is, I think, hard to be impressed by this illustration of a link between a person and his body. It seems superficial to view those reponses to situations which are constitutive of personality as not expressible in different ways. Even if inexpressible, could they not still be his reactions? Further, even if part of the personality must be acknowledged to have been lost, it seems a relatively insignificant loss.[19]

The general claim which will need to be supported if it is to provide a criticism of (6) is that, in brain transplants too much is lost of what the particular person was (lost, because it requires the body which was left behind) to make it acceptable to think that the person (or the same self) remains. Now, it would be wrong, I think, to dismiss out of hand this way of resisting (6). My criticism is, rather, that Williams's illustration of it does not make it seem very strong. On one view, what is at issue is the very close identification of philosophers with their mental life, so that the artificial preservation of the organ for that makes them suppose *they* survive. The present counter-suggestion is that this is simply a part of what there is in us, and we would lose, in brain transplants, too much of the body-linked elements to survive. I have not tried to refute such a bold conjecture, but no one has satisfactorily supported it.

[18] 'Personal Identity and Individuation', in *Problems of the Self*, p. 12.

[19] A vivid way of revealing what this suggestion is up against is to imagine us urging it (by some communicating channel) on the conscious subject housed in the brain in the vat (something about which this objection to (6) is not being sceptical) as a basis for that subject's concluding he (or it?) is not identical with the person who donated the brain. The remarks do not seem particularly powerful for that role. (A remark of Professor Dummett produced this way of putting the problem.)

## IX

That is as far as I want (or am able) to take the question as to where exactly the argument based on (5) and (6) goes wrong. I find myself thinking that the resolution must lie in such a criticism since attempts to deny (3) seemed futile. However, before considering a rather different sort of argument which might be thought to help us, I want to note and try to counteract a certain rigidity in my discussion so far of the argument based on (5) and (6). My approach (in section VII and VIII, may have given the impression that there might be such a thing as *the* reply to that argument (that is, to the argument identified as containing (5) and (6)). In fact, if (5) is accepted, then the appropriate reply may, indeed surely will, (see note 6 above) depend upon what the supposed circumstances are which are being taken by a proponent of the argument to support (6). The present (unsuccessful) discussion should therefore be thought of as directed against (6) *as supported by full brain transplant cases*. (6) might be supported by, amongst other things, less than full brain transplants (e.g. split-brain or hemisphere transplants), or by transplant of more than the brain (e.g. complete head transplants). Bearing this in mind, it seems that a reply of the sort I claimed to find in Williams's paper, and which was considered in section VIII, has a better chance of working against (6), as supported by cases where less is transplanted, than it has of working against (6), as supported by cases where more substantial animal-parts are involved. My general point, though, is simply that a defender of (3) need not expect there to be a *single* criticism which will counter all the different sorts of transplant cases which have been taken to support (5).

The conviction that (3) is true would be strengthened if there were other arguments for it. I want to enquire whether there is another way to support (3), namely on the basis of the account of being a person advanced by Wiggins in chapter 6 of *Sameness and Substance*. If this account, which he calls the animal attribute theory and which asserts that necessarily persons are sorts of animals, is accepted, then, given the undoubted truth of (1) we can infer (3). What then, is the animal attribute theory (which I shall call AAT)? Here is (an abbreviated form of) what is proposed:

'(Perhaps) X is a person if and only if X is an animal . . . of a

> kind whose typical members perceive, feel, remember, etc. . . . conceive of themselves as perceiving, feeling, etc. . . .'[20]

We can best explain the significance of the account by contrasting it with Locke's account. There are three features of Locke's elucidation which are abandoned. First, Locke did not restrict in any way the sort of thing that can be a person, except as a thing possessing the specified set of mental capacities. The AAT restricts persons to animals. Second, the AAT has an open-ended list of psychological capacities required for personhood. Third, the AAT allows that an actual creature can count as a person without it having the relevant psychological capacities, namely if it is a member of an animal kind whose typical members have those capacities. We should also note that these three dimensions of modification (or difference) are independent. For example, we could adopt the limitations to animals, but retain Locke's list of psychological characteristics (with or without linking the psychological characteristics to the kind). Other combinations are obvious. A full discussion of the proposal would, therefore, be a matter of real complexity.

How should we react to this theory? I want to express a difficulty with one of its aspects. The short Lockean list of cognitive features supposedly required for personhood is replaced by a more complex list which is, as it stands, open-ended. We are told to 'note carefully these . . . dots'.[21] By what route, by gaining what knowledge, shall we be able to complete the definition and eliminate the dots? It is clear that the psychological attributes are supposed to be those of a typical human being; the dots will get eliminated, therefore, when psychology and biology tell us what the characteristic mental capacities of human beings are. There is, that is, a (surely, unobjectionable) commitment in the approach to something which may be called human psychological nature. Understood this way, the proposal invites the question: why is it necessary to have the typical psychological capacities of a human in order to be a person? I do not myself see what the answer to this question is.

This line of thought queried the list of cognitive capacities offered in the animal-attribute theory. We can also question, with some justification, the idea that for an object S to be a person, it need not

[20] *Sameness and Substance*, p. 171. [21] Ibid.

itself possess the characteristic capacities, but must be a member of kind which typically does. In one respect this is an illiberal proposal. The second element in it rules out the possibility of being a person for a freakishly gifted member of a kind the typical members of which do not attain personhood. If an experiment in foetal development produced a highly intelligent and self-conscious orang-utan, I think we could count it as an (unfortunate) person. In another respect the proposal is liberal, for according to it human beings who are incapable of any advanced cognition are, by virtue of being human, to count as persons. There are uses of 'persons' which fit this suggestion. Thus in assessing the claim that a person dies in a certain hospital each day we would count it as true so long as a human being, however cognitively endowed at the time of death or, at any stage in their life, died each day. Such a use of 'person' is not sensibly defined in Locke's way. It is not clear, however, that it is sensibly defined in the animal-attribute way, since it seems to mean little more than 'individual human being'. There are however other uses for which this liberal suggestion fails to account. We say (or some do) that the very young are not yet persons, have not reached personhood, and that people suffering irreversible and severe loss of mental capacity are no longer persons. It is, in part, the existence of such claims (or at least the tendency for such claims to be made) that grounds the conviction that there is a distinctive and interesting person-concept.

I want to leave this problem unresolved and ask the crucial question: is it correct to require that all persons are of necessity animals? We can bring against this suggestion the willingness of many to think there can be persons who are not animals: for example, God, Satan, and angels. It may be said that these are impossibilities. That is, I agree, not ruled out simply because people believe in them. The existence of a willingness to think this way suggests, however, what—as I want to claim—is the correct conception of the issue. However precisely the contrast is to be drawn, there is agreement that persons are, at most, a sub-class of mentally endowed subjects. Cats are mentally endowed (with perception and sensation, etc.) but are not persons. So we can represent the concept of a person as involving at least both the notion of a mentally endowed subject and possession of some further mental qualities. Call these further mental properties the P-factor. The necessary animality of persons might be viewed as required either by the general notion of mental endowment or by the P-factor, or by its being a further restriction on the person-notion that a mentally endowed and P-factor possessing entity counts as a person only if it is also an animal. This third idea is the one which looks implausible given the widespread belief in non-animal persons. We cannot treat such believers as making the same sort of mistake as would be made by someone who failed to see the connection between kennels and dogs (or between pigs and sties). It would, also, surely, be implausible to allow that things other than animals can be mentally endowed (in the basic ways) but that only animals can possess the extra P-factor. If non-animals can perceive and feel, why cannot they also think, reflect, have self-consciousness, and so on?[22] This means that a defender of the animal-attribute view of persons is committed to defending the claim that necessarily only animals are mentally endowed. (I shall call this psychological animalism PA, in contrast to the animal-attribute theory of persons).

If this identification of the issue to be fought over is correct, then some comments are appropriate. (i) The difference between Locke's and the animal-attribute theorists's account of persons is, on the animal-attribute view when considered in its full commitment, not large. For Locke's definition, couched as it is in psychological terms, defines a notion which, given PA, could only apply to animals. (ii) PA will need to be supported by its proponents. However, they have, I think, a prior task—that of explaining how the claim *could* be true. In what way might the essential tie between mental state and animal nature arise? This will not be easy since it runs counter to well-entrenched psychological and philosophical dogmas. (iii) I think it becomes sensible, if I am right, to hold that the animal-attribute theory of persons is not a theoretically interesting claim. It is not a thesis which it is appropriate or valuable to argue for. Rather, the debate should be, in part, about psychological animalism.

We can confirm this by considering one passage from Wiggins's (extremely rich) argument. He is, in this passage as I interpret it, trying to support the animal-attribute view of persons. He says

[22] There are some who think that this question is not unanswerable. They think that it is possible to find grounds for restricting the P-factor to animals which are not grounds for restricting sentience to animals. A proper consideration of this approach would need to be much more thorough than the very brief one I have provided.

To these claims I think that the animal attribute theorist who embraces their conservative implications will want to add that here at last we begin to see the proper grounds for what has sometimes appeared to be only fear or prejudice, but now starts to seem the plainest good sense. This is our defensible or indefensible conviction that, however we may conceive of higher animals such as dolphins or horses or apes, such artifacts as robots and automata have no title to any kind of civil right—or even to the consideration that we ought to accord to the lowlier sentient creatures . . . No weaker claim than that entered by the animal attribute view could do justice to the depth and passion of most people's resistance to the idea that automata can approximate to life or sentience, and it is certain that we still believe that, to have genuine feeling or purposes or concerns, a thing must *at least* be an animal of some sort.[23]

The suggestion made here is that there is some confirmation of the animal-attribute view of persons in its being a ground for certain fundamental convinctions we have. The idea is that the combination of some firm opinions, together with its being the case that a certain theory would, if true, be an explanation or ground for them, is a sort of support for that theory. What opinions, however, are to be grounded? They are:

(i) artefacts have no rights;

(ii) automata cannot approximate to life and sentience;

(iii) only animals have genuine feelings and concerns.

The suggested ground for them, it seems, is AAT, a theory about what it is to be a person. Now (i) might be grounded in AAT only if the auxiliary assumption is made that persons alone have rights. The natural question would then be: why assume that only persons have rights? The answer must be that only persons possess those morally important attributes which support rights. This means that (i) is properly grounded by convictions of sort (ii) and (iii). But convictions of sort (ii) and (iii) are not consequences of a necessary link between personhood and animality; rather any assertion of such a link must be grounded on independent defences of (ii) and (iii).

I hope that consideration of this passage reveals that PA is the crucial claim (and not AAT). Of course, PA itself, if true, will ground (3), which is what we were looking to AAT for. However, a defence of PA would be an enormous task.

[23] *Sameness and Substance*, pp. 174–5.

## X

The strategy explored in the last section was that of attempting to show we must think of ourselves as possessing a certain feature (being animals) by showing that the feature must belong to persons. But it is obvious that there may be crucial features we must acknowledge ourselves as possessing, which have nothing to do with our being *persons*. There are, then, two questions which should be distinguished:

(7) how should we elucidate the notion of a person?
(8) how should we think of ourselves?

I shall make some remarks on (and in response to) these questions, and conclude the discussion of our antinomy.

In his discussion Wiggins claims that unless we think of persons as animals (having a determinate, biological nature which can be discovered only by empirical investigation) there are very serious consequences. For example, he says:

> one is bound to wonder what changes it would bring to the theory and practice of politics, if all inquiry and all description came to be organised by a conception of human personality that was focussed only by a systematic specification, rather than the idea of something that we can try to discover about, and may even be surprised by.[24]

By a 'systematic specification' he means one setting out the conditions for being a person by specifying, in a relatively a priori manner, a finite list of functional requirements (as in the Lockean definition). What is puzzling in this passage is the assumption that adopting a 'systematic' account of what is necessary for personhood will have any implications at all for our conception of human nature, or for the idea that we are essentially human. What is dangerous here is rather ways of thinking of *ourselves*, ways which are nothing to do with what we think of as conditions for personhood. Wiggins's remark neglects the important distinction between issue (7) and issue (8). We can have a relatively 'systematic' concept of personhood because we can allow that the things which qualify (ourselves for one) have a real nature not implied by or involved in that concept.

[24] Ibid. 179

It may be replied: if this 'systematic' account is combined with the view that persons, as a sort, have distinctive criteria of identity, we cannot dismiss the problems raised by a 'systematic' account so easily. Leaving aside the question whether that reply is cogent, it merely acts as an incentive to suggest that, in so far as personhood is a more general notion than that of simply being human, the notion is not one tied to, or implying, criteria of identity. That is to say, I think we should seriously consider abandoning proposition (2) of section 1. Here, I shall do no more than put the idea forward. Locke, and many people who discuss criteria of personal identity, assume that a person is a type of continuant, a different type from animals, and the aim is to articulate the requirements for persistence of such things. Wiggins rejects the contrast between person and animal, but still holds that (2) is true, because being a person is being a sort of animal. If we are suspicious both of the tie between person and animal, suggested by Wiggins, and the contrast between them suggested by Lockeans, we can resolve the problem by allowing that different kinds of things (animals and maybe non-animals) can equally be persons, and for them to be so is not for them to share persistence requirements. One reason for thinking that this is not totally unacceptable is the chaotic mess, and the evident arbitrarinesses, exhibited by the debate about criteria of personal identity. Maybe this is not so much a result of the great difficulty of the search, but rather of there being nothing to find.[25]

It may also be fair to see this proposal linked with another; namely, that the extant notion of being a person is not susceptible of a clear and tight analysis. We have a use of the term which applies it to a range of creatures (and not necessarily to all human beings at all times) which is guided by two things. The first is the aim of marking a class important from the moral point of view; and the second is that this importance derives from their sharing certain higher cognitive and psychological capacities. It is being claimed that it is simply untrue to say that our attributions are guided by

[25] It should not be assumed that dropping (2) dissolves all these issues called 'problems of personal identity'. On the contrary, there will, of course, remain problems about our human, animal identity. The suggestion is rather that the mistaken conviction that as well as these problems there are also problems about the identity of another fundamental kind of thing, persons, has led to an unrestrained field day for groundless and subjective fantasies. It should not be assumed, either, that adoption of the view being recommended is necessarily inconsistent with some of the revisionary conclusions about what is of value in human life which, as normally argued for, seem to depend on (2).

much in the way of agreed conditions. If this is roughly correct, then it supports the rejection of (2) in two ways. First, if to be a person is to be capable of certain morally important, psychological functions, it will apply to things, of whatever sort of continuants, which are capable in the right way. Second, in being an imprecise notion, it can hardly mark out a distinctive and theoretically important sort of continuant.

Having queried (2) we can query (1E). If I had been brain-damaged at birth, I would not have become a person (taking the notion along the lines of the previous paragraph). Since I might never have become a person, I am not essentially a person.

Returning to our original six propositions, the combination I am proposing, although in no sense properly arguing for, is that (1), (3), (3E), and (4) are true; (1E) and (2) are dubious. However, this combination includes (3) against which there is a powerful objection which has not been properly answered. That important task is one for another occasion.

# 5
# Stoic Philosophy and the Concept of the Person

*Troels Engberg-Pedersen*

Like so many other time-hallowed concepts, that of the person is constantly under attack in modern philosophy, and one may be rather tempted to give it up altogether. Has it in fact any specific function at all? Does it add anything that is not already, and better, being done by other concepts in ethics and the philosophy of mind and action? Also, it may be suggested that the concept of the person is a specifically Christian idea. The Greeks did not have it, and therefore, so it may be said, with the demise of Christianity the concept of the person too will disappear.

Both claims, I believe, are right up to a point. It is true that the concept of the person is in a way parasitic on ideas in ethics and the philosophy of mind and action. There is no 'philosophy of the person' as such, and the work that must be done in order to elucidate the concept of the person belongs in those other philosophies. Still, I shall argue that the concept of the person has valuable work to do in bringing together a number of ideas developed in the other philosophies.

As for the second claim, it is true that classical Greek philosophy (Plato, Aristotle, the Stoics) had no special term for 'the person'—just as, and not unrelatedly, the Greeks had no exact term for 'freedom' of will nor indeed for 'will'. It also seems true that when the term *persona* came to have its full theoretical content in later ancient philosophy, one important factor behind this development was reflection on the Trinity and Christ's two natures. Still, it is decidedly false to suggest that the classical Greek philosophers had

This is an extensively revised version of the paper I read at the Aberystwyth conference. A later version was read to the Copenhagen Aristotelian group. I am grateful to the audience on both occasions for criticism that helped to clarify a number of points. Adam Morton, Finn Collin, Peter Sandøe, and the editor also provided written comments, for which I am most grateful.

no concept of the person. On the contrary, it seems fair to say that whatever they said in ethics and those parts of their philosophy which we would include under philosophy of action was intended to bring out precisely what defines a person, namely a 'human being' (*anthrōpos*) in the rather exclusive sense in which the Greeks understood this. Therefore, when around AD 520 the Christian philosopher Boethius defined the person (*persona*) as 'an individual substance of a rational nature',[1] he was summing up the whole ancient tradition rather than being innovatory.

If, then, ancient Greek *and* Christian thought agree in their understanding of the person, and if it is also the case that this understanding finds expression in their doctrines in ethics and the philosophy of action, then the modern attack on the concept of the person will presumably not be an insignificant affair. Rather, it will be part of a very general attack on central elements in what may (in spite of individual differences) fairly be called *the* common tradition in European thought in ethics and moral psychology. The aim of this essay is to diagnose what is, as I hope to show, a fairly important element in that clash between the ancients and the moderns, and moreover an element which seems to me to lie at the centre of the concept of the person. If that concept is to have any future, the element that I shall point to must prove capable of resisting attack.

What concerns me is an understanding of the function and power of reflection (rationality) in relation to an agent's desires which in spite of great individual differences is shared by Plato, Aristotle, and the Stoics. This is the view that the power of reason is such that it may in principle change a man's desires. I say 'in principle' mainly because of Aristotle. Although the matter is debated, it seems reasonably clear that Aristotle developed a view of the antecedents of action according to which two independent roots, namely belief and desire, are in the final analysis required in order to give a full explanation of it.[2] In spite of this, however, Aristotle insists, in his chapter in the *Nicomachean Ethics* (hereafter *EN*) on moral psychology, that 'the desiderative part' is made so as to 'obey' 'the rational part', which in turn 'gives commands' to the other one

[1] *Liber de persona et duabus naturis*, ch. 3, in J.-P. Migne (ed.), *Patrologia Latina*, lxiv. 1343c: *Persona est naturae rationalis individua substantia.*

[2] I have argued for this in *Aristotle's Theory of Moral Insight* (Oxford, 1983), pt. II.

(*EN* 1. 13. 1102b25–1103a1). One may, but need not, find an inconsistency between these two views, but the point is that, no matter whether there is one or not, Aristotle himself apparently wished to claim that reason does have the power to change a man's desires—even when he held views which (at last initially) seem to point in a different direction. In Stoicism, not only is it explicitly claimed that reason is 'a craftsman of impulse' (Diogenes Laertius, 7. 86), but we shall see that a great deal of Stoic ethics and philosophy of action is intended to explicate the ramifications of this idea. This idea, I suggest, is 'common knowledge' down through the history of European thought on these matters. It begins to be questioned, famously, in Hume; and Kant's moral philosophy (with its distinction between the empirical and the noumenal world) may to a large degree be seen as an attempt to reinstate it in the face of criticism made of it by Hume and others. But Kant's attempt to stem the tide was unsuccessful and throughout the two last centuries it has come under constant attack, not only in philosophy, but also in new intellectual disciplines like psychology, so that by now it has more or less lost its hold on the general imagination.

I wish to discuss the idea here in the form given to it in Stoic philosophy. This is not merely for the reason that, historically, the Stoic formulation is particularly important. It *is* this: the Stoics confronted the question of the power of reason more directly than Aristotle did, both in their analysis of desire (impulse) and in their analysis of human freedom of the will. In other words, Stoicism contains the classic formulation of the idea, to which Plato and Aristotle may be said to lead. Furthermore, although the formulation of the idea given by Boethius in his definition of the person is reached by him through a series of dichotomies which are common Platonic, Aristotelian, and Stoic heritage,[3] I believe that the exact point of 'individual' in the definition is in fact specifically Stoic. So this definition, which stands at the gateway to medieval and later European thought, reflects a specifically Stoic understanding.

The other reason why I concentrate on the Stoics is that they developed the idea of reason as a craftsman of impulse in a way that invites comparison with certain ideas put forward in two quite recent and important books on ethics, Bernard Williams's *Ethics and the Limits of Philosophy* and Thomas Nagel's *The View from*

[3] See *Liber de persona*, ch. 2, in Migne (ed.), *Patrologia*, lxiv. 1342c–1343c.

*Nowhere.*[4] These two books are not directly concerned with the person in the sense in which I am working with the notion here,[5] but I have already stated my view that any valid assertion about the person will be made in ethics and other philosophical disciplines. The two books are also very different in their basic attitude towards morality. Still, as I shall try to show, they share an understanding of individuality or subjectivity which, irrespective of any differences between them, opposes them to the traditional view, as exemplified here by Stoicism, and in fact casts doubt on the general validity of the concept of the person.

My procedure here is as follows. I first mention the ideas in Williams and Nagel that interest me. Then I set forth certain relevant ideas in Stoicism with the following aims in view: (1) elucidating the view of subjectivity that Williams and Nagel share, by distinguishing it from the kind of subjectivity we find in Stoicism; (2) suggesting that the view of subjectivity that is found in Williams and Nagel, and the corresponding view of rationality in relation to individuality, threatens to erode the traditional concept of the person; (3) suggesting, with appropriate caution, that there may not, after all, be sufficient grounding for their view, and hence for its far-reaching implications.

Before starting I should perhaps emphasize that my topic here is not just the familiar one of the relationship of reason to desire (although I referred to that theme earlier). That theme is part of the topic, but not the whole of it. Rather my topic is the more general one of the relationship in a human being of rationality and individuality. On reason and desire, as is well known, Williams and Nagel disagree, Williams avowing himself to be 'sub-Humean' in the explanation of action[6] and Nagel adopting a more Kantian position.[7] On the wider and more fundamental question, however, I believe that they agree—thereby displaying their modernity.[8]

The point that I find significant in Williams and Nagel is their dissociation of what Nagel calls 'the good life' from what he calls

[4] *Ethics* (London, 1985); *View* (New York, 1986).

[5] Nagel, of course, discusses extensively the question of personal *identity*.

[6] See esp. 'Internal and External Reasons', in *Moral Luck: Philosophical Essays 1973–1980* (Cambridge, 1981), 101–13.

[7] *View*, pp. 149–52—and of course in Nagel, *The Possibility of Altruism* (Oxford, 1970), *passim*.

[8] In spite of Nagel's professed reactionary stance, *View*, pp. 9ff.

'the moral life.'[9] In the end Williams would hardly find any use at all for the notion of 'the moral life'. For one result of his sustained attack throughout *Ethics* on 'morality, the peculiar institution' is clearly that the idea of the moral life, in the basically Kantian sense in which I employ it, is discredited as being at all a useful one.[10] But Williams and Nagel agree in denying a view which was fundamental to ancient ethics, namely that the moral life *is* the good life. The Greeks (Aristotle and the Stoics) started out by asking about the *telos*, i.e. about the good life for a man, and then by various routes ended up by saying that a life consisting in behaviour that is ordinarily said to be moral is (at least part of) what the good life *is*. Furthermore, they more or less explicitly understood the moral life in that sense, that is a life in accordance with virtue and 'the noble', as one that is impersonally good in a way that points in the direction of the Kantian conception.[11] In Williams and Nagel, by contrast, the moral life, to the extent that it is allowed for at all (by Williams), is dissociated from the good life not just logically (as it is in ancient ethics too), but in fact: in certain situations concern about the good life will require one type of behaviour whereas concern about the moral life will require another, *and the two requirements are not to be reconciled.* We may note some of the underpinnings of this idea in Williams and Nagel, taking the two philosophers in that order.

As already noted, in Williams the dissociation of the good life and the moral life has the form of a 'challenge', which Nagel has christened 'Williams's Question',[12] 'to the claims of impersonal

[9] *View*, ch. 10, *passim*. Nagel himself declines to define the two terms in advance, since 'their analysis is part of the problem' (p. 193). In this chapter I understand 'the moral life' as 'a life that complies with moral requirements' (so Nagel, p. 193), but understand moral requirements as being impersonal requirements. 'The general opposition we are concerned with is that between the claims of impersonal morality and the personal perspective of the agent to whom they are addressed' (Nagel, p. 192).

[10] Williams has a lot to say throughout *Ethics* about a life which he calls an ethical life. But this life is defined precisely in opposition to the moral life as I understand it here.

[11] This may seem a very strong claim. I have argued for it, as regards Aristotle, in *Aristotle's Theory*, chs. 2–3; and the affinity of the Stoic theory with Kant's will become apparent later in this essay. Williams, who is very sympathetic to Aristotle and wishes to enlist his theory in support of his own attack on 'morality', does not confront this aspect of the Aristotelian theory in his otherwise excellent discussion of Aristotle in *Ethics*, ch. 3. But then, in the final analysis he of course stands back from the Aristotelian theory when he comes near to its view of human nature and its function in the theory. (See *Ethics*, ch. 3, pp. 52–3.)

[12] *View*, pp. 189–93. The quotation is from p. 191.

morality from the point of view of the individual agent to whom those claims are addressed. . . . The general objection [sc. Williams's] is that impersonal moralities demand too much of us, and that if we accept and act on those demands, we cannot lead good lives.' Behind this challenge there lies a view of man which finds expression in a number of different, but connected ideas. I mention some of them.[13]

There is first Williams's adoption of a 'sub-Humean' understanding of practical reasoning according to which so-called 'external reason statements, when definitely isolated as such, are false, or incoherent, or really something else misleadingly expressed. . . . The only real claims about reasons for action will be internal claims.'[14] This view, however, is not in itself sufficient to question the legitimacy of connecting the good life and the moral life. For as already hinted, whereas Aristotle may have subscribed to a Humean understanding of the explanation of action, he certainly did not dissociate the two lives.[15]

Next there is Williams's insistence on the plurality, and in fact the genuine incommensurability, of values.[16] This insistence is part of his general attack on utilitarianism, but it is also connected with two claims of his which take us nearer to the root idea behind his challenge to impersonal morality. One is his thesis that a man has 'a *ground* project or set of projects which are closely related to his existence and which to a significant degree give a meaning to his life', 'the idea of a man's ground projects providing the motive force which propels him into the future, and gives him a reason for living'.[17] With this idea comes, according to Williams, the possibility of 'radical conflict'[18] between the claims of a man's ground projects and those of moral impartiality of the Kantian kind, and once this possibility is allowed for, one is forced to admit

[13] In what follows I often refer to Williams's writings previous to *Ethics*. This is because some of the formulations of particular aspects of Williams's general view seem sharper there. I do not find any fundamental change from these writings to *Ethics*. If one wants to spell out the *basis* for Williams's position in *Ethics*, e.g. for his final rejection of the Aristotelian theory (cf. n. 11 above), which turns on the possibility of a gap between 'the agent's perspective', or 'personal aspirations', and 'the outside view', one will often find it helpful to go back to the earlier writings.

[14] 'Internal and External Reasons', in *Moral Luck*, p. 111.

[15] Williams of course knows this and brings out well in *Ethics*, ch. 3, the difference between Aristotle and himself.

[16] See e.g. 'Conflicts of Values' in *Moral Luck*, pp. 71–82.

[17] See 'Persons, Character and Morality' in *Moral Luck*, pp. 1–19. Quotations are from pp. 12 and 13. (Williams's emphasis.)

[18] Ibid. 12.

that it is not a reasonable demand on the agent that the requirements of impartial morality should always win. 'There can come a point at which it is quite unreasonable for a man to give up, in the name of the impartial good ordering of the world of moral agents, something which is a condition of his having any interest in being around in that world at all.' Williams sums up this idea in the notion of 'having a character' and claims that 'the Kantians' omission of character is a condition of their ultimate insistence on the demands of impartial morality, just as it is a reason for finding inadequate their account of the individual'.[19] With the very last word in this quotation we are, I believe, at the heart of the matter.

The other claim that is linked with the idea of the incommensurability of values is that we need the concept of moral individuality if we are to give an adequate account of personal relations. People have dissimilar characters and projects and one context where this becomes of vital importance is that of personal relations. For these are precisely cases of commitment or involvement with a particular other person regarded as being different from others. Moreover, since personal relations fall under a man's ground projects, they too may come into conflict with impersonal morality, and this conflict too will be radical and in fact insoluble: 'somewhere . . . one reaches the necessity that such things as deep attachments to other persons will express themselves in the world in ways which cannot at the same time embody the impartial view, and that they also run the risk of offending against it'.[20]

A third idea behind Williams's challenge to impersonal morality is his historicist and relativist view of the ontological status of values. In 'The Truth in Relativism',[21] he argued for an understanding of relativism which allows it to be a logically coherent claim that relativism 'for ethical outlooks at least' is a correct standpoint. In *Ethics* he argues extensively[22] that relativism (for such outlooks) is in fact the correct standpoint. For my purposes the most important feature of this argument is Williams's repeated claim that philosophers have misconceived the power and role of reflection (reason). Instead of assuming that reflection can provide a universal justification of morality, which can then be applied to

[19] Quotations, ibid. 14.

[20] Ibid. 15–19. Quotation from p. 18.

[21] In *Moral Luck*, pp. 132–43. The quotation is from p. 142.

[22] See esp. ch. 9.

everyday practice, one should recognize that 'reflective criticism' should work in the opposite direction. 'Critical reflection should seek as much shared understanding as it can find on any issue, and use any ethical material that, in the context of the reflective discussion, makes some sense and commands some loyalty'[23] and on this basis it should 'help us to construct a world that will be our world, one in which we have a social, cultural, and personal life'.[24] The opposition that is brought to play here is well known from the history of ethics. There are similarities (but decidedly not more than that) in Aristotle's reaction against Plato's theory of the good and in Hegel's against Kant's theory of morality. It is important, however, to see the particular basis on which Williams argues for this view. I believe this comes out very clearly in the following, already famous, passage:[25]

> Any attempt to see philosophical reflection in ethics as a jump to the universalistic standpoint in search of justification, which is then brought back to everyday practice . . . makes in some degree a Platonic assumption that the reflective agent as theorist can make himself independent from the life and character he is examining. The belief that you can look critically at all your dispositions from the outside, from the point of view of the universe,[26] assumes that you could understand your own and other people's dispositions from that point of view without tacitly taking for granted a picture of the world more locally familiar than any that would be available from there; but neither the psychology nor the history of ethical reflection gives much reason to believe that the theoretical reasonings of the cool hour can do without a sense of the moral shape of the world, of the kind given in the everyday dispositions.

On the next page Williams refers to 'the differences between practical and theoretical reason'. I shall take this up, in connection with Williams's final rejection of the Kantian argument for morality in *Ethics*, chapter 4, once I have introduced the relevant Stoic material.

With the long quotation from Williams we have reached what I take to be the root idea behind Williams's challenge to impersonal morality, namely the insistence on the non-transcendable character of 'the local view'. The question that calls for an answer is whether there is sufficient philosophical backing for this insistence, or whether it is rather an expression of a combination of Williams's

[23] Ch. 6, p. 117. [24] Ibid. 111. [25] Ibid.

[26] In Sidgwick's phrase, which Williams has discussed on p. 105.

own openly professed liberal individualism[27] with a more widely shared, general modern sentiment to the same effect.

I may be somewhat briefer on Nagel's version of the view that I am tracking, since on the relevant points it is closely similar to Williams's. Nagel differs radically from Williams, of course, in that Nagel's whole book is premissed on the view that the idea of a 'point of view of the universe' is not, as Williams once put it,[28] 'memorably absurd', rather it brings out a vital property of a human being, which is that the human individual has an impulse and a capacity to transcend the subjective viewpoint and to adopt an objective viewpoint from which one sees oneself as just an individual among others. This viewpoint, so Nagel claims, is to be thought of as being 'centerless',[29] it is the viewpoint of 'someone considering the world in detachment from the perspective of any particular person within it'[30] or 'from no particular point of view'.[31] But the other side of Nagel's overall picture is that the objective view will need to recognize that the world that it is considering contains subjective points of view which cannot be replaced by the objective view, and this idea turns out to be closer to Williams's than might immediately appear.

In its first appearances in *The View from Nowhere* Nagel's claim takes up his old view[32] that there are subjective features of conscious mental processes which cannot be captured by objective thought, but only (if at all) by some kind of subjective imagination. Thus we shall never know exactly how scrambled eggs taste to a cockroach even if we develop a detailed objective phenomenology of the cockroach's sense of taste.[33] But Nagel broadens this idea considerably when he goes on immediately to declare: 'When it comes to values, goals, and forms of life, the gulf may be even more profound.' Later in the book, in the chapters on value, ethics, and living rightly and living well, the gulf is taken to be an established fact precisely with regard to values, goals and forms of life. And here the pages are full of formulations that seem to fit in completely with Williams's view. Let me give a few examples:

[27] Although in fairness to Williams this should be combined with a very serious concern about man's social side.

[28] *Moral Luck*, Pref., p. xi.

[29] *The View*, pp. 18, 140.

[30] Ibid. 153.

[31] Ibid. 161.

[32] From 'What is it Like to Be a Bat?', in *Mortal Questions* (Cambridge, 1979), 165–80.

[33] *View*, p. 25.

> Some aspects of practical reason [note, not just of what it feels like to be somebody] may prove to be irreducibly subjective, so that while their existence must be acknowledged from an objective standpoint their content cannot be understood except from a more particular perspective.[34]

> The task of ethical theory is . . . to reconcile the apparent requirement of generality that objectivity imposes with the richness, variety, and reality of the reasons that appear subjectively.[35]

> It is not easy to follow the objectifying impulse without distorting individual life and personal relations. . . . In some respects it is better to live and act not for reasons, but because it does not occur to us to do something else. This is especially true of close personal relations. Here the objective standpoint cannot be brought into the perspective of action without diminishing precisely what it affirms the value of.[36]

There are 'pockets of unassimilable subjectivity'.[37] There are 'specific projects and concerns of the agent'.[38] 'Each of us must live in part from his own point of view',[39] as 'individuals who have their own lives to lead',[40] and so on. Impressed by these ideas, Nagel therefore tackles the difficult question of how to align the claims of the good life and the moral life once 'the possibility of a conflict between morality and the good life'[41] that is inherent in those ideas is fully recognized. He even takes this possibility of conflict as 'a prime example of the clash between the personal standpoint of each individual and the more objective, detached standpoint' of impersonal morality.[42] His discussion is illuminating, but he ends by noting (rightly to my mind) that 'there remains something deeply unsatisfying about conflict between the good life and the moral life and the compromises between them'.[43] As in the case of Williams, I believe that the question should be whether there is in fact enough philosophical backing behind the insistence on individuals 'having their own lives to lead' (and so on)—or whether here too this insistence may not rather be an expression of a modern pluralistic individualism to which Nagel too declares his adherence.[44]

I now turn to the Stoic material. I shall not, of course, engage in any detailed exegesis, but I shall have to present the relevant Stoic ideas

[34] Ch. 8, p. 149.
[35] Ibid. 151.
[36] Ibid. 155.
[37] Ibid.
[38] Ch. 9, p. 178.
[39] Ibid. 187.
[40] Ch. 10, p. 189.
[41] Ibid. 192.
[42] Ibid. 193.
[43] Ibid. 205.
[44] Ibid. 188, 207.

in such detail that it will become clear to the reader who is unfamiliar with them exactly how they are relevant to the modern ideas that I have presented so far.

The Stoic doctrine that interests me is their account of *oikeiōsis*, i.e. of a mental process by which a human being will, if things go rightly, arrive at the true grasp of the good, namely that it is 'living in accordance with nature' (*convenientia naturae*) or rather, as we shall see, 'in accordance with the real'. The Stoic account has two stages. It first provides an account of the explanation of pre-rational action (of animals and infants), which is thought of by the Stoics as a non-normative account of pre-rational 'impulse' (Greek *hormē*). Next it gives an account of a change in understanding of the goals of action that comes with reason and issues in a grasp of what is truly good. The account of the second stage is itself twofold. At first the process results in the grasp that the true good is *convenientia naturae*, where the latter is understood in such a way that it does not coincide with anything *we* would include under 'the moral'.[45] (By contrast, the Stoics themselves did connect *convenientia naturae* with 'virtue' and 'the noble', i.e. with *to kalon*, which from Aristotle onwards is the common Greek expression for what belongs in the 'moral' sphere as opposed, for example, to considerations of prudence.)[46] Later, then, the process results in a grasp of something that we too will immediately call a moral good, normally the goodness of justice.

Let me explain these stages in more detail. The essence of the first stage is this.[47] Any pre-rational action that is governed by impulse is to be explained in the following terms. (1) The immediate logical starting-point is the animal's love of self, and impulse is then to be

[45] I take it to be constitutive of the ordinary modern notion of the moral that it has to do with an individual's relations with others.

[46] The distinction that I am implying here between the Greek understanding of the 'moral' sphere and the modern one should not be pressed. It is precisely a question whether 'the Greek' understanding, as expressed in their use of the term *kalon*, does differ so strongly as it is often taken from 'the modern' understanding with its strong emphasis on the relationship with others and on considerations of justice.

[47] I have discussed all the Stoic topics that I touch on in this essay much more extensively in a book entitled *The Stoic Theory of Oikeiosis* (forthcoming). In the present essay I incorporate from the book some fairly important changes in relation to my earlier paper, 'Discovering the good: *Oikeiōsis* and *kathēkonta* in Stoic Ethics', in M. Schofield and G. Striker (edd.), *The Norms of Nature: Studies in Hellenistic Ethics* (Cambridge, 1986), 145–83. The main textual evidence on *oikeiōsis* on Cicero, *De Finibus* (*Fin.*), 3. 5. 16–7. 25.

explained in terms of an awareness on the part of the animal that things in the world either 'belong' or are 'alien' to the self, of whose 'constitution' or structure the animal is also aware. A child, for example, will have some instinctive awareness of its own bodily structure and, due to its love of self, it will consider certain things, e.g. food, which tend to preserve that structure, as 'belonging' to itself, whereas other things, e.g. lack of shelter, will be considered to be 'alien' to it. In the appropriate circumstances such awareness will issue in action. (2) This account of pre-rational impulse seems, at first glance, to be based on the familiar idea that an animal's response to its environment combines an evaluative component (love of self) with a certain set of non-evaluative beliefs in the form of an awareness of the structure of the self and of the relationship of certain things in the world to that structure, namely whether they will tend to preserve or destroy it. However, underlying what immediately appeared to be the logical starting-point (love of self), the Stoics postulated another kind of relation to the self, viz. self-awareness (*sensus sui*, in Cicero's formulation) (*Fin.* 3. 5. 16). In fact it appears that they worked with a logical triad which (starting from what is most basic) consists of (*a*) 'being aware of oneself', (*b*) 'seeing oneself as belonging to oneself',[48] and (*c*) 'loving oneself'.

The idea of this may be that self-awareness (*a*)—even of the rudimentary kind attributable to animals—implies a recognition of two entities, the self that is aware and the 'bearer' of that consciousness, i.e. what the self is aware *of* in self-awareness. But then self-awareness (*a*) will presumably imply seeing the self of which one is aware as logically 'belonging' to 'oneself', i.e. to the self that is aware. In other words (*a*) will imply (*b*). But once (*a*) is seen to imply the fuller form of (*b*), it seems to follow that self-awareness (*a*) *creates* a *complex* self (*b*) *from* which, as an ineliminable viewpoint, everything *outside* the self will henceforth be seen. But in that case (*a*) and (*b*) will add up to (*c*), 'loving' oneself; and self-awareness (in this fully developed form) will be sufficient by itself to explain why an animal's beliefs that things outside the (full) self either belong or are alien to it will also be action-guiding. This interpretation of the Stoic doctrine may seem contrived, but it is the only one that gives any real sense to Cicero's remark that animals 'could not feel desire towards anything unless they possessed self-awareness *and consequently* felt love for

[48] '. . . ipsum sibi conciliari', ibid.

themselves' (*Fin.* 3. 5. 16). What the Stoics seem to be saying is that one cannot think of a being who is aware of himself, and hence of the fact that he is distinct from the rest of the world, but who is not also concerned about himself or about maintaining in existence the distinct being that he is.

What the Stoics have given us so far is an analysis of pre-rational impulse with the following main features. Such impulse is to be understood in terms of the idea of what we may call a subjective viewpoint, and there are two aspects of this claim. First, the viewpoint is *subjective* in the sense that it is ineradicably based in the agent's awareness of his own self. Whatever is seen is seen *from* the particular perspective that is created by self-awareness in the way I suggested. Secondly, the subjective viewpoint is to be understood precisely as a *viewpoint*, as a perspective from which things are *seen*. The Stoics are analysing impulse, which is a generic term for desire, but they are claiming that impulse should be understood in terms of two mental states which are not evaluative: (1) awareness of individual identity and (2) belief about the 'constitution' of the self and about what things in the world preserve and destroy the self as so constituted.

The Stoics give no extended argument for the truth of this way of understanding pre-rational impulse. Rather, their claim is an a priori one.[49] It is, however, based on an understanding of the relation of sentient beings to the world which is of crucial importance to the whole doctrine. According to the Stoics, when an animal or infant starts 'dividing' the world between that which belongs and that which is alien, the logical starting-point, as we have seen, is self-awareness. But this does not mean that it is the self which in some sense posits how it is constituted and how, consequently, the world should be divided. On the contrary, even in its most rudimentary state of awareness the self is concerned from the start with judging the truth about its own constitution and the divisions of the world. The animal's mental equipment is right from the start adapted towards discovering how things are. This view is a naturalistic one, and it coheres closely with, and is indeed a part of, Stoic epistemology. It is also, as I think we should say, a normative view, in the sense that it presupposes without argument a certain description of sentient beings at a fundamental level which while

[49] Cf. in the sentence from Cicero quoted above: 'they could not feel desire towards anything unless . . .'.

being taken to be true is also understood as having normative consequences (at least potentially): if a sentient being does not fulfil the process of development described in this account, it goes wrong and should in principle be corrected. I am not going to argue that this view is true (though I believe it is), merely to note that on this view sentient beings are from the start operating in an area of what may be called 'public discourse', an area where the presupposed aim is truth or being right and where the criteria for truth-assertions are shared or public.[50]

The main point is that although the Stoics saw every case of intentional behaviour as being based in a subjective viewpoint that is ineliminable, they would not have understood (or at least would have pressed for further information on) the notion of ineradicable subjectivity as regards the *content* of the subjective viewpoint. The Stoics stressed the importance of the notion of the self to such an extent that one may be tempted to claim that they even discovered it. But they did not allot to it any ineradicably subjective content. On the contrary, whatever content it has was thought by them to be in principle public and accessible to rational discourse.

The next stage in the Stoic account of *oikeiōsis* comes with the arrival of reason. Essentially this stage consists in becoming aware, by a process of self-reflection, of the value that underlies behaviour at the first stage. Once a man has acquired reason he will come to see two things. The first is that, although at the first stage the various particular objects appeared to be valuable and good since they 'belong' to the self, what is truly valuable (and hence the only thing that truly deserves the predicate 'good') is in fact the single 'value' which underlies those particular judgements, namely truth or being right about what belongs. That, then, is the good for man, *convenientia naturae* in the sense of being right about 'nature' or about what is the case (as regards belonging or being alien to somebody). The second thing that will become clear to a man during this process of self-reflection is that in reflecting on his own earlier acts and discovering in that way the single underlying value of being right about what belongs, he is making use of a special

[50] This way of putting it may seem both anachronistic and somewhat ludicrous once it is thought to apply to cockroaches and the like. The first objection I shall merely waive. As for the second, the Stoics fairly clearly wished to understand non-rational animals (and infants) as *pre*-rational, i.e. to understand them *on the basis of* their understanding of rational animals.

property of his, namely his rationality. In other words, in exercising his rational capacity and thus acquiring a belief about the good for man, he also becomes aware of his own rationality and comes to see rationality as a constituent of his own self. The result is that the belief about the good that he has acquired becomes a belief about his own good, and hence it becomes (at least potentially) action-guiding.

The good that is so grasped is not yet what we would call a 'moral' good. It is, in Stoic terms, as we already noted: they call it *to kalon* or *honestum*, and the grasp of it is virtue. And so they are entitled to say that what in the process of *oikeiōsis* began as a search for 'the good', in the sense of one's *telos* (and evidently one's own *telos*), has ended up by identifying that good as moral virtue. The reason why the Stoics could understand *convenientia naturae* (in the sense in which I have explained it) as a 'moral' good is that they saw the defining property of those mental states that were ordinarily called moral virtues as lying in the dissociation from the immediate, subjective view of values—and this dissociation is the essence of *oikeiōsis* at the rational level as I have just described it.[51] This dissociation is the result of what Nagel calls man's 'objectifying impulse'. It is not yet a dissociation from oneself in relation to others (and hence not moral in our sense). Rather, it is a dissociation from oneself in the sense of one's immediate, subjective view, and an adoption of a view of oneself that is external since it draws on public or objective criteria in order to determine the truth or falsity of one's immediate view of what is valuable. Let us consider further the exact form of this dissociation, thereby bringing the Stoic material to bear on some of the ideas we noted in Williams and Nagel.

The Stoics drew a fundamental distinction between what is good, which is one thing alone, as we have seen, and things that are *proēgmena*. The good alone is 'choiceworthy' (*haireton*). The *proēgmena* consist of most of those particular objects that appeared choiceworthy at the first stage of *oikeiōsis*. At the mature stage they are no longer considered choiceworthy (and rightly so), but they are still *proēgmena*. How should we translate this term? In two ways. (1) Such things are 'preferable' in the sense of 'objectively to be preferred'. For in many cases these things are the goals pursued in

[51] See e.g. Cicero, *Fin.* 3. 7. 25.

actions which are objectively right since they are directed towards procuring what (in the objective view) genuinely belongs to a given individual. Here the objective view *confers* value on the things that are *proēgmena*. (2) But such things are also 'preferable' in the sense that they will also be *actually* 'preferred' by an individual who is applying the objective view. For he sees them as belonging to himself *qua* individual, and hence as worthy objects of pursuit: he would rather have them than not.

The two senses of *proēgmenon* that I have distinguished clearly correspond, to some extent, to the two points of view that give rise, in Williams and Nagel, to the distinction between the moral life and the good life. It is also well known that whereas Williams and Nagel insist on the possibility of conflict, the Stoics denied this possibility. Why this difference? I believe that the reason is to be found in a different understanding, in the two cases, of individuality and rationality and of their mutual relationship.

Take first the case of (practical) rationality. As we saw, Nagel understands the objective viewpoint, which he associates with practical rationality, as centreless. Williams ridicules this idea. In fact, Nagel's formulation may be only a *façon de parler*,[52] but why is it necessary? Presumably because of Nagel's assumption that if one does not understand the objective view as centreless, if practical rationality remains *somebody's*, then it will necessarily lose its rational and objective character. Contrast with this the Stoic understanding of practical rationality. In Stoicism, practical rationality is consistently regarded as belonging to *somebody* and to somebody who has, and retains, an individual self throughout the development of the objective view. The objective view is a view *on oneself*, and this fact has a number of welcome consequences. One is that we can avoid the idea, which when taken literally is in fact absurd, of a 'point of view of the universe'. Another consequence, which I hinted at when explaining the theory, is that there is now no difficulty in understanding how one should come to *act* on the insights gained in applying the objective view. Most importantly, however, in Stoicism, in contrast to Nagel, there is no suggestion that the connection of the objective view to the individual makes it any less objective or rational.

Take then the other pole, individuality. Why should Nagel in fact assume that once we locate the objective view in an individual it

[52] See his qualifications, *View*, pp. 4–5.

will lose its objective character? It seems fairly clear that this is because in Nagel, and in Williams too, the notion of the subjective or individual is heavily loaded in some way that one would wish to see further specified. The Stoics, by contrast, did have the notion of the subjective or individual, namely the theoretically crucial concept of the self, but they understood it in such a way that it is not opposed to the notion of objectivity and rationality. In Stoicism the subjective viewpoint is not allotted any *content* that cannot in principle be taken over by the objective view. Here what is 'radically subjective' is nothing beyond the sheer fact, the importance of which cannot admittedly be overstated, of the indexicality of the objective view, i.e. its being ineradicably bound up with a given individual. So, just as practical rationality and objectivity are conceived by the Stoics as being logically inseparable from individuality and as 'matching' it, so individuality and subjectivity are conceived as being logically inseparable from rationality and objectivity. On the Stoic conception, the former two presuppose the latter two.[53]

The Stoic conception of man is therefore that of a being who is, so to speak, intermediate between being merely individual (a 'thing') and no longer individual (God). His intermediate status is bound up with his sentience, for sentience already marks a step from the object-like status of pure individuality, and yet his continuing sentience marks his continuing status as an individual. What defines the middle ground is an unbreakable, logical connection of individuality and rationality.

Against the background of this conception of the adult human being, how should one understand the Stoic category of the *proēgmena*? It has often been suggested that, after introducing their radical view that there is only one thing that is good, the Stoics bowed to human nature, so to speak, by bringing in the *proēgmena* as things of secondary value. Nothing could be further from the truth. We noted above that things are *proēgmena* in two ways that correspond to the two points of view that an adult human being may adopt. Note then that in an adult human being his dual view of the *proēgmena* is 'fused' in such a way that he retains his subjective interest in them, when this is allowed by the objective view, but

[53] Recall that pre-rational individuality (the self-awareness of non-rational animals and infants) is precisely understood by the Stoics as pre-rational, i.e. it is understood on the basis of their view of rational individuality.

loses that interest, when this is required by the objective view. In a way, things that are *proēgmena* remain 'preferable' both objectively and subjectively even when the objective view tells one to act in ways that will *not* procure such things for onself;[54] but in these cases they are subjectively *proēgmena* in the sense that the agent *would* rather have had them. There is an actual loss of interest in those things, but not of such a kind as to render the agent's attitude 'impersonal'. Once more the suggestion is that the subjective and the objective views should be kept together. The Stoics managed to do this in the way I have attempted to explain.

In order to explore the Stoic conception of the relation between the two views we may consider the second phase of their account of the development towards objectivity in an adult human being. This is the phase that results in a grasp of the moral good proper (in our sense of 'moral'), namely the goodness of justice.[55] In its essence the theory is very simple. Just as in the first phase (the development from the primitive to the mature grasp of value), so in the second phase the starting-point is something the Stoics took to be a pervasive empirical fact: that parents love their children. This love is both intelligible as an expression of the basic instinct of self-love, since children are an 'extension' of the parents, and also a genuine case of an altruistic attitude, since it is love of the children for their own sake.[56] All children, then, have experienced this attitude and they reciprocate it through love for their parents. As reason comes, along with adulthood, the human being extends his love for his parents (whom he, in turn, saw as 'belonging' to himself) to all other human beings, whom he now sees as also 'belonging' to himself since they share in the rationality that he now realizes in himself. This newly acquired affection for all mankind is the attitude that underlies justice.

The details in this picture may appear unpersuasive, but the point that is relevant in the present context is that the doctrine is one more example of how the Stoics aimed to start from a subjective perspective and to develop it in the direction of a genuinely

[54] This has to do with the fact that *proēgmena* are *types* of thing. They may therefore retain their character of being valuable even though reason may in particular cases order one to abandon them.

[55] The main textual evidence is in Cicero, *Fin*. 3. 19. 62–20. 66.

[56] The term in Cicero is 'care' (*cura*), e.g. in *De Officiis*, 1. 2. 12.

objective one in such a way that there is no loss of personal content once the objective view has been reached. It would surely be perverse to suggest that on the Stoic view children would (or should) stop loving their parents (or vice versa) once they have reached the objective view. Rather, as in the case of *proēgmena*, we should take it that in the adult human being the two types of concern are fused into a single one; and although, in this fused concern, the objective aspect must always win, room is still left for personal concern. The reason why the Stoics could make both claims is that they saw no discrepancy between the subjective and objective viewpoints, but saw them as essentially united.

I now propose to consider two arguments in Williams and Nagel (one in each) that seem to me to depend crucially for their validity on what is (when contrasted with the Stoic view) a heavily loaded understanding of subjectivity. First I discuss an argument of Williams's in *Ethics* and next a line of thought of Nagel's, the consideration of which will require a brief discussion of the Stoic doctrine of freedom of the will.

In chapter 4 of *Ethics*, Williams proposes to show that Kant's attempt to ground morality in practical reasoning is unsucessful, by appraising the claim that ethical considerations are somehow presupposed by rational freedom. He first[57] constructs a (very Nagelian) argument in support of Kant's claim. The freedom of a rational agent consists of the freedom to act on reasons (as opposed to acting in a way that is to be explained merely in terms of beliefs and desires). Acting on reasons, in this view, implies reflecting on oneself as an agent, seeing oneself as one agent among others, and standing back from one's own desires and interests in order to see them from a standpoint that is not that *of* those desires and interests. It implies, in short, the standpoint of impartiality, which also implies, in turn, that the rational agent will seek to harmonize the interests of all rational agents.

Next[58] Williams proceeds to argue why this line of thought does not work. Basically, his argument turns on a distinction between factual and practical deliberation. The latter is 'essentially', even 'radically', 'first-personal' and involves an *I* which is in some important sense 'the *I* of my desires'. Factual deliberation, by

[57] *Ethics*, pp. 65–6.
[58] Ibid. 66–9. The quotations that I give in what follows are all from these pages.

contrast, is '*about the world*'[59] and the *I* that may be involved here[60] is 'impersonal'. In factual deliberation one is indeed 'committed, by the nature of the process, to the aim of a consistent set of beliefs, one's own and others' ', so here one will take up a standpoint that is 'impartial and seeks harmony'—'but this is because it seeks truth'. In factual deliberation there is a 'unity of interest with prereflective belief: each in its way aims at truth, and this is why the prereflective disposition to believe yields so easily, in the standard case, to corrective reflection'. In practical deliberation, by contrast, 'the *I* that stands back in rational reflection from my desires is still the *I* that has those desires and will, empirically and concretely, act; and it is not, simply by standing back in reflection, converted into a being whose fundamental interest lies in the harmony of all interests. It cannot, just by taking this step, acquire the motivations of justice.'

It will be immediately clear how one should react, on Stoic premisses, to this objection to the Kantian project. First one should applaud everything Williams says about factual deliberation—that it is concerned with the world, that it seeks truth, and that it shares a 'unity of interest' with pre-reflective belief. Secondly, one should insist that exactly the same holds for practical deliberation. And thirdly, one should claim that everything that Williams takes to be specific to practical deliberation is in fact specific to it—but that this does not prevent us from aligning practical with factual deliberation (the latter being understood as Williams—correctly—characterizes it). Thus it is true that practical deliberation involves an *I* that is the *I* of my desires; it is true that the *I* that stands back in rational reflection from my desires is still the *I* that has those desires and will, empirically and concretely, act; and it is true that practical deliberation is essentially first-personal. All of this holds good on the Stoic view too, as we have seen—but without making practical deliberation any less 'about the world' than factual deliberation. So the Stoic conception can give Williams all that he requires for practical deliberation (to judge from his actual words) while preventing the dichotomy between factual and practical deliberation that Williams takes to show the inadequacy of the Kantian attempt.

But, it may be asked, is practical deliberation '*radically*' first-

[59] Williams's emphasis.

[60] e.g. in 'What should I think about this question?'.

personal, on the Stoic conception, in the sense intended by Williams? Well, what *is* that sense? In the argument that I have been discussing nothing more is said to make clear any special sense that Williams may attach to the 'first personal' view, which would enable us to distinguish his conception of practical deliberation from the Stoic one, and hence see how his conclusion is justified. So perhaps we should look elsewhere in his book for further illumination, remembering that the supposed differences between practical and theoretical reason are invoked elsewhere, e.g. in chapter 6 on 'Theory and Prejudice'.[61] But I believe that we could go on in this way until we decided to stop at what seems to be the root idea of the individual or personal viewpoint as some kind of sacred zone not to be intruded upon by any kind of invasion from the outside.[62] One may agree with Williams' claim on the final page of the book that we should uphold the belief in 'the continuing possibility of a meaningful individual life, one that does not reject society, and indeed shares its perceptions with other people to a considerable depth, but is enough unlike others, in its opacities and disorder as well as in its reasoned intentions, to make it *somebody's*'.[63] One may agree with this, particularly with reference to the idea of opacities and disorder that characterize human beings as they actually are. But, on Stoic premisses, one would like to see more by way of philosophical justification of the claim that there is some *inherent* property in individuality (other than indexicality, the importance of which is obvious) that makes it appropriate to speak of radical first-personhood in a very strong sense.

Williams rejected the project of grounding ethical considerations in rational freedom. One might perhaps paraphrase his argument as claiming that, in the case of practical deliberation, there is not a

[61] *Ethics*, p. 111.

[62] This observation may seem unfair to Williams, who has done so much to spell out the many different philosophical contexts in which the notion of the individual viewpoint turns up, in his view, as basic. But the aim of the present essay is precisely to point to an overall alternative understanding of some, at least, of these contexts with the implication that there are distinctions within the notion of the individual viewpoint that should be drawn but which are not drawn by Williams. Once these distinctions have been drawn, we may go on to ask which general understanding is the better one. Whether in answering this question we are still doing 'philosophy' in a strict sense of the term or rather (to the extent that it differs) in a broader sense which includes reflection on the history of European man, is a question to which I have at present no answer.

[63] *Ethics*, pp. 201–2.

sufficient degree of freedom for the project to get off the ground precisely because of the irreducibly first-personal elements in such deliberation. I now turn to a line of thought in Nagel that appears very similar and leads Nagel to deny not only that human beings have freedom of the will, but also that there is any coherent notion of the freedom of the will at all. First, however, I shall outline, very briefly, the Stoic view on this matter. Their doctrine here is extremely complex[64] and I shall concentrate on those elements that are immediately relevant to the present discussion.

The doctrine has two parts, one intended to account for freedom of action and one for freedom of the will. I am concerned only with the latter. On one influential interpretation of the Stoic doctrine of moral responsibility and freedom,[65] when the Stoics say that human actions are 'up to us' they are saying that our actions are 'ours' in the sense that they are not directly caused from the outside; rather the single most important causal factor lies in ourselves, in our own 'character', 'personality' or 'individual nature'.[66] But then, it is sometimes asked, how will a reference to the individual's character or individual 'nature' (understood as both determining the particular action and being themselves determined by the external factors of heredity and environment) in fact make the individual morally responsible and even free?[67]

I believe that it can be shown that the Stoics both wished (and were able) to claim that the human being is free even in relation to his own character and also that in a different respect human freedom is bound. This comes out best in certain Stoic passages in the Christian philosopher Origen. In one of these[68] Origen contrasts animal movement at large with the intelligent behaviour of a rational being. The rational agent, so he says, is capable of 'somehow following his own movement'. This is clearly another formulation of the basic element in *oikeiōsis*, namely self-reflection. A man has the capacity for being distanced from his own immediate impulse or understanding, and it is this capacity which enables him, as Origen says elsewhere,[69] to 'judge his presentations and reject

[64] I have discussed it in detail in *Stoic Theory*, ch. 6.

[65] C. Stough, 'Stoic Determinism and Moral Responsibility', in J. M. Rist (ed.), *The Stoics* (Los Angeles, 1978), 203–31.

[66] Stough, p. 219.

[67] Cf. e.g. B. Inwood, *Ethics and Human Action in Early Stoicism* (Oxford, 1985), 68.

[68] H. von Arnim (ed.), *Stoicorum Veterum Fragmenta*, ii (Leipzig, 1903, repr. Stuttgart, 1964), fr. 989.

[69] Ibid. ii. 988, 990.

some or accept some as a guide to action', 'to handle them in this or the opposite way by using reason as a judge and inquirer into how one should react to these particular external things.' What Origen describes here is of course practical deliberation, and it is precisely the capacity for practical deliberation, as the Stoics understood this, which makes a man morally responsible, because free—even in relation to his own character. For on the Stoic view, just as an impulse is at base a (practical) belief about the world, so an agent's character is a set of beliefs, and in practical deliberation a person is capable of raising in a way that is genuinely new the question whether his previous understanding was in fact correct.

But note two ways in which, if human freedom is the freedom of deliberation, such freedom will also be bound. It will be bound, first, in that it is essentially committed to discovering what the world is like. As Origen says:[70] we *ourselves* reject certain impressions *as false*. Elsewhere[71] he says that the mind assents to something *because of* certain plausibilities. This is the point at which the freedom of reason is bound no less than anything else; it is determined by the way the world is, that is by fate. In a splendid remark,[72] Origen explicitly distinguishes his Stoic understanding of what is 'up to us' from what looks like a more modern notion of freedom. 'If', he says, 'somebody should want what is up to us to be *detached from the (world as a) whole* so that we do not choose something *because* something has happened to us, then he has forgotten that he is part of the universe and that he is contained in a community of human beings and of what contains.' Reason does not exist in a vacuum. Reason is *about the world* and its point lies in grasping the world. It would be a complete misunderstanding of the role of reason in binding human beings and the world together, were one to understand what is 'up to us', and hence the freedom that reason gives us, as being completely detached from any relation to the world. Rather the freedom that reason gives is a freedom to reach a *better* understanding of the world, to reach a grasp of the world that is more likely to be *true*.

There is a second way in which human freedom (understood as the freedom of deliberation) will be bound. As reason works in deliberation it is a capacity to extend infinitely towards objective truth, but the specific understanding of any given individual will necessarily be limited, and therefore his assent and decision will in

[70] Ibid. 989. [71] Ibid. 988. [72] Ibid. 996.

fact be bound by the actual limitations on the scope of his reach towards the whole of truth. The Stoics would evidently admit that at some point any given individual will necessarily have to decide for himself about how the world appears to him, but I conjecture (it cannot be more) that they would insist that this fact does not diminish his freedom; *for*, since he is rational, such an individual will *know*, first that he may be wrong about the world, and secondly that he *could* have made further attempts to find out about it. This knowledge, indeed, seems implied in the very ability to deliberate.

How does this account of moral responsibility and freedom compare with Nagel's interpretation of freedom? I cannot do full justice here to the complexity of Nagel's chapter on freedom,[73] but a brief sketch is required.

According to Nagel we have an intuitive conception of autonomy according to which we are, in some fairly strong way, the authors of our own actions. This belief implies that the ultimate explanation of an autonomous action is wholly intentional and essentially connected with the agent's point of view. This intuitive and pre-reflective belief in autonomy is initially strengthened when the external view, by increasing our objectivity and self-awareness, gives us a better understanding of the external circumstances of our actions and enables us to control those circumstances better. But when the objective view turns inwards and wishes to examine also the 'desires, beliefs, feelings and impulses of the agent',[74] and when, as a result of this expanded objectivity, 'the unchosen conditions of action are extended into the agent's make-up and psychological state',[75] then these unchosen conditions seem to engulf everything, and the area of freedom left to the agent shrinks to zero. And so the intuitive idea of autonomy and freedom breaks down. The external view, which operates only by causal explanations, has ousted the idea of autonomy, which was based in the subjective view, and has shown the latter to be unintelligible. But since we cannot, according to Nagel, give up our belief in an autonomy of the kind sketched, we are, he concludes, at a dead end.

Seen through Stoic eyes, it is fairly clear that Nagel combines in his conception of subjectivity two types of content which should be kept distinct. There is first his point about the intentional, as opposed to causal, character of action, a point that is connected

[73] *View*, ch. 7. [74] Ibid. 119. [75] Ibid. 125–6.

with Nagel's general insistence on the irreducible character of the subjective. But then there is another point, one that Nagel shares with Williams: that there are 'individual' desires, beliefs, feelings, and impulses (and unchosen conditions of these) that are inherently inaccessible to rational discourse. Whereas a Stoic might conceivably accept the first point (and so enrich his theory by it), he would see the second point as a premature expression of despair and would press for further argument in its defence. For the Stoics there is no inherent property in the subjective view which makes it unfit as an object of rational reflection. For, although the subjective view is ineliminable as the starting-point of deliberation and the basis of action, it is restricted to being just that. As for its content (first-personal practical beliefs), these are of the same type as the beliefs formulated by the objective view, and so descriptive in form. There is nothing in the subjective view that the objective view will show to *be* nothing.

This concerns the pole of individuality in the dual scheme of the individual and the rational. Here, as we have seen, although the Stoics insisted, and very strongly, on the notion of the self, they also regarded any content that is ascribed to it as being public, rather than private, and therefore as open to rational examination by other rational beings. Nagel's despair that ultimately human beings cannot transcend themselves would not, therefore, be theirs. As regards the other pole in the scheme, in particular Nagel's suggestion that reason at first leads us to believe that we can, in an absolute sense, choose 'everything about ourselves, including all our principles of choice',[76] and that this is the content of our intuitive idea of autonomy, the Stoics would, if anything, find the suggestion preposterous. For on the Stoic view human beings are bound to the world and so is human reason. Still it gives them freedom of the only intelligible kind, by making them capable of understanding the world and themselves better, which is what they have been trying to do all along. Human freedom is having or exercising this capacity, nothing more nor less.

I believe that the Stoic conception of the human being as one in whom individuality and rationality are logically connected, and their concomitant views on impulse, practical deliberation and freedom, are worthy of further exploration with a view to assessing

[76] Ibid. 118.

their independent, philosophical merit. This has not been my aim in this essay. Rather, I have wished, as it were, to impersonate Stoic philosophy and to present certain central tenets of that philosophy in the form of a challenge to a view of human subjectivity that seems to be shared by Bernard Williams and Thomas Nagel, but which one might wish to see further clarified and argued for.

The perspective of my argument will be clear. I suggested initially that there is a single concept of the person which runs through centuries of European thought; and that this concept, as formulated by Boethius, for instance, on the point of transition between the ancient and the medieval world, is specifically Stoic in its insistence on the connection between individuality and rationality in a person. I then introduced into my picture claims of Williams and Nagel in ethics and in the philosophy of mind which are incompatible with the Stoic conception of the person even though the two philosophers do not set out to dispute that conception explicitly. The perspective was that if these claims are correct, then the concept of the person that has reigned for centuries should fall.[77]

But should it not be allowed to fall? Even if the Stoic conception can be upheld against the individualistic views of Williams and Nagel, it may seem that it presupposes, without defence, an unchanging conception of human nature, and that it is, in any case, too generalized to be of much practical use. As for the first objection, although the Stoics did not themselves work with the idea of historical change, one may fairly easily extend their conception of a person to take account of this idea too. For as I have explained it, their conception is a second-order notion, which allows for changes in human nature at the first-order level and correspondingly for changing views of what 'belongs' to a human being. And as for the second objection, while the Stoic notion of the person (and their concomitant view of the good as living in accordance with the real) is in fact general and does not determine, in specific detail, how human beings should live, it seems likely that it was never intended to do this, in any strong sense of 'determine'. What it gives is the formula for a general view of human beings which may serve as a framework for reflection on how to live one's

[77] In fact it is not clear what the position of Williams and Nagel is in relation to the person. Williams has some derogatory remarks on the concept in *Ethics*, p. 114, Nagel has none (on the idea of a person as opposed to questions of personal identity) in *View*.

own life—but which will also place important moral constraints on the result of such reflection. It is not clear that the property that is conveyed in this formula is itself subject to historical change, nor that the formula may not do valuable work in reflection on the good life.

# 6

# The Human Being as an Ethical Norm

*Christopher Gill*

In the Introduction to this volume, I suggested that the most obvious analogue in ancient philosophy for the modern concept of person was that of 'human being' (*anthrōpos*).[1] I want to explore that suggestion here by examining two rather celebrated uses of the 'human' as a normative concept in ancient ethical theory: Aristotle's use of the notion of the human function in the *Nicomachean Ethics* (hereafter *EN*) and the Stoic use of that of human nature, as formulated in two key passages of Cicero.[2] In particular, I want to question the rather common view that the notion of human nature or function is conceived in these theories as having a superordinate normative status, in relation to other ethical norms, which enables intractable ethical problems to be settled or the whole ethical framework to be confirmed; and that this status derives from the fact that the conception so deployed is 'objectively' grounded in an extra-ethical metaphysics or world-view. I will argue for the alternative view that these notions function rather as a means of articulating ideals which are already part of an ethical framework; and that, even if they figure (more than other ethical norms) as part

I am grateful for the responses given to previous versions of this chapter at the conference on 'Persons and Human Beings', at a meeting of the Aberystwyth Philosophy Society, and at a philosophy seminar at the University of Arizona at Tucson. Julia Annas, Troels Engberg-Pedersen, David Gill, Christopher Rowe, and an anonymous reader for the OUP made helpful comments on an earlier written version. I am also grateful to Julia Annas and to Martha Nussbaum for showing me, after the completion of this chapter, copies of forthcoming papers, whose general line of approach to Aristotle is similar to that adopted here: J. Annas, 'Naturalism in Greek Ethics: Aristotle and After', *Proceedings of the Boston Colloquium in Ancient Philosophy*, 4 (1988), 149–71 and M. C. Nussbaum, 'Aristotle on Human Nature and the Foundations of Ethics', in R. Harrison and J. Altham (edd.), a volume of essays on the work of Bernard Williams (Cambridge, 1989).

[1] Cf. p. 7 above.

[2] Aristotle, *EN* 1. 7; Cicero, *De Finibus* (*Fin.*), 3. 5. 16–7. 26 (also discussed by T. Engberg-Pedersen, ch. 5 above) and 19. 62–20. 68.

of a world-view, the world in question is one that is viewed from an ethical standpoint. My account is intended only as an interpretation of these two ancient theories, and not as a formula which is designed to fit all such theories in ancient philosophy.[3] However, I think my interpretation could be applied more broadly; and at the close of the essay I consider briefly two other cases, in Plato and Aristotle, which, in spite of some significant differences, lend themselves to the same general type of interpretation.[4]

It is clear, I think, that the issue I have outlined could also be raised in connection with the use of the notion of human nature—or of the person—in modern ethical philosophy. Without tackling that question in so general a form, I do ask whether the kind of approach to the topic which I discern in Aristotle and the Stoics is still a conceptual possibility for us today. I discuss ways in which the treatment of Aristotle's account of the human function by two modern thinkers, Bernard Williams and Alasdair MacIntyre, serves to indicate their own views on this type of theorizing. I also consider an essay on the person by David Wiggins which seems to me to exhibit certain striking points of analogy with the approach of the ancient thinkers, as I understand this, and which thus suggests that this ancient approach is—to put it at its weakest—not a conceptual impossibility for us.[5]

Let me begin with the famous passage in Aristotle's *EN* 1. 7 in which he suggests that specifying the function (*ergon*) of the human being may help us to define the kind of happiness that constitutes our highest goal (1097b24 ff.). He then specifies this function, first as 'an activity of the psyche ('mind', 'soul', 'personality') in accordance with reason (*logos*)', and then as one 'in accordance with virtue (*aretē*)'.[6] I want to raise two questions in connection with this passage. One is whether Aristotle introduces the notion of a distinctively human function here in order to provide a criterion for distinguishing between (what he takes to be) credible rival

[3] Since this type of theorizing develops out of the fifth-cent. debate on the relationship between *nomos* and *phusis* ('law' or 'morals' and 'nature'), in which a wide variety of positions were adopted, no single formula is likely to fit all such cases. See further on this debate W. K. C. Guthrie, *A History of Greek Philosophy* iii (Cambridge, 1969), pt. 1, ch. 4.

[4] Plato, *Republic* (*R.*) 9, 588b ff., and Aristotle, *EN* 10. 7–8; cf. app. to this ch. below.

[5] Cf. refs. in nn. 8–9 and 61 below.

[6] *EN* 1098a7, 16–17, the latter specification is further qualified in a17–18 ('or, if there are several virtues, in accordance with the best and most perfect one').

candidates for the notion of supreme happiness. Aristotle is often taken to be doing this, and is sometimes criticized for the attempt. David Wiggins, for instance, speaks dismissively of 'the unconvincing speaking part' (as an arbiter of happiness) 'assigned to [human nature] by Ethical Naturalism and by Aristotelian Eudaemonism'.[7] The second question is whether Aristotle, in offering this specification of the human good is, so to speak, stepping outside the ethical framework in which he normally operates in order to take up an extra-ethical position from which to substantiate his account of the good life. Bernard Williams, for instance, suggests that Aristotle is here seeking to articulate what 'an absolute understanding of nature' would yield in support of his account. Aristotle, on his reading, believes that an ethical agent who 'stands back' reflectively 'from his own dispositions' and who adopts a view 'from outside' will find nothing but confirmation of the inside view from 'the best possible theory of humanity and its place in the world'.[8] A. MacIntyre's description of Aristotle's procedure seems to presuppose a similar reading:

> Human beings, like the members of all other species, have a specific nature; and that nature is such that they have certain aims and goals, such that they move by nature towards a specific *telos*. The good is defined in terms of their specific characteristics. Hence Aristotle's ethics, expounded as he expounds it, presupposes his metaphysical biology.[9]

The comments cited reflect a common interpretation of *EN* 1. 7. But this interpretation, in both of the relevant aspects, has been questioned by John McDowell. Responding to Wiggins's complaint that Aristotle allocates to human nature an 'unconvincing speaking part' in the debate about happiness, he disputes the assumption that Aristotle uses human nature as criterial in the way that is often supposed. As he points out, in 1.7 (as distinct from 10. 7–8),[10] Aristotle does not use the notion of humanness to adjudicate between what he takes to be plausible candidates for supreme happiness. The only candidate ruled out by Aristotle's brief survey of natural kinds and their correlated functions is, as McDowell notes, the 'life of unreflective gratification of appetite', and that is

[7] 'Truth, Invention, and the Meaning of Life', *Proceedings of the British Academy*, 62 (1976), 331–78; quotation from p. 375 n. 1.

[8] *Ethics and the Limits of Philosophy* (London, 1985), 52, cf. 43–4.

[9] *After Virtue: A Study in Moral Theory* (2nd edn., London, 1985), 148, cf. 158, 162–3.

[10] On the latter passage cf. app. to this ch. below.

only ruled out by inference (because of Aristotle's stipulation of rationality as the distinctive human quality) rather than being explicitly eliminated.[11] Thus McDowell has good grounds for questioning whether I. 7 constitutes (as it is often supposed to) 'a sketch of a decision procedure for disputes [such as the one about the nature of happiness] ... and hence a program for the justification for his own substantive view of eudaimonia'.[12]

Also, reviewing Williams's *Ethics and the Limits of Philosophy*, McDowell questions his assumption that 'Aristotle's remarks about the significance of human nature . . . reflect a conviction of harmony between the inside and the outside views, as opposed to being themselves made from within Aristotle's own ethical outlook and reflecting a healthy lack of concern with how things would look from outside it.'[13] McDowell's comment may need some qualification, in the light of the fact that Aristotle's brief taxonomic survey of natural kinds and correlated psychological functions in I. 7 (1097b24 ff.) has a certain studied neutrality, avoiding overtly value-laden characterizations of functions in terms such as 'bestial' or 'brutish'.[14] The passage thus seems to mark some kind of reflective detachment from the standpoint of ethical engagement adopted elsewhere in the *Ethics*. But it is not clear, on the other hand, that Aristotle's position here is quite that of someone who (in Williams's words) 'stands back from his own dispositions' in an attempt to view them 'from the outside'.[15] There is, for instance, no indication that the notion of virtue which figures in Aristotle's characterization of the human function is intended to be understood in some special value-neutral sense, that is, as the excellent performance of the human 'craft' *and not* as ethical virtue.[16] Also, as Aristotle emphasizes, earlier in the discussion and later in this same chapter, ethical enquiry presupposes as its starting-point a

[11] 'The Role of *Eudaimonia* in Aristotle's Ethics', in A. O. Rorty (ed.), *Essays on Aristotle's Ethics* (Berkeley, 1980), 359–76, quotation from p. 366. We may take it that this is what is denoted by the 'sensory' life (*aisthētikos*), ruled out in 1098a1–3 because it is common to men and beasts rather than being peculiar (*idion*) to men. But the criterion of 'brutishness' has already been used, and in a much more overtly discriminatory way, in I. 5 (1095b19–22), in the claim that the life of sensual enjoyment (*apolaustikos*) is 'the life of cattle'.

[12] '*Eudaimonia*', p. 371.

[13] *Mind*, 95 (1986), 377–86, quotation from p. 385. I am grateful to Julia Annas for drawing my attention to this review.

[14] Cf. n. 11 above.

[15] *Ethics*, p. 52, cited above.

[16] See *EN* 1098a7–18; similarly *spoudaios*, applied to a human being as distinct from a lyre-player, seems to have its usual ethical sense of 'good'.

grasp of 'the that' (or 'the fact'), by which he seems to mean, at the very least, a practical understanding (based on a sound upbringing) of what is meant by 'virtue' and 'the fine' (*to kalon*).[17] In other words, to understand what 'in accordance with virtue' means in Aristotle's characterization of the human function, we need to bring to bear our 'inside' view as ethical agents, drawing on our ethical experience and engagement.[18]

But is it more plausible to suggest—and is this what Williams really has in mind—that Aristotle, in this passage, tries to *combine* the inside and outside views, thus confirming the perspective of ethical engagement by 'an absolute understanding of nature'? This is perhaps a more promising proposal, since it answers to the distinctive style of the argument, with its combination of reflective detachment and presumed ethical engagement. But, on this interpretation, what could be meant by an 'outside' view (if it is one which does not rule out the retention of an 'inside' view)? What, presumably, gives rise to the talk of an 'outside' view in this connection is the fact that Aristotle briefly adopts a quasi-biological perspective from which he maps the distinctive function of human beings in relation to other natural kinds (1097b24–1098a20). At the same time, he seems to presuppose a framework of thinking we find in his writings on psychology and metaphysics, according to which each species has a natural disposition to fulfil its distinctive 'form' or essence, and that to do so is its goal (*telos*), as a species.[19] From this perspective of (what MacIntyre calls) 'metaphysical biology',[20] and in line with this general framework of thinking, which is not peculiar to ethics, Aristotle—it may seem—reconceives rationality and virtue as species-specific characteristics, validated by their place in a natural order.

However, on such a reading, Aristotle's procedure still involves a shift, albeit a temporary one, from the ethical agent's inside view to an outside view of virtue (as a species-specific characteristic), even

[17] *EN* 1.4, 1095b4–7, 1. 7, 1098b2–8; cf. M. F. Burnyeat, 'Aristotle on Learning to be Good', in Rorty (ed.), *Aristotle's Ethics*, pp. 69–92, esp. 71–3.

[18] For a much more adequate defence of a related claim, cf. Wiggins, 'Truth', pp. 350–5.

[19] Cf. T. H. Irwin, 'The Metaphysical and Psychological Basis of Aristotle's Ethics'; id., 'Reason and Responsibility in Aristotle'; and K. V. Wilkes, 'The Good Man and the Good for Man in Aristotle's *Ethics*', in Rorty (ed.), *Aristotle's Ethics*, pp. 35–53, 117–55 (esp. pp. 126–9),and 341–5 respectively; also J. Lear, *Aristotle: The Desire to Understand* (Cambridge, 1988), ch. 4, and pp. 160–4.

[20] Cf. refs. in n. 9 above.

if that view is taken to confirm the inside one. But it is not clear that Aristotle envisages the abandonment of the inside view at any point in this passage. Is there any interpretation which both allows for the retention of the inside view and does justice to the indications of exceptional reflective detachment? McDowell argues that Aristotle's characterization of the human function is not to be seen as marking the interposition of an outside perspective but simply as a striking way of prefacing his contribution to the debate (a debate within ethics) about the nature of supreme happiness. As McDowell sees it, Aristotle's contribution to this debate (that is, his account of the relationship between virtue and happiness) is gradually unfolded in the course of the *Ethics*. He sees the reference to the idea of a human function at this early stage in the exposition simply as 'a sort of rhetorical flourish', added to an argument which is 'already complete without it', or (rather more positively) as 'a natural focus for the rhetoric with which one might naturally try to recommend a particular conception of eudaimonia'.[21] This interpretation allows for the retention of the ethical agent's inside view but at the cost, perhaps, of understating the role of the notion of human function in the argument. However, McDowell makes some other suggestions which, if developed a little, could bring one closer, I think, to a just assessment of this role. He suggests at one point that the question 'what is the business of a human being?' is a perfectly proper question for inclusion in ethical debate between participants who answer it by drawing on their ethical understanding and engagement. Such a question forms part of the way in which, as an ethical agent, one tries to make sense of one's 'world', and to see how it 'hangs together', a project which is distinct from that of trying to confirm one's ethical understanding by appealling to the facts of an (independently viewed and value-neutral) world.[22]

These latter suggestions seem to me to offer the most promising route to understanding the passage. The notion of a human function is introduced into the argument in order to enable Aristotle to present the question of the nature of supreme happiness as being one about the 'world' shared by the participants in this ethical enquiry. The theme is developed to the point where we can

[21] '*Eudaimonia*', pp. 371, 375 n. 27.

[22] I have juxtaposed points made separately (ibid. 371, 372), which seem to be connected, by implication at least, in his argument. For a similar suggestion by MacIntyre, cf. p. 154 below.

(from a reflective but ethically engaged standpoint) conceive 'an activity of the psyche in accordance with virtue (and reason)' as the human being's distinctive 'function'; but no attempt is made to develop it to the point where virtue is fully *re*conceived (from a standpoint of 'metaphysical biology') and thereby 'grounded'. Although Aristotle's move does not, on this reading, involve abandoning the standpoint of ethical engagement, it is important to appreciate (as I think McDowell does) that the 'world' so explored is the actual world (as viewed from an ethical standpoint), and not some distinct, hermetically sealed, 'world' of ethical experience. The question thus raised in ethical debate is a question about actual human beings, understood as Aristotle understands them elsewhere. Indeed, the very fact that the question is raised in this context—taken in conjunction with Aristotle's opening remarks in *EN* 1. 1—implies the belief that men are, as a species, uniquely capable of directing their lives towards certain general goals, and also of conceiving such a goal-directed life as being the proper life for a human being to lead. Such a belief has implications outside ethical enquiry;[23] but this does not mean that the exploration of what this belief entails for ethical life is not a reasonable move to make within ethical enquiry. On such a reading, the validity of the distinction between the 'inside' and 'outside' views of the ethical agent may begin to blur; but such blurring may be a necessary part of getting to grips with the way the notion of a human function is actually used by Aristotle, as distinct from the way in which (misled, perhaps, by certain modern preconceptions) we might expect him to use it.[24]

If this account of Aristotle's use of the notion of a human function is a correct one, I think it can also serve as a starting-point for understanding some important Ciceronian texts on a related theme.[25] These texts treat aspects of the familiar Stoic thesis that it is natural for human beings to acquire the conviction that the moral good has priority over other goods and to express this conviction in other-related actions. I want to explore the sense in which this development is thought to be 'natural' for human beings, and to do so in terms of the issues raised in connection with Aristotle's

[23] Cf. refs. in n. 19 above.

[24] See further discussion of Williams and MacIntyre below.

[25] Cicero, *Fin.* 3. 5. 16–7. 26 and 19. 62–20. 68.

description of the human function. That is, I want to ask to whom, and from what viewpoint, the claim of the 'naturalness' of this development is envisaged as being intelligible and convincing.

Both of the relevant passages figure in contexts in which characteristically human behaviour is, in certain respects, both associated with, and distinguished from, the characteristic behaviour of other living creatures. The general theme of the first passage is that all living creatures have a natural inclination to pursue their own good, and of the second that they have a natural inclination to care for others of their own kind.[26] It is plausible for us to associate these claims with the Stoic claim made elsewhere that human nature is characterized by the rationality which functions as the 'craftsman' (*technitēs*) of the common animal impulse to pursue one's own good (Diogenes Laertius (hereafter D.L.), 7. 86). And it is plausible for us to associate these claims in turn with the Stoic belief that it is valuable to study the nature of the universe in order to understand the place of human nature in that larger scheme of things and so to order one's own life in the light of that understanding.[27] But this general line of thought is difficult to appreciate properly. On the face of it, these Stoic claims seem to be liable both to the charge of circularity and question-begging (in so far as they seem to build into the concept of nature the value-laden content that enables it to play a normative role) and of simple falsehood (in so far as they misdescribe the mundane reality of human and animal propensities).[28] The liability of the Stoic thesis to these objections underlines the importance of trying to be clear about the kind of argument being advanced in the relevant texts (if they are properly described as 'arguments'),[29] and about the ethical standpoint presupposed by the arguments.

The first passage on which I want to focus is one in which Cicero describes a crucial stage in human development. It is one in which man's instinctive attraction to what is naturally beneficial becomes converted into a deliberate and rational selection of what is

[26] Both themes form part of the Stoic doctrine of *oikeiōsis* (an untranslatable term which implies both assimilating oneself to the world and making the world one's own); cf. S. G. Pembroke, 'Oikeiōsis', in A. A. Long (ed.), *Problems in Stoicism* (London, 1971), 114–49, and other refs. below.

[27] See e.g. D.L. 7. 88; Cicero, *Fin.* 3. 22. 73; and N. P. White, 'The Basis of Stoic Ethics', *Harvard Studies in Classical Philology*, 83 (1979), 143–78, esp. 153–9.

[28] Cf. G. Striker, 'The Role of *Oikeiōsis* in Stoic Ethics', *Oxford Studies in Ancient Philosophy*, 1 (1983), 145–67, esp. 161–5.

[29] Cf. below on this point.

recognized as being in accordance with one's nature and a rejection of what is not. It is at this stage, Cicero says, that 'what is truly called the good' (as distinct from the natural goods pursued at an earlier stage) 'begins to be present and to be understood). In explanation of this point, Cicero says that 'man's first attachment is to the things in accordance with nature', but that when he acquires 'rational understanding' (of the good), he sees that this inheres in 'the order and, as it were, harmony of actions' (also described as 'consistency' or 'conformity', *homologia*). Then, Cicero continues, man concludes 'by rational argument' that it is this good alone that is genuinely desirable for its own sake and not the primary natural goods. This supreme good is also identified in moral terms, as constituting 'right actions and the right itself' (*honeste facta ipsumque honestum*), and is said to be the 'standard of reference' for the selection of everything else, including the primary natural goods (*Fin.* 3. 6. 20–2).

Cicero's account is very compressed, and needs to be supplemented from related Stoic texts to be comprehensible.[30] But it seems clear that the development described involves at least three aspects:

1. There is a change from an unreflective pursuit of what seems good (that is, the primary natural goods, such as health and physical strength, to a deliberate and rational selection of these goods as being 'in accordance with (one's) nature (as a human being)'.

2. There is a recognition that this type of rational selection and, in particular, the self-consistency and conformity (with one's nature) it embodies, is more valuable than any other apparent good. In fact, this is recognized as being *the* good, by comparison with which the natural goods (the objects of one's earlier unreflective pursuit) come to seem relatively unimportant.

3. An essential feature in this process is the recognition that 'right actions and the right itself' constitute the supreme criterion of selection and rejection; such recognition is an integral part of a human being's understanding of what is 'in accordance with nature'.[31]

[30] For related texts and exegesis, see A. A. Long and D. N. Sedley, *Hellenistic Philosophers*, i (Cambridge, 1987), 354–68, including a tr. of Cic. *Fin.* 3. 6. 20–2 on pp. 360–1.

[31] See further on this passage, White, 'Stoic Ethics', pp. 154–7 (and also the texts he cites on 170–3), Striker, '*Oikeiōsis*', pp. 156–8, and T. Engberg-Pedersen, 'Discovering the Good: *Oikeiōsis* and *kathēkonta* in Stoic Ethics', in M. Schofield and G. Striker (edd.), *The Norms of Nature: Studies in Hellenistic Ethics* (Cambridge, 1986), 145–83, esp. 156–8.

My concern with this passage is, as I say, to try to establish to whom, and from what viewpoint, it can reasonably be thought to be intelligible and convincing. An initial difficulty lies in determining the exact function which the passage is designed to serve within Cicero's exposition of Stoic ethics. Should we interpret it (as A. A. Long interprets a related Stoic text) as containing, albeit elliptically, a formal argument for the central Stoic theses about the goal of life?[32] Although the passage may be taken to imply such an argument (namely, the reasoning that leads the developing human being to reach the conclusion he does), no actual argument, either formal or informal, seems to be given here. Correspondingly, the passage is taken by Gisela Striker not as 'an argument for the thesis that accordance with nature is the human good' (a thesis whose truth seems to be simply assumed) but rather as a description of the process of development by which someone might plausibly be supposed to adopt such a thesis. That is to say, if someone came to see that the fundamental characteristic of one's instinctive pursuit of the beneficial lay in acting 'in accordance with nature', then he might plausibly be expected to see consistency with nature as the good.[33] Troels Engberg-Pedersen, qualifying this view, maintains that, while the passage 'does not in itself *contain* an argument for that claim [that man's end is living in conformity with nature] . . . still if it contains an indication of how a man will reach his new insight, then it will also contain an indication of a rational argument for the Stoic claim about man's end', an argument he attempts to reconstruct.[34]

On either reading of the passage, Cicero articulates, even if he does not argue fully for, the Stoic thesis that acting in accordance with nature is the human good. But the passage is much less explicit about one of its central presumptions: namely, that such development consists in coming to regard moral good (*honestum*) as an absolute priority and as the criterion of all other choices. It is true that the passage makes it plain that such recognition is a crucial part of moral development; and it also adds certain illustrative parallels to clarify what is involved in acting in the light of such

[32] See A. A. Long, 'The Logical Basis of Stoic Ethics', *Proceedings of the Aristotelian Society*, 71 (1970–1), 85–104, esp. Long's reformulation of D.L. 7. 85–8 in logical terms (pp. 97–101).

[33] '*Oikeiōsis*', pp. 158–61.

[34] 'Discovering the Good', pp. 158 ff., cf. ch. 5 above.

recognition.[35] But there is no attempt to mount a full-scale argument to support this conception of moral development (any more, to take a parallel case, then Aristotle attempts to argue for his assertion that virtuous acts are done 'for their own sake' or 'for the sake of the fine', *to kalon*).[36] In other words, the passage presupposes that the person receiving this account will find such a conception of moral development intelligible and plausible, presumably because it answers to his own experience and understanding as an ethical agent. The main focus of the exposition is not on trying to substantiate this conception, but on presenting moral development (as so conceived) as being *also* a realization of what is 'in accordance with nature'. As a matter of fact, there is no attempt to argue fully for the claim that moral development, as so conceived, *is* 'in accordance with nature'. It seems to be presumed that, as the idea of consistency with nature is explored, it will become apparent that treating the moral good as an absolute priority is a supreme example of such consistency.[37] The assumption seems again to be that the recipient of the account (like the subject in the description of moral development)[38] will be able to draw on his own ethical experience, and will see his own choices as consistent with nature in so far as they treat moral good as a priority.

The point of my remarks is not to suggest that Cicero's account of this aspect of Stoic ethics is muddled and incomplete (although it certainly is compressed at certain key points). It is rather to bring

[35] e.g. aiming to shoot 'well' (skilfully) rather than to be successful in hitting the target, or practising an art, such as dancing, for its own sake and not for an ulterior end, Cicero, *Fin.* 3. 6. 22–7. 24. Cf. G. Striker, 'Antipater, or the art of living', in Schofield and Striker (edd.), *Norms of Nature*, pp. 185–204.

[36] Cf. *EN* 2. 4, 1105a31–2, 3. 7, 1115b11–13; see further R. Sorabji, 'Aristotle on the Role of Intellect in Virtue', in Rorty (ed.), *Aristotle's Ethics*, pp. 201 ff., and, for connections between the Aristotelian and Stoic conceptions of virtue and happiness, T. H. Irwin, 'Stoic and Aristotelian Conceptions of Happiness', in Schofield, and Striker (edd.), *Norms of Nature*, pp. 205–44. For a comparable modern account of virtue, as pursuing the goods 'internal to practices', see MacIntyre, *After Virtue*, pp. 187–96.

[37] Cf. the line of reasoning in *Fin.* 3. 7. 23–4: as one understands one's own nature better (i.e. the natural function of one's human impulses and reason), one understands that one's nature is conducive to treating the practice of virtue as an end in itself.

[38] This is to take 'the order and ... harmony of actions' (*Fin.* 3. 6. 21) as consisting of, or including, the order in the person's own selection of goods, esp. when this has become 'fixed and consistent with nature' (6. 20). Cf. Engberg-Pedersen, 'Discovering the Good', pp. 162 ff.

out more clearly the kind of person, and the kind of viewpoint, presupposed by such an account. We certainly should not suppose that, because the passage presents giving absolute priority to moral good as consistent with nature, the account is therefore expected to be inherently plausible to anyone, regardless of his ethical state. The passage presupposes a recipient who has (or who can come to have) the kind of conception of 'nature' that is compatible with such a belief. It is a premise of the whole account that a person's understanding of what 'nature' means develops hand-in-hand with (and as part of) his moral development. Thus, I take it that the subject of the described process of moral development will initiallly assume that it is natural (whether or not he articulates the assumption) to pursue the primary natural goods. It is only later that, partly by reflecting on his own instinctive pursuit of the beneficial, he comes to have an understanding of 'nature' such that the adoption of moral good as an absolute priority comes to seem in accordance with it. It is for this reason that, as Long puts it, 'there are grounds for taking "according to Nature" to be primarily an evaluative expression'; although, as he also emphasizes, this does not mean that the expression is not also designed to describe a factual state of affairs, as seen from the standpoint of the developing moral agent.[39] In this respect, Cicero's account of moral development, like Aristotle's account of the human function, appeals to the 'inside' view of the ethical agent for its intelligibility and plausibility, although it invites the agent to enlarge and develop his understanding of the world, or 'nature', from that ethical viewpoint.

I think that the idea that there is a direct correlation between a person's state of moral development and his understanding of nature is the key to understanding the second Ciceronian passage (*Fin.* 3. 19. 62–20. 68). This passage is usually taken as being a continuation of the account of human development which is started in the first passage; and as illustrating how the active, other-related expression of virtue (like the ethical agent's realization of the absolute priority of virtue) can be understood as being 'in accordance with virtue'.[40] And, like the earlier passage—indeed,

[39] 'Stoic Ethics', p. 99; cf. also his claim that Stoic 'statements about Nature do not need to be construed as assimilating facts to values, or values to facts . . . [but] as *combining* statements of fact and value'.

[40] Cf. Pembroke, 'Oikeiōsis', pp. 121 ff.; Engberg-Pedersen, 'Discovering the Good', pp. 175–7.

even more so—it needs to be interpreted with care if we are to avoid misunderstanding the character of the claim about the ethical implications of the facts of nature.

For instance, the fact that the passage so obviously presents itself (by extensive use of logical connectives) as an argument,[41] and one in which ethical inferences are based on (what are presented as) natural facts may lead one to misconceive the aim of the passage. Since, by contrast with the earlier passage, both the conception of nature presupposed and the ethical inferences are fully spelled out, we may be tempted to take the passage as intended to convince *anyone* (regardless of his ethical state) of the 'naturalness' of other-related virtue. Some of the observations of nature are striking and unobvious (such as the instances of animals who are said to act co-operatively on behalf of *other* species (3. 19. 63)); and it is noteworthy that both here, and in the earlier passage, human patterns of ethical behaviour are seen as an extension of animal patterns and not as fundamentally different in kind.[42] Even so, we should not take the passage as attempting to prove 'scientifically', as it were, that other-related virtue is natural for anyone. For one thing, the argument is much too elliptical and underdeveloped to bear that type of interpretation. For instance, the passage moves from the fact that animals and humans love their own offspring to the inference (if we call call it such) that: 'From this arises the mutual attraction men have naturally for one another, so that, because of their common humanity, no man should be seen as a stranger to another' (3. 19. 63). Again, the observations about cross-specific co-operation among animals are taken to support the conclusion that: 'Much closer is the bound between men. And so we are fitted by nature to come together in groups, communities and states' (3. 19. 63). Although Cicero has almost certainly

[41] See e.g. in the first para. (*Fin.* 3. 19. 62): 'This should be understood in the first place from. . . . Yet it would of course be inconsistent . . . While clearly it is natural for us . . . it is equally obvious that . . .'. Translations here and elsewhere in this passage by M. R. Wright, from Cicero, *Fin.* 3, forthcoming; I am grateful to her for allowing me to use her translation.

[42] Hence, in the fact that animals devote such effort to procreating and bringing up their young, we can hear 'the very cry of nature' ('naturae ipsius vocem') and one which has implications for us (*Fin.* 3. 19. 62; cf. the earlier claim that all living creatures instinctively pursue what is beneficial to them as members of their species, 3. 5. 16). (This is not, of course, to overlook the very substantial implications of the fact that human beings, alone of animals, are 'rational'; cf. below, and Long and Sedley, *Hellenistic Philosophers* i. 352.

reduced the cogency of this argument by compression (for instance, he seems to have omitted the important point that the basis for the bond between mankind is their shared rationality), there is no reason to suppose he has omitted stages in the argument which would make it convincing to anyone, regardless of his ethical presuppositions.[43]

In any case, there are clear inclinations in the passage that its aim is more restricted, and more compatible with the earlier passage, than it might seem at first glance. When Cicero draws out the inferences of the picture he gives of the universe as a single 'world-state', governed by divine will, he presents his conclusion (that one should 'look to the general interest rather than . . . his own') as one which should be drawn by 'the man who is wise and good, obedient to the laws and conscious of his duty as a citizen' (3. 15. 64). and, although Cicero may have accentuated the 'civic' character of the person who should draw these inferences, it seems that his general presentation is true to the spirit of his Stoic sources. Thus, this whole passage, like similar observations in a parallel Stoic source, is embedded in a larger discussion of the nature of the wise man who is standardly regarded as the ethical norm in Stoicism.[44] Indeed, the whole passage seems to be intended, at least partly, as a contribution to the debate (which figured in some form in virtually all ancient philosophical theories)[45] about whether human happiness was constituted by the practical life, understood here as the life of other-related virtue, or the theoretical life, a topic which is treated here as part of the delineation of the supremely happy wise man. The general drift of Cicero's discussion is to suggest that, notwithstanding the value of studying natural philosophy (which is itself presented here as valuable primarily for its ethical implications (3: 22. 73)), the life of other-related virtue is to be seen as a proper expression of the wise man's wisdom. Hence, the fact that 'it is the natural condition of bulls to fight with all energy and force against lions in defence of their calves' is taken to carry the inference that 'men of exceptional gifts and great ability . . . have a

[43] On the omission of the point about human rationality, see Engberg-Pedersen 'Discovering the Good', p. 176 and refs.; and on the early Stoic basis for Cicero's account, see Pembroke, 'Oikeiōsis', pp. 122–3.

[44] The larger passage is Cicero, *Fin.* 3. 18. 59–22. 76. See D.L. 7. 117–31; cf. esp. D.L. 7. 120 and *Fin.* 3. 19. 62 (with the qualification noted in n. 48 below), D.L. 7. 121 and *Fin.* 3. 20. 68, D.L. 7. 129 and *Fin.* 3. 20. 67.

[45] Cf. e.g. Aristotle, *EN* 10. 7–8, discussed below in app. to this ch. below.

natural impulse to protect the human race' (3. 20. 66). And the passage as a whole concludes with the general assertion (based on man's natural inclination to protect and perpetuate the human race), that 'the wise man should be ready to take part in politics and government, and also to live according to nature by taking a wife and wanting to have children by her'.[46]

Despite the radical difference, as the Stoics see it, between the moral state of the wise man and the rest of us (the 'foolish'), the wise man is normative precisely because he embodies the state of character to which all people should aspire.[47] My point is that the Stoics do not suppose that the claim that such virtuous activity is 'natural' will have exactly the same force, or even the same meaning, for everyone, regardless of his ethical state.[48] These observations of nature are not presented here with the delusive hope that these *bare facts* will exert some moral leverage in anyone's calculations about the pursuit of happiness. The study of the natural universe, and especially of the informing principles and 'order' embodied in the pattern of human and animal behaviour, is certainly taken by the Stoics to form a proper part of the moral development of the human being. But it does so, not by providing a body of facts whose moral implications nobody could fail to recognize; but rather by enabling the person who has already seen the 'order' in his own moral conduct and character to recognize the same ordering principles at work in the universe and its components' parts.[49] As in the case of Aristotle's (much briefer) taxonomic survey of natural kinds in *EN* 1. 7, it is taken to be valuable for the ethical agent to situate his understanding of virtue in the context of the world as a whole. But, as also in Aristotle's case, the exercise is not deemed valuable because it involves the agent in trying to stand 'outside' his own ethical position, but because it enables him to survey the world (including his own place within it) from an enlarged but still ethical standpoint.

[46] *Fin.* 3. 20. 68; for the line of thought, cf. D.L. 7. 130, taken in conjunction with 120–1.

[47] Cf. Long and Sedley, *Hellenistic Philosophers Hellenistic Philosophers* i. 352.

[48] This point may underlie the claim in D.L. 7. 120 that 'parental affection is naturally present in the wise [i.e. good] but not in the bad', a claim apparently in conflict with that alleged 'naturalness' of parental concern (Cic. *Fin.* 3. 19. 62); cf. Pembroke, 'Oikeiōsis', p. 132.

[49] This is to connect the recognition of the 'order and harmony of (one's) actions' in Cic. *Fin.* 3. 6. 21 with the other-related principles and 'order' of 3. 19. 62 ff., esp. 64 (the divinely ordered 'world-state'); cf. White. 'Stoic Ethics', pp. 170–8.

In the remainder of this essay, I want to take up a question which has been, so to speak, lurking just below the surface of the discussion, and which anyone who reflects on these matters is bound to raise at some point. This is the question whether the way of thinking about the human function and nature that I have ascribed to Aristotle and the Stoics is still a conceptual possibility for us today. The question I have in mind—to state it more precisely—is not whether the substantive content of the Aristotelian and Stoic accounts are still conceptual possibilities for us. It is rather whether the *kind of* thinking that I have ascribed to them, that is, the combination of an ethically engaged standpoint and an (in some sense) empirical study of the place of humankind in the world, is still an acceptable one to us. I want to approach this question by re-examining the treatment by Williams and MacIntyre of Aristotle's account of the human function, to see how far they recognize, and respond to, this question. I shall also discuss an essay on the person by Wiggins which seems to me to exhibit certain striking parallels to the ancient approach (as I have described this), and which thus suggests an answer, of sorts, to the question I have raised.

Williams seems to come close to demarcating, and answering, the question, in speaking of the 'many modern doubts' occasioned by Aristotle's account of human nature:

> Our present understanding gives us no reason to expect that ethical dispositions can be fully harmonised with other cultural and personal aspirations that have as good a claim to represent human development . . . Aristotle saw a certain kind of ethical, cultural, and indeed political life as a harmonious culmination of human potentialities, recoverable from an absolute understanding of nature. We have no reason to believe in that . . .[50]

William's misgivings are partly about the substance of Aristotle's theory: but he is also concerned about the form of the argument. In the same context, he speaks of the difficulty of believing 'that an account of human nature—if it is not already an ethical theory itself—will adequately determine one kind of ethical life as against others. Williams is clearly concerned with the question whether Aristotle's account of human nature (as he interprets it) constitutes the kind of account which can reasonably be thought capable of

[50] *Ethics*, p. 52.

playing a useful role in ethical inquiry. But what kind of account *does* he think capable of doing so? His views on this matter are clarified later in the book, when he describes two different forms of the project of trying to achieve ethical objectivity at the reflective level. The first form (which he regards as, ultimately, incomprehensible) is that of moving from localized ethical judgements to general ethical truths by the use of ethical theory alone. The second form (which he regards as at least intelligible) is that of 'giving to ethical life an objective and determinate grounding in considerations about human nature', considerations, that is, which are not themselves ethical and which are based on, *inter alia*, 'social and psychological science'.[51] It would seem that he regards Aristotle's account of human nature as a version of the latter project; hence his apparent presumption that Aristotle's account 'is not an ethical theory itself', and that it purports to ground 'a certain kind of ethical life . . . from an absolute understanding of nature'. And it is as an exercise of this kind that Williams judges this account to be unacceptable to modern thinking, because it incorporates assumptions 'we have no reason to believe'.[52] However, I have already argued that this is not the best way of interpreting Aristotle's use of the idea of human nature;[53] and that Aristotle's project is rather that of helping the ethical agent to make sense of the world (including human beings and their distinctive characteristics) from an explicitly ethical standpoint. Whether I am right to hold this view is, of course, open to dispute; but it means that Williams' statement of discontent about the character of Aristotle's account, suggestive though it is, does not quite focus on the question I have in view.

The position is rather different in the case of MacIntyre's treatment of Aristotle's account of human nature, in part because MacIntyre has fewer misgivings about this aspect of Aristotle's theory. In fact, his overall project in *After Virtue* might well be described as recreating the form of Aristotle's approach to the topic

[51] Ibid. 151–5 (quotations from 153–4), discussed and criticized usefully by McDowell, in his *Mind* review, pp. 378 ff.

[52] Quotations, ibid. 52. It is perhaps because of the fact that he reads Aristotle in the light of this project that (in spite of his general sensitivity to Aristotle's ethical aims) he—as I think—misinterprets Aristotle's thinking on human nature.

[53] Not at least as regards Aristotle's use of this idea in *EN* 1. 7 (which is what Williams seems to have in mind); Aristotle's use of it in *EN* 10. 7–8 is rather different (cf. app. to this chapter below).

of human nature, but without its specific content. He rejects, as he thinks modern thinkers must reject, the 'metaphysical biology' which he takes to provide the basis for Aristotle's account of the human function; but he argues for the retention of the teleological approach associated with that account.[54] I have already given reasons for thinking that MacIntyre rather misinterprets Aristotle's account (since, like Williams, he seems to regard it as purportedly based on a non-ethical 'science' of human nature).[55] Indeed in some respects—though not quite all—MacIntyre's revised teleological approach seems to me closer to the spirit of Aristotle's use of the notion of human function than is MacIntyre's actual description of Aristotle's procedure. MacIntyre, like Aristotle (on my reading), sees the question, 'What is the good for man?' as a properly ethical question, and one that can play a key role in helping an ethical agent to give unity and focus to his life. But it can play this role only if the person responds to the question in the light of the understanding of virtue he has acquired from his involvement in a nexus of socially cooperative and morally meaningful activities (or 'practices').[56] In emphasizing this point, MacIntyre adopts a position which is close to that which I ascribed to Aristotle and the Stoics.[57] The same is true, to some extent, of his stress on the essential linkage between the questions 'What is the good for man?' and 'What is the good life?', questions which he, like them, sees as centrally ethical questions.[58] Where MacIntyre differs from Aristotle, and still more from the Stoics, is in abandoning the attempt to answer this question by reference to the nature of man and his place in the universe. The idea that such an attempt could

[54] *After Virtue*, pp. 148, 158, 162–3, 175, 184, 196–7, 201.

[55] Cf. text to n. 9 above.

[56] *After Virtue*, pp. 218–19, *cf.* 186–7 and 273–5 (in the Postscript to the 2nd edn.).

[57] This position may be less obvious in Stoicism than in Aristotle's theory, given their stress on living 'in accordance with nature'; but for them too, moral development is envisaged as normally occurring within the ethical life of one's own particular community. Indeed, they sometimes present ethical life as consisting *both* of enacting one's social roles *and* of living 'according to (one's human) nature'; see further I. G. Kidd, 'Stoic Intermediates and the End for Man', in Long (ed.), *Problems in Stoicism*, pp. 150–72, and C. Gill. 'Personhood and Personality: The Four-*Personae* Theory in Cicero, *De Officiis* 1'. *Oxford Studies in Ancient Philosophy*, 6 (1988), 169–99. MacIntyre wholly elides this social dimension of Stoicism (168–70); cf. A. A. Long, 'Greek Ethics after MacIntyre and the Stoic Community of Reason', *Ancient Philosophy* 3 (1983), 184–99.

[58] *After Virtue*, pp. 218–19.

still be regarded today as a valid part of ethical enquiry is not one he seems to consider. Instead, in his teleology, he places great stress on the morally informing role of the social context, and on the idea of a moral tradition underlying that context. He also emphasizes the idea that one can give one's life unity by conceiving it as a kind of narrative or quest. Indeed, he sees the enquiry about the good for man as one which can help to sustain this quest, and can do so, in principle, throughout one's life.[59] His emphasis on these latter points, together with his abandonment of concern with human nature, makes his version of the teleological approach, in the end, rather different from that of the ancient theories I have discussed, in spite of the important point of contact that he too sees the enquiry about the good for man as a fundamentally ethical one.

It might be argued that MacIntyre's version of teleology is the only one we can take seriously at the present time; and that any attempt to combine an ethical and an empirical approach to the subject of human nature is incompatible with current thinking about what is involved in these approaches. But before embracing that conclusion, we should need to take account of contemporary studies of human nature, and of the concept of person (in medical ethics, for instance) in which there is an attempt to combine these approaches.[60] However, rather than embark at this stage in this essay on exploring such a large body of material, I will focus wholly on a recent essay on the person by Wiggins.[61] It may seem curious that I should introduce a discussion of the concept of person, rather than of human nature, at this point. But it is a feature of Wiggins's treatment that he insists on the fact that we cannot give any determinate content to the notion of person without drawing on 'our understanding of "human being" and our empirical notions of what a human being is'.[62] It is a related feature of his essay that he

[59] On the idea that 'the good life for man is the life spent in seeking for the good life for man', and the claim that this idea is not as existentialist and relativistic as it seems, see *After Virtue*, pp. 219–20, 275–6 (Ps).

[60] See e.g. M. Midgley, *Beast and Man: The Roots of Human Nature* (Brighton, 1979); and (on the question whether the job of defining the concept of person in medical ethics is a scientific or moral one) D. Wikler, 'Concepts of Personhood: A Philosophical Perspective', in M. W. Shaw and A. E. Doudera (edd.), *Defining Human Life: Medical, Legal, and Ethical Implications* (Ann Arbor, Mich., 1983), 12–23.

[61] 'The Person as Object of Science, as Subject of Experience, and as Locus of Value', in A. Peacocke and G. Gillett (edd.), *Persons and Personality: A Contemporary Inquiry* (Oxford, 1987), 56–74. This essay summarizes and develops ch. 6 of *Sameness and Substance* (Oxford, 1980).

[62] 'The Person', p. 60.

argues that it is possible (though difficult) to hold 'in a single focus' three different ideas of what it is to be a person, that is:

(1) as an object of biological, anatomical, and neurophysiological inquiry;

(2) as a subject of consciousness; and

(3) as a locus of all sorts of moral attributes and the source or conceptual origin of all value'.[63]

Wiggins has a number of arguments for both these theses; but the key to his account is, I think, the idea of interpretation. These ideas of the person are intelligible to us because, and in so far as, we deploy (or at least presuppose) them in the process of interacting with, and making sense of, other human beings.[64] Similarly, it is worthwhile for us as thinkers to try to hold these different ideas 'in a single focus', because, in our ordinary relationships with other human beings, we are capable of treating them as 'persons' in the three relevant senses, and of doing so in an inter-connected way.[65]

A crucial point in Wiggins's argument is that this type of interpretation is mutual and reciprocal. Human beings, considered as persons, 'are the subjects of fine-grained interpretations *by* us and are the would-be exponents of fine grained interpretations *of* us'.[66] We interpret persons, that is to say, as beings like ourselves (and as capable of interpreting us as beings like themselves); and this fact has implications for our understanding of human beings as persons in all three of the senses Wiggins identifies as well as in their interconnection. In particular it helps to explain the moral scruple with which we treat those we regard as persons: we think of them as being (like ourselves) consciousness-bearing, embodied individuals, capable of originating action and of interacting with us as persons. This explains our proper sense of moral constraint at the thought of treating a human being as a thing, or non-person, whose presence can be ignored or (at worst) deleted by wilful killing.[67]

Wiggins's approach here is clearly an interesting one;[68] but in

[63] Ibid. 56 (adapted), cf. 66–7.

[64] Hence, from our experience of human-beings-viewed-as-persons, we are able to piece out the necessary incompleteness of any philosophical definition of the 'person', such as Locke's (ibid. 68–9).

[65] Ibid. 70, 72. [66] Ibid. 71. [67] Ibid. 72–4.

[68] On Wiggins's approach, cf. P. Smith, ch. 3 above, text to nn. 11–12 (on 'The Person'), and P. F. Snowdon, ch. 4 above (on *Sameness and Substance*).

what respects, and to what extent, is it comparable to that of Aristotle and the Stoics, as described earlier? The essential point, I think, is that both approaches are ethical-cum-empirical, in two respects. One is that both approaches emphasize the ethical relevance of our empirical understanding of the human being as a natural creature in the world, but in a way that does not involve trying to use this empirical understanding to provide an external foundation for ethical theory. The ancient theorists, as I argued, suggest that grasping what it is to be a human being (an actual human being in the world, as disclosed by empirical study) can make a significant contribution to ethical debate. Analogously, Wiggins wants to draw together the concept of the embodied human being (an entity which is, in principle, amenable to biological inquiry) with that of the person as subject of consciousness, and to draw those concepts together with that of the person as locus of value. But he also insists that, in so doing, he does not seek to *reduce* any one concept to another (or to *ground* one in another). He specifically excludes the idea of reducing the psychological dimension of personhood to the physical.[69] He also specifically rules out any attempt to draw up a definitive set of psychological criteria of personhood which can be used to determine what is valuable in non-human as well as human forms of life. Even if the concept of human being is not coextensive with that of person, personhood is something which we (as human beings) recognize—and only recognize—in creatures of our own kind, whom we can genuinely 'interpret' as persons in the physical, psychological, and moral sense.[70] Wiggins's insistence that we can combine an understanding of ourselves as a determinate class of natural living creatures with that of ourselves as persons, in the sense of loci of value, has thus a more than superficial resemblance to the Aristotelian and Stoic claim that our conception of human nature can be both based on empirical understanding and ethically normative.

There is a second way in which both approaches are ethical-cum-empirical. Neither Wiggins nor the ancient thinkers suppose themselves to be supplying ideas to their respective audiences *ab initio*. They recognize that for their account of human nature or

[69] Cf. his distinction between 'the reducibility of psychological concepts to concepts that pull their weight in the sciences of matter' and 'the fact that the elucidation of psychological concepts seems to be essentially *matter-involving*', 'The Person', p. 66.

[70] Cf. ibid. 68–70, 72–3.

personhood to be intelligible and convincing, some answering chord must be struck in the experience and ethical understanding of the listener. The aim is not to *initiate* the process of seeing oneself as a human being (or as a human being who is also a person) but to advance the process, and to focus, by articulation, the kinds of thinking that already inform such a view of oneself. This point comes out clearly in the following quotation from Wiggins's essay, in which, as I think, he is commenting both on his own attempt to correlate the concepts of person and human being and on the way in which we (moderns) generally do so:

> We reach these marks of the person not by an unprincipled transcription of all the marks of being a human being no matter what, but by letting our conception of human being and our conception of person come together so that each will supply the conceptual lacunae in the other. Our grasp of what it is to be a human being gives matter and substance to our conceptions of persons . . . while our conception of persons, and our apprehension of persons as subjects of consciousness and objects of reciprocity and interpretation, is what directs and animates our search for those marks of human beings in virtue of which we have to see them as the bearers and sources of value.[71]

The fact that Wiggins is able to distinguish the concepts of person and human being (even while affirming their close interdependence) enables him to define the procedure he has in mind more easily than can the Greek theorists, for whom the notion of *anthrōpos* ('human being') functions both as a descriptive and normative term. But the kind of connection Wiggins wants to affirm, between our sense of ourselves as members of our natural kind and as (partial) embodiments of our own ideals (of personhood), is very much the kind of connection the ancient theorists want to affirm too. While I do not want to exaggerate the degree of convergence involved (or to understate the difference in their conceptual frameworks and terminologies), I think the extent of similarity shown here indicates that the empirical-cum-ethical approach I described in the ancient thinkers is by no means necessarily unavailable to modern thought.

## APPENDIX

In earlier versions of this chapter, I also discussed two other ancient passages (Plato, *R.* 588b ff., and Aristotle, *EN* 10. 7–8), whose treatment

[71] Ibid. 74.

of the human being exhibits some similarities to the Aristotelian and Stoic passages already treated here. I am still impressed by those similarities (which I will note later); but I am now more struck by certain points of contrast. These are (1) that the characterizations of the human being are not empirical and 'world-guided' in the same way as the ones we have considered; (2) that the characterization in question is not so much of the human being (or human nature) but of an element within human nature (or the human psyche) which is given a supreme or privileged status; (3) that the status so given is designated as that of being divine rather than (or at least as much as) being human. Correspondingly, these two passages illustrate a rather different approach from the one I have examined so far. I will illustrate these differences briefly (because to do so brings out the wide range of approaches to this topic we can find in the ancient material),[72] before pointing to the respects in which these passages seem to me comparable with the others.

The *Republic* passage seems at first glance to be fundamentally different from those so far considered in that Plato there presents a model of the human psyche (as a composite of inner man, lion, and many-headed beast) which is apparently designed to show anyone, even an immoralist, that 'justice pays'. However, Plato soon abandons this fiction; and the full (sometimes paradoxical) implications of the model are explored in dialogue between Socrates and his ethically well-disposed interlocutor Glaucon.[73] There is no attempt to provide any empirical grounding, however sketchy, for the model presented; indeed, even to make sense of the model, one needs to interpret it in the light of the preceding arguments of the *Republic*.[74] Unlike *EN* 1. 7 and the Stoic passages discussed, the model is not used to define distinctively human characteristics by contrast with (or in relation to) those of other living creatures, but to isolate one element within the human psyche (the rational) which is specified as being truly 'human' (or, sometimes, as divine).[75] It is made plain that, on this understanding of 'humanness' some—perhaps most—actual human beings will not possess this truly 'human' feature, at least not in a fully effective form.[76] In effect, then, the aim of this passage is not to offer a characterization of what is distinctively human, but to promote a certain

[72] Cf. n. 3 above.

[73] See *R.* 588b ff., esp. 589d–590a (where the fiction of addressing an immoralist is gradually abandoned), and 590d, 591b (where Socrates brings out the full, paradoxical implications of his model). On the ethical character of Glaucon (and Adeimantus), see *R.* 368a–b.

[74] Esp. the account of the tripartite psyche, *R.* 439–42, and of the management and mismanagement of pleasures in 586.

[75] Human in *R.* 588d–589b; human or divine in 589d1–2 (the shift coincides with Glaucon's taking over more overtly the role of addressee from the imagined immoralist); divine in 589e4–5, 590d1–4.

[76] *R.* 590c–d (a notorious passage).

type of self-understanding, according to which one values the 'human' (or 'divine') aspects of oneself and devalues the bestial.[77] The form of dialogue in which this model is presented suggests that the model is only likely to perform this function for a person of a certain kind, a Glaucon (a person of good ethical character who accepts the conclusions of the argument), not an immoralist like Thrasymachus.[78]

Many of these points also apply to the second passage: Aristotle, *EN* 10. 7–8. The relationship of this passage to 1. 7 (as regards its account of human happiness) is intensely controversial;[79] but I think some points germane to my concerns here can be made briefly. This passage differs from 1. 7 in its general aim, the earlier passage offering a general characterization (a 'sketch') of the human function (as distinct from that of other kinds) and human happiness as a whole, while the later passage distinguishes different strands (the 'human' and 'divine') *within* the general class of activities designated as human.[80] (It follows that 'human' does not have quite the same content in the two passages[81]). The later passage uses the notion of 'the human' in a criterial way in the debate about happiness whereas (I argued) the earlier one does not. As in the passage from Plato's *Republic*, the 'human' and 'divine' are used to distinguish functions or elements falling *within* the capacities of the human mind, although in the Aristotelian passage the 'divine' function is contrasted (favourably) with the 'human'. These characterizations are not defended (as is the account of the human function in *EN* 1. 7) by a taxonomic sketch of natural kinds; indeed, given the nature and aim of these characterizations, that would hardly be possible or appropriate. It is often claimed that the characterizations reflect Aristotle's thinking elsewhere (in his works on metaphysics and psychology) about god and about man's highest functions.[82] (In the

[77] Cf. the psychology of *Phaedrus*, 253d–254e, discussed by C. Rowe, ch. 10 below; on Plato's psychology in general, esp. its promotion of self-identification and self-alienation with certain 'parts' of oneself, cf. A. W. Price, ch. 11 below.

[78]. Cf. nn. 73–5 above (Thrasymachus is noted by name, dismissively, in *R* 590d). I plan to make a closer study of the use of the dialogue form in this passage in another context.

[79] See e.g. the contrasting accounts of T. Engberg-Pedersen, *Aristotle's Theory of Moral Insight* (Oxford, 1983), 94–121, and M. C. Nussbaum, *The Fragility of Goodness: Luck and Ethics in Greek Tragedy and Philosophy* (Cambridge, 1986), 373–7.

[80] See esp. *EN* 1. 7, 1097b24 ff., 1098a20 ff.; 10. 7, 1177a12 ff., 1177b26–1178a8; 10. 8, 1178a9–23.

[81] See *EN* 1. 7, 1098a3–5, cf. 1. 13, 1102b13 ff., 1. 7, 1098a16–18, cf. 1. 8, 1098b22–5, and refs. in 10. 7–8 in n. 80 above.

[82] Cf. Aristotle, *Metaphysics*, 12. 9 *De Anima*, 3. 4–8; Rorty, 'The Place of Contemplation in Aristotle's *Nicomachean Ethics*', in Rorty (ed.), *Aristotle's Ethics*, pp. 377–94 esp. pp. 387–8; J. M. Cooper, *Reason and Human Good in Aristotle* (Cambridge, Mass., 1975), 175–7; Lear, *Aristotle*, pp. 293–320; see also S. R. L. Clark, ch. 8 below, who places the divine/human contrast of *EN* 10. 7–8 in a wider conceptual framework.

same way, this account of the human function in 1. 7 seems to reflect his thinking in those works.[83]) However, in neither case is Aristotle in a position simply to 'read off' these characterizations from a presupposed and determinate world-view, vouchsafed from 'an absolute understanding of nature' (to reuse Williams' phrase).[84] In each passage, the characterizations need to be argued for within the context of ethical debate.[85] As for the question of the person for whom such characterizations are likely to seem convincing, Aristotle's general stipulations for his intended listeners (as ethically 'mature' and capable of rational self-direction) apply fully here if the characterization of the 'human' aspect of our capacities is to seem credible.[86] But, in addition, Aristotle presupposes an ability to see the capacity for theoretical contemplation as being 'divine'; and it goes without saying that this narrows still further the circle of intended addressees.

This latter point brings out what I see as the essential element of similarity between these two passages and those I discussed in the main body of the essay. Like those passages, these are written in full consciousness of the kind of audience to whom the characterizations of the human (or animal, or divine) can be expected to be convincing and ethically useful. The passages do not set out to use the notion of the human being, and related notions, in order to convince those who would not otherwise be convinced of the truth of certain ethical claims. The characterization of what is human, animal, or divine, is not presented as something which can be simply 'read off' from a determinate picture of nature and its kinds whose truth is obvious to anyone (even an immoralist). Rather the thinkers in question presuppose a certain degree of ethical experience and understanding as a precondition of making sense of the characterizations offered. The aim of the characterizations is to provide a larger intellectual framework in which the person concerned can place his own ethical experience and understanding, and so better make out (from an ethical viewpoint) his picture of the world and of the self. The passages noted in this Appendix differ in laying stress on the understanding of the self rather than the world;[87] but in other respects they make similar presumptions about the type of person addressed and the aim of the address.

[83] Cf. refs. in n. 19 above.

[84] *Ethics*, 52.

[85] See *EN* 1. 7, 1097b33–1098a5 and (much more elaborately argued, and, inferentially, more open to dispute), 10. 8, 1178b7 ff. (on the 'divine' character of theoretical contemplation).

[86] Cf. *EN* 1. 3, 1095a2–13, 1. 4, 1095b4–8, and 10. 9, 1179b4 ff.

[87] In so far as we can separate these two notions in such a context (Clark suggests reasons why it is difficult to do so, ch. 8 below).

# PART II

## The Human and the Rational Mind: Models of Self-Understanding

# 7
# Human Nature and Folk Psychology

*George Botterill*

Is there really such a thing as human nature? If we understood the question it would be easier to settle on an answer. One thing that can be agreed is that, as Mary Midgley puts it, 'There is simply no need to take sides between innate and outer factors.'[1] Even the blankest of pages needs to have a certain texture if it is to be receptive to the imprint. So perhaps 'human nature' should be held as a label in waiting for common innate factors, whatever they may be found to be? Under the influence of Kripke, we may well be persuaded that there are properties, to be discovered a posteriori, which every member of humankind necessarily has. Is it this biological species-essence that should be identified with human nature? Against this it might be said that in speaking of human nature we have in mind something at a psychological, rather than a biological, level. The objection can be reinforced (or is it just reiterated?) by pointing out that, if the essence of a species is taken to lie in its DNA, then it will be shared with the unborn foetus who has the *potential* for human nature, but may not survive to enjoy the realization of that potential. There is also the simpler, less contentious, thought that human nature is not a specialist topic; that, so far from awaiting scientific discovery, it is the commonest subject of participation and encounter.

At any rate, the idea that a conception of human nature informs our psychological understanding of our fellow human beings seems to be worth exploring. In exploring it, I will proceed on the assumption that a conception of human nature can be constructed within the resources of a psychology couched in the categories of ordinary, pre-scientific thinking. There are arguments, which seem

---

I would like to thank my colleagues O. R. Jones, Peter Smith, and Christopher Gill for reading earlier drafts of this paper and making many valuable suggestions.

[1] *Beast and Man: The Roots of Human Nature* (Brighton, 1979), 21.

to me to be strong ones, against the possibility of a scientific theory being developed which might explicate what human nature consists in, while abandoning the intentionalistic idioms of ordinary language.[2] But, in any case, even if that were a possible project, we would still have to acknowledge that we are not currently in a position to avail ourselves of its results.

On the other hand, it would be naïve to rely uncritically on ordinary, colloquial appeals to 'human nature'. We do make such remarks as 'It's only human nature to . . .' and we do describe certain appetites and attitudes as 'natural'. There are two obvious dangers involved in paying heed to what common sense may explicitly say about human nature. The first is lack of serious intent. When we comment, most likely on some descent into temptation, that 'It's only human nature, after all!' there are several things that we might mean to imply. Often the implication intended will amount to no more than this: that some agent is not to be singled out for blame, because lots of other people are up to the same thing. Perhaps truthfulness would be better served if we were less ready to speak of any sufficiently common misdemeanour as the product of a basic human tendency. But, on the whole, it is no bad thing that there is a place in ordinary discourse for charitable fictions. The second danger, a far more important one for our purposes, is parochialism. Where such judgements are seriously intended, they may be the product of a sort of myopia: we may be quite wrong about the 'naturalness' of what are in fact the attitudes and appetites of our own society or our own set. Emile Durkheim went too far in his emphasis on the dependence of the psychological upon the societal, but we should certainly heed his warning against neglect of the social setting:

a certain religious sentiment has been considered innate in man, a certain minimum of sexual jealousy, filial piety, paternal love, etc. And it is by these that religion, marriage, and the family have been explained. History, however, shows that these inclinations, far from being inherent in human nature, are often totally lacking. Or they may present such variations in different societies that the residue obtained after eliminating all these

[2] I am thinking esp. of *the argument from interpretation* advanced in G. Macdonald and P. Pettit, *Semantics and Social Science* (London, 1981), 72–4. It is not necessary to our present purposes to exclude the possibility of the theoretical development of a psychology that is both genuinely scientific and also couched in an intentionalistic vocabulary, although F. Collin presents a persuasive argument against this possibility in his *Theory and Understanding* (Oxford, 1985), esp. ch. 5.

differences—which alone can be considered of psychological origin—is reduced to something vague and rudimentary and far removed from the facts that need explanation.[3]

One might wonder whether there is any hope of avoiding parochialism when treating of human nature within a common-sense scheme of thought. For it might be suggested that one of the chief marks that distinguishes common sense from scientific theory is its restricted range, either with regard to the topics in which it takes an interest or the scope of its applications. While we might admit that the common-sense approach has its limitations and that its concerns can seem petty when measured against the impersonal perspective of science, it can still work well enough for practical purposes. Mistakes as such only emerge when we attempt to convert it into a theory, and even then a generalization of limited application (and so, strictly speaking, false) may serve as well as a true one, if we stick to familiar territory—as when someone believes that all swans are white and never ventures out of the northern hemisphere. But what do we expect a conception of human nature to consist in? Does it have to be comprehensively applicable to all humankind? In that case it would seem that we are looking for some sort of general formula, and really deserve to be disappointed. For there is certainly something peculiar about taking human nature as a potentially theoretical subject that could be adequately reduced to general principles and written down on paper. After all, this is not the sort of area in which one could well imagine precocious virtuosity, because there is really no substitute for experience, including encounter with diversity of character. For the time being, I will leave the question of what might be involved in 'a conception' of human nature in convenient obscurity. In order to see what might be needed from a conception of human nature by way of an aid to our understanding of other people, let us consider how it might be connected with the general structure of explanations of human action.

## *Folk Psychology and R-Explanation*

It has become fashionable in the philosophy of mind to talk of *folk psychology*, by which is meant a common-sense theory that is

[3] *The Rules of Sociological Method*, tr. S. A. Solovay and J. H. Mueller (Chicago, 1938), 107.

implicitly understood and practised by anyone capable of using the psychological vocabulary of a natural language. Perhaps there is room for dispute as to whether there is a core of common-sense beliefs about states of mind sufficiently systematic, orderly, and comprehensive to be referred to as a 'psychology', folk or otherwise. But we do seem obliged to acknowledge that there is a standard form for the explanation of actions—namely, explanation in terms of the agent's reasons.[4] These reasons are constituted of psychological states of two sorts: beliefs (or, more broadly, cognitive states) and desires (or, more broadly, pro-attitudes). Pairs of belief-like and desire-like states qualify to be cited as explaining actions if and only if these two conditions are met:

(1) they caused the agent to act as he did—otherwise they would not be *the* reason for which he acted (the *causal condition*);[5]

(2) they make the action an appropriate or intelligible thing for that agent to do, in that they represent it as being likely to satisfy the agent's desires in the light of his beliefs—otherwise they would not be a *reason* for the agent to act as he did (the *rationalizing condition*).

The quiet ubiquity of belief-desire accounts of action is readily illustrated by the way in which half of the account may be left to lie dormant, a sleeping partner tacitly understood. For example, the

[4] For the delineation of the basic structure of folk psychology we are indebted, above all, to Davidson. Cf. esp. the papers that have been collected together in D. Davidson, *Essays on Actions and Events* (Oxford, 1980).

[5] There has been a considerable controversy over condition (1), and rightly so, since it is of decisive importance to our understanding of the nature of mental states in general whether beliefs and desires are to be thought of as inner causes. However, we need not enter into this debate in the present paper, since, whatever the theoretical importance of condition (1) for the philosophy of mind, it plays only a background role in the provision of ordinary action-explanations. Its position might be described as that of an *ideal posit* and likened to the requirement for a correct scientific explanation of a phenomenon, that the occurrence of the phenomenon be displayed as the consequence of a *true* law-like generalization. To this requirement of truth, explicit formulations of model scientific explanation sometimes awkwardly append some such rider as 'or, at any rate, well-confirmed'. It is not, however, to be supposed that scientists are being encouraged to make do with well-confirmed theories, as a substitute for discovering true ones. Rather, we hope that our most highly corroborated theories are true, as a high degree of confirmation is the best intimation of truth that our epistemic situation allows. Similarly, we hope to penetrate to the psychological causes of action in those token-beliefs and token-desires by which, on the basis of the evidence, we may most plausibly suppose the agent to be motivated. But the causal activity of those intentional states will not itself be a part of the evidence available to us.

explanation 'She caused a scene at the party because she wanted to embarrass her husband' leaves it to the audience to ascribe to the agent a belief that causing a scene *would* embarrass her husband. It works the other way round too, with desires that one need not make explicit. Thus, when the captain of a cricket team wins the toss and puts the other side in to bat, the commentator who explains that he did this because he thought that the initial dampness in the air might assist his swing bowlers, is taking it for granted that the captain wants his bowlers to take wickets, and taking it for granted that the audience take this for granted too. Sometimes, indeed, we can go even further and omit any explicit reference to thoughts or wants as such, as in 'He put on his greatcoat because there was a biting frost that night'.

The tidy-minded muse of analytic philosophy may frown at the degree of vagueness in the claim that explanation of action in terms of the agent's beliefs and desires (call this *R-explanation*—'R' for 'agent's *reason*') is the *standard* form of action-explanation. Yet, in as much as vagueness is only to be expected in common-sense theorizing, this seems no ground for objection against an account of common-sense psychology, and we need not dwell on it further. There are, however, two matters which deserve further consideration.

### *Is folk psychology only about folk?*

The first is the range of agents to which folk psychology is applicable. This is an issue which is connected with the question of what sort of concept the concept of a person is. One answer is the *liberal-functionalist* view of persons,[6] according to which the

[6] The term 'liberal-functionalist' perhaps requires a few words of elucidation, since I believe it is here introduced for the first time. It is, I suggest, a useful name for an important position which links topics in moral philosophy and the philosophy of mind. In moral philosophy this position can appropriately be termed 'liberal' in so far as it is opposed to the 'conservative' position on issues concerning the right to life, of which abortion has been the most strenuously debated. The conservative holds abortion to be wrong because taking innocent human life is wrong. Against this the liberal insists that a foetus is not a person, and that, on pain of speciesism, we should recognize that it is the person that is the bearer of rights. The position also deserves to be called 'functionalist' because it needs to be supplemented by some account of what it is to be a person. And that account, both in order to hold the concept of a person apart from the concept of a human being and also in order to provide an account of what it is about persons that grounds the special rights ascribed to them, is bound to represent personhood as consisting in the possession of certain functional capacities (in particular, for self-awareness, reflective thought, and second-order intentional states).

concept of a person is a quite different concept from the concept of a human being, and that, although it may be a contingent truth that all the persons we encounter are human beings and all the human beings we encounter are persons, it cannot be assumed that the two concepts are coextensive. We can align ourselves with this view by maintaining that folk psychology shows a majestic indifference to species-membership. The range of subjects whose activities may be accounted for by reference to their beliefs and desires is not limited to what one would ordinarily call 'people'. It is not just human beings whose actions can be explained in this way. If asked to specify the class of subjects for folk psychology, we would have to say something like 'rational agents' or 'purposive agents'. But that would be just a label, as we have no other way of picking out this class except the criterion: those agents are rational/purposive whose actions are R-explicable. Thus, if there are any intelligent extra-terrestrial agents, their actions would also have to be interpreted within the same basic scheme, as they are routinely in science fiction. So the actions of persons other than human beings could be the *explananda* for R-explanations.

What is to be said against the liberal-functionalist view of the concept of a person? Opposition consists not so much in a single rival account, as in a tradition of warnings against supposing that we can understand a concept whilst extending it to cases far removed from the only applications to which it has ever been put.[7]

[7] Authority for such opposition is regularly sought from Wittgenstein. I am not sure how much can be made in this context of the intriguing remark: 'The best picture of the human soul is the human body,' which is to be found on p. 178 of L. Wittgenstein, *Philosophical Investigations*, tr. E. Anscombe (Oxford, 1963). After all, it has still to be argued whether the concept of a person must always reproduce the contours of the human soul. D. Wiggins might also be regarded as an influential source for the opposition case, as in his *Sameness and Substance* (Oxford, 1980), 169–82. The opposition he provides does not always appear very resolute, e.g.: 'The suspicion cannot help but arise that, if indeed *person* collects up natural kinds under a functional or systemic specification, and we do not rush things by ignoring the dots that we have left there, then this specification has to be constantly referred back to the nature of the particular class of actual persons who are men' (p. 174). Delete the word 'constantly' and this fits in comfortably enough with the idea that a functional concept can be derived from exemplars within a single natural kind. But, of course, Wiggins would by no means agree to that deletion, as he has made clear in a more recent paper ('The Person as Object of Science, as Subject of Experience, and as Locus of Value', in A. Peacocke and G. Gillett (edd.), *Persons and Personality: A Contemporary Inquiry* (Oxford, 1987), 56–74). However, his readers may well feel that he exaggerates the difficulty of arriving at a satisfactory functional characterization of the conditions of personhood.

It can be made to seem that there is robust good sense in this opposition. Surely such understanding as we have of what it is to be a person is an understanding of what it is to be a human person. No amount of fiction about extraterrestrials can alter this. Indeed, the point is rather reinforced by the way that these creatures turn out to be little more than human beings in fancy dress.

Those who take this line are likely to be disinclined to accept fictional cases as legitimate thought-experiments. Still, I would have thought that the liberal-functionalist could attempt to refute the opposition case by reaching for a copy of *Frankenstein* or *The Island of Doctor Moreau*. For instance, is it not logically possible that, starting out with a human person, a sequence of spare-part surgery operations could produce an individual that was no longer a member of the human species, but was from first to last a person (the same peson)? If this is possible, then, since the individual in question would persist as a person while ceasing to be a human being, the concept of a person is species-transcendent, as the liberal-functionalist view claims. And on what grounds could the opponent of liberal-functionalism claim that such a transformation is not even logically possible? I will add another point that seems to me to count in favour of liberal-functionalism. So far from a functionalist concept of a person derived from human exemplars being an instance of wanton extrapolation and unsound linguistic practice, it can be argued that it is quite in accordance with a useful and ancient tendency to functionalize concepts. We encounter an object occurring in nature that interests us because of some important capacity that it possesses. We then develop a concept of a *thing with this capacity*, whether it be of the same kind or not. Are hearts, for example, a natural organic kind? Originally, yes. But that does not mean that any conceptual confusion need be involved in the idea of an artificial heart.

While there is a connection between the questions about the scope of application of folk psychology and the nature of the concept *person*, they are different questions. For, whether or not there can be persons other than human beings, it seems that we do recognize 'rational/purposive agents' other than persons, in so far as the actions of terrestrial animals of species other than Homo sapiens, in particular of mammals such as dolphins and apes and cats and dogs, are also quite frequently made the subject of R-explanations. Of course, it is possible that such explanations should at times be quite fanciful, especially if they involve an excessively anthropomorphic view of what motivates these creatures. Yet anyone maintaining that they must always be mistaken would be opposing the general consensus amongst both philosophers and laymen. So should we conclude that folk psychology applies to 'higher' terrestrial animals other than humans? An answer qualified in terms of degree seems to be called for, since some animal agents are clearly less rational than others. It is not surprising that the question is difficult since it touches our central concern—namely, the extent to which the working of folk psychology depends upon a conception of human nature. In fact, the scheme of explanation applicable to non-human animals seems to be a sort of diluted version of folk psychology in which the cognitive states and pro-attitudes ascribed are shadowy analogues of human beliefs and desires. We can indicate the content of the intentional states, but only in a rough sort of way, without any hope of further refining what exactly it is this creature thinks and wants.

Does it, then, count against any useful employment for a conception of human nature that folk psychology should be applicable to a wider category than humankind? Hardly, for although R-explanations may in principle be supplied for the actions of members of other species, in practice this is either just an imaginative projection of the human case (in the guise of extraterrestrials, hobbits, robots, etc.) or else something that we would not claim to be particularly adept at (in the case of other species of terrestrial mammals).

*How is an R-explanation singled out from the multitude of possible motivations?*

The second issue leads us to an indication of the workspace in which I think a conception of human nature must operate. Although there may yet be some matter to dispute in a Davidsonian characterization of the basic structure of folk psychology, what should most forcibly strike us about it is its lack of detail, its highly abstract and schematic character. To be told that actions can be explained by being attributed to the agent's beliefs and desires is rather like being informed that words are spelled out in letters, without being given any indication as to what the alphabet is, let alone how any particular word is spelled. So far we have only the barest of frameworks: what beliefs people are likely to have, whether some desires are stronger than others, and what factors constrain possible or plausible assignments of such intentional states, are all areas that we have not even started to shade in.

To put it another way, one might say that we have hardly begun to tackle the *non-sceptical* problem of other minds. The old familiar *sceptical* problem of other minds raises the question of how, given that our range of observation is limited to overt behaviour, we can ever have a rational justification for supposing others to have thoughts and feelings. The non-sceptical problem is this: given that other people do have thoughts, beliefs, feelings, desires, and pro-attitudes, how can the attribution to an agent of a *particular set* of beliefs and/or desires ever be warranted? It would seem to be a reasonable answer to say that such an attribution is warranted where it is an indispensable part of the best explanation of something that the agent does. But now, here is the rub: how is one R-explanation, out of the many possible, to be singled out as the uniquely best explanation?

In practice we are (or at least we think we are) sometimes able to do this. And yet it seems a very remarkable feat, for it is theoretically possible for an action that we take to be R-explicable in terms of one set of intentional states to be 'rationalized' by an indefinitely large number of other combinations of beliefs and desires. The *causal condition* and the *rationalizing condition* (conditions (1) and (2) above), presented as the basic framework of folk psychology, are of no further help on this score. Indeed, they generate the problem. The underlying principle of rationalization might be formulated as follows:

> if an agent desires that $p$ and believes that by $\phi$-ing he will bring it about that $p$, then *ceteris paribus* the agent will $\phi$,

or alternatively:

> if an agent desires that $p$ and believes that by $\phi$-ing he will bring it about that $p$ and if that agent has no overriding desires, then the agent will $\phi$.

But these formulae have a bland formality that leaves so much flexibility in R-explanation as to be compatible with an agent doing almost anything for almost any reason. I might scratch my nose to stop the stars in their courses, if I wanted to and thought it would. Indeed, quite generally, one can produce rival R-explanations simply by what might be called 'flipping over the motivation'—attributing to the agent the negation of a given belief combined with a desire that is the opposite of some initial attribution. Suppose, for example, that on a table in front of some man there is a glass which contains a poisonous fluid. He picks up the glass, drinks from it, and dies. We have, given just that information, at least these two possible explanations (actually, of course, among many others):

(1) that he wanted a drink and thought the liquid in the glass was innocuous;
(2) that he wished to die and believed the glass contained a poison virulent enough to kill him.

Now, so far from this flexibility indicating an inadequacy in contemporary philosophical accounts of the framework of folk psychology, it rather tends to confirm their correctness. For there really are examples of actions that are *ambiguous*, in that, given available evidence, more than one equally good R-explanation can be provided for them.[8] What it does indicate is that between the framework of folk psychology and the understanding of a particular action performed by a particular agent there is a very large gap to be filled. We are not always confident of our ability to fill this gap. The whole point of calling this the *non-sceptical* problem of other minds is that we are under no obligation to show that we can invariably tell what motivated an agent to perform a particular act. Solipsism, the sceptical hypothesis that all these other beings around me are zombies, is certainly not compatible with common sense. But common sense can and does live with the idea that we are sometimes a mystery to each other.

## *The Non-Sceptical Problem of Other Minds*

For many years the non-sceptical problem escaped attention through being confounded with, and overshadowed by, the sceptical problem. A symptom of this confusion was a failure to distinguish between the questions:

[8] Piquant examples of ambiguity of interpretation can be constructed from cases in which it is practically impossible to decide whether an agent acts out of virtue, or out of a desire to appear virtuous.

(Q1) How do we know *that* other people have thoughts and feelings?

and:

(Q2) How do we know *what* thoughts and feelings other people have?

There is a temptation to this confusion in the worry that a proposed justification for our general belief in the existence of other minds ('a defence of common sense', albeit common sense translated into metaphysics) would be useless if it left us without any rational grounds for confidence in individual cases as to what the contents were. Unfortunately, this worry brings the old bugbear of certainty into the game, to be followed all too swiftly by concentration on the sort of case (e.g. a victim of recent injury showing symptoms of acute pain) which seemed to come closest to making a mistaken attribution entirely inconceivable. This approach amounted to an adoption of the methodology of *naïve falsificationism*, as if the sceptical hypothesis could best be refuted by advancing a single, incontestable counterexample. It would have been far better to have followed Karl Popper in his strictures against taking absolute certainty to be a plateau lying above the foothills of good reason.[9]

The Argument from Analogy offers a particularly striking example of the conflation of the sceptical and non-sceptical problems. The usual presentations of that notorious argument started by stating (1) that I observe other people behaving in similar ways to me when placed in similar circumstances, and (2) that I know that in such circumstances I have (or: my behaviour is due to) certain thoughts and feelings. But what is the *conclusion* of the argument suuposed to be? Is it:

(AA1) Other people are like me in that they too have thoughts and feelings?

Or is it:

(AA2) Other people have thoughts and feelings which are like the thoughts and feelings that I have?

Only the conclusion (AA1) is required in order to rebut solipsistic scepticism. But the conclusion which appears to be intended is the

[9] *Objective Knowledge: An Evolutionary Approach* (Oxford, 1972), 78–81.

much stronger (AA2). That, however, so far from being obviously what is needed against the sceptic, is a contention to which the defence of common sense should not, in general, be committed. It may be plausible enough to suppose that if the circumstances in question are bricks being dropped on toes, fingers trapped in doors, and such like, then the feelings experienced will be similar. But as soon as one moves away from brute sensation to the complexities of motivation the plausibility of the claim declines.

A rational reconstruction in the style of Lakatos would require that this point be detected, and that investigation should then commence into the differences between psychological attributions that could be made with confidence and those which were bound to be tentative and conjectural. Unfortunately, things did not go that way. Instead, a popular verdict was that the Argument from Analogy was hopelessly feeble in as much as it was, at best, a rash generalization from a single instance. What ensued was the search for some strong sense in which we had *criteria* for ascribing mental states: criteria which would somehow be constitutive of the meaning of such an ascription. This whole approach involved overlooking that the strength of the criteria in certain cases (most strikingly in the case of the favourite example, pain) was best appreciated through a contrast with the weakness of the criteria for a unique psychological attribution elsewhere.

Now that the emphasis in the philosophy of mind has shifted from sensations to intentional states, we are beginning to outgrow our fixation with the example of pain. That makes it possible to confront the non-sceptical problem of other minds without being hell-bent on proving that the contents of other minds are perfectly transparent. Subtler investigations of how we know and how much we know about the minds of others, with an appreciation of the theoretical and interpretive character of such knowledge, can replace desperate assurances that we do know.

What has been established so far is the heading under which these investigations are to proceed—*the holism of the mental.* The best-known epitome of the *holistic* character of intentional states and R-explanation is Davidson's declaration that: 'Beliefs and desires issue in behaviour only as modified by further beliefs and desires, attitudes and attendings, without limit'.[10] But this quota-

[10] *Actions and Events*, p. 217. In fairness to Davidson we should note that the context in which this sentence was written was a rejection of behaviouristic theories,

tion actually highlights only one dimension of the holism of the mental. A general characterization of what is meant by saying that attributions of intentional states to an agent are *holistic* would go something like this: they are dependent upon a system of explanation in which an R-explanation in respect of a particular action by a particular agent (and hence the attributions such an explanation involves) are confirmed by means of entrenching the R-explanation in question within a wider context. This form of holistic explanatory confirmation contrasts with the case, familiar in the natural sciences, in which an explanation is best confirmed by a closer analysis of the link between *explanandum* and *explanans*. If this is right, it explains why 'the holism of the mental' seems to function as a label which has come to subsume several rather different, though interconnected, ideas.[11] It is a pointer to the way in which the non-sceptical problem of other minds is resolved in practice, and as such can point to a number of different contexts against which a particular action can be viewed.

## *How Human Nature Informs Folk Psychology*

But what of our original question? Have we not strayed rather a long way from the topic of human nature? Not really, for, stripped of distracting complications, my central suggestion is a simple one: we need the assistance of a shared conception of human nature in order that the non-sceptical problem of other minds should be adequately resolved in the ordinary practice of folk psychology. Our original concern with a common conception of human nature can now be reformulated in this way: can the mere humanity of the agent be counted amongst the contexts that help to pin down R-explanation? One might approach this question by attempting to eliminate the contributions made by other forms of context in which an action is situated, with the idea that the residue should be attributed to human nature. But in this case the method of elimination would be an overwhelmingly laborious procedure. The contexts to be considered would include circumstances, conduct of

on the grounds that they could not deal with the complexity of the connections between psychological state and overt behaviour. So, although he goes on to refer to 'this holism of the mental realm', he is only invoking one aspect of holism.

[11] There is more than one way of being holistic. See the appendix on the varieties of mental holism.

the agent (both before and after the action),[12] character, and career, and everything that culture contributes. I do not have the time to take that route, however interesting the scenery might be. Instead I will take the short cut of considering various ways in which a conception of human nature might help in determining what is the right R-explanation. In this way a very necessary limitation is imposed on the inquiry, since it is restricted to those aspects of our knowledge of human nature which function as an interpretive resource for folk psychology. Indeed, if there is more to folk psychology than R-explanation, that also falls outside our present remit.[13]

One suggestion to be considered is that there is an important asymmetry between beliefs and desires, in that attributions of belief are subject to constraints which have no parallel in the attribution of desire. The existence of wishes—that is, pro-attitude counterparts of desire in cases where we realize the achievement of the object is not within our power—is testimony to this asymmetry between the cognitive and the affective. Stood in front of a palpably solid wall, a normal human being can hardly believe that he can walk through it. But that does not prevent him from wishing that he could. Because the function of belief is to represent things as they are, we cannot take a creature to have a system of beliefs without also taking those beliefs to be responsive in some way to the creature's environment. In theory at least, we have an aid to pinning down the beliefs of others in the fact that ultimately they must be tethered to reality.

In some respects this has more to do with the nature of belief than the nature of human beings. The most obvious constraint upon belief, logical consistency, is species-transcendent. If there is such a thing as a maximum tolerable level of inconsistency within a belief-system, it applies to extraterrestrials as well as to us. But the particular ways in which human beliefs are responsive to the environment are due to the sensory organs with which we are equipped, and that is a part of human nature. Normal human

[12] This is why an action that causes the agent's own death is particularly liable to ambiguity of interpretation. The behavioural context is bisected and the agent can no longer do anything that might resolve the question of motivation.

[13] So I am not trying to do in one paper what has previously been attempted in lengthy volumes on human nature or human understanding. Whereas in the past philosophers have been prone to the error of treating philosophical issues as if they were psychological ones, I am treating as philosophical a question about folk psychology.

beings all possess a similar set of transducers which convert other forms of energy into electrochemical energy; e.g. the ear transduces the mechanical energy of sound waves into signals within the auditory nerve. Of course, although the perceptual aspects of our conception of human nature depend upon these processes of transduction, we do not need to know the neurophysiological facts in order to know what other people are seeing and hearing. In the ordinary course of events we receive a vast supply of information about other people's beliefs. For, as we see them around us, we take it unreflectively that they are aware of the things we see, hear, and feel—such things as the tarmac beneath our feet, the grey skies above, stars twinkling in the night, bird-song, music, and police sirens, the wind blowing against our cheeks, the roughness of broken brick, pebbles worn smooth by the sea.[14] This is a great help, for in the interpretive formula *belief* + *desire* → *action* we will be able to find the second term if the first and third terms are known. Imagine, by contrast, some intelligent alien life-form with a radically different set of senses (bat-like sonar, chemically sensitive pads, or whatever). There is no reason why such creatures should not be rational agents whose actions are in principle subject to R-explanation. However, the inscrutability of their beliefs about their alien sensory world would make their motivation extremely difficult, if not impossible, to interpret. Reverting to our question about the subjects of R-explanation, we should note that there can be no guarantee that other purposive/rational agents will in practice be intelligible to us.

I do not think any further argument is needed to establish that common perceptual beliefs provide a vast input that is vital to the functioning of folk psychology. That much is surely undeniable. But if it were the only relevant contribution that human nature made, then our conception of human nature would be exclusively

[14] It is these ordinary, everyday perceptions that reminded Orwell of the common human nature which, in his view, should persuade us of 'the unspeakable wrongness' of capital punishment: 'It was about forty yards to the gallows. I watched the bare brown back of the prisoner marching in front of me . . . once, in spite of the men who gripped him by each shoulder, he stepped slightly aside to avoid a puddle on the path . . . His eyes saw the yellow gravel and the grey walls, and his brain still remembered, foresaw, reasoned—reasoned even about puddles. He and we were a party of men walking together, seeing, hearing, feeling, understanding the same world; and in two minutes, with a sudden snap, one of us would be gone—one mind less, one world less.' From G. Orwell, 'A Hanging', *Collected Essays, Journalism and Letters of George Orwell*, edd. S. Orwell and I. Angus, i (London, 1968), 66.

cognitive. Yet surely there is something to be said about the constraints that human nature places upon the range of possible pro-attitudes?

I am inclined to begin by dismissing as too crude any claims that there are certain basic desires that are universal amongst human beings, even if such qualifications as 'adult', 'sane', or 'rational' are added. The obvious consideration to advance is that if the desire for self-preservation is sometines absent (as it may be, e.g., in our example of drinking from the poisoned glass), we can hardly hope to find anything else in the category of desire that is invariably present. However, so swift a rejection would be erroneous, and would involve a fallacy of equivocation over the term 'universal'. The extreme claim for the universality of basic desires would generalize over times as well as people, i.e. it would assert that there are desires that all humans have throughout their lives. That claim is certainly unacceptable. But more moderate variations are possible. Thus, basic desires might be taken to be universal in so far as all human beings have them, either most of the time, or some of the time. More interestingly, it might be pointed out that desires of different kinds have different patterns of persistence, and that accordingly their possession will take rather different forms. Some might have a very high degree of stability and be attributable to a human agent most of the time, even when having little or no current effect on conduct (e.g. the desire to go on living), while other desires may be produced by specific triggering occurrences (such as sexual desires) or by recurrent physiological conditions (such as a desire for food or sleep). No doubt we can find some sense in which it is true that there are basic human desires, particularly if we reduce the boldness of the claim still further (e.g. by introducing talk of 'defeasibility'). So I have no objection to the idea that such basic desires are part of human nature nor to the idea that our awareness of them in others is part of a shared conception of human nature. But what is not satisfactory is the suggestion that appeal to these basic desires might suffice as a contribution to resolving the non-sceptical problem of other minds. For that problem derived from a quite general under-determination of R-explanation by behavioural evidence, and I think we can take it that basic desires can only be invoked for the purposes of explaining certain areas of conduct.

A refinement that might be proposed at this juncture would

remind us that the 'interpretive formula' *belief* + *desire* → *action* was over-simplified. According to the holism of the mental, actions do not spring from discrete belief-desire pairs but rather result from the interaction of whole complexes of intentional states. So we really ought to regard a *conflict of desires* as being the normal state of affairs, since any action will have an 'opportunity cost', to use the economists' phrase. In other words, no matter what you are doing, there is always something else that you could be doing, thereby satisfying some different pro-attitude. So when we explain an action by citing a desire, the imputation is not just that the agent had that desire, but also that it was, on this occasion, stronger than other, competing pro-attitudes. This prompts the reflection that, although there may be no universal desires, some kinds of desire are such that, if present at all, they will be stronger than others. People do not always want to go on living. Yet, so long as they do, this desire must be accorded a certain precedence. It might be outweighed by some other objective that was sufficiently momentous or valuable. But it must prevail over a whim to do press-ups on a motorway, a hankering to taste poisons, a desire to cut a dash before one's friends, and practically any other pro-attitude one can think of.

One might try to exploit this point by claiming that there are restrictions on possible humanly normal or intelligible pro-attitudes that parallel the constraints upon belief. A belief-system is composed of elements which stand in relations of consistency, coherence, and evidential support, whereas the system of pro-attitudes is organized in terms of the subordination of what is less important to what is more important. Now, of course, what people regard as important may certainly vary enormously. Yet it may be that such variation must always occur within a general architectural frame of what is permissible in the way of relative importance and affective strength. Recalling our case of the poisoned glass, consider the following attempt at R-explanation:

> 'Why did he drink it?'
> 'He wanted to see if he could taste what vintage it was.'
> 'Oh, so he wasn't aware that it had been poisoned?'
> 'No, he certainly knew that it contained a lethal poison. But he wanted to find out if he could taste the vintage all the same.'

This seems a very queer explanation of the agent's reasons, and perhaps we should say that it is unacceptably queer precisely because the implied influence of desires upon action offends against a humanly permissible ordering of importance.

However, I am not inclined to press this idea of general structures of importance or affective influence. Although there may be something in the idea, I doubt whether it can be carried much beyond such a commonplace as that the desire for self-preservation is unlikely to be weak.[15]

The question remains: is there a common attribute or possession of mankind which is of particular assistance to mutual comprehension? I submit that the answer has been before us all along, for it is folk psychology itself. The very scheme that is used to interpret the intentional states of others can also be used by an agent to inform other people of his intentional states. So long as the roles of interpreting observer and interpreted agent are treated separately a major part of the resolution of the non-sceptical problem of other minds will be overlooked. But when dealing with a human agent we are dealing with someone who, in addition to being an object of interpretation, is also an interpreter of motivation and in the process of interaction with other people a *presenter* of his or her own beliefs and attitudes. Naturally, it cannot be claimed that a desire to display the intentional states that motivate action is always present. However, that conforms to what we are looking for in the way of a resolution of the non-sceptical problem, for we have acknowledged that it may be difficult to tell why an agent acted as

[15] Another proposal that might be considered is that a significant role is played by *simulation* or, as I would prefer to call it, *ego-projection*. According to this proposal our ability to predict what someone else will do in certain circumstances, or how a conflict of desire will be resolved, is at least in part dependent upon our ability to say what we would do if we were similarly situated or had similar attitudes. For this approach see R. Gordon, 'Folk Psychology as Simulation', *Mind and Language*, 1, (1986), 158–71. If folk psychology did operate by means of ego-projection, each of us would have a sort of conception of human nature in that each would take himself or herself as an exemplar of humankind. There is at least this to be said for the proposal: that in the case of folk psychology each and every one of us has access to a working model which instantiates the theory, and it would be strange if this were of no help to us in applying the theory. So I would be reluctant to reject the proposal. But there are many difficulties. What I reckon that I would do or think or feel is likely to be what someone with my social background, education, age and sex would do or think or feel. So ego-projection may seem to work smoothly close to home, but break down as soon as we try to interpret agents at a greater cultural or historical distance. Besides, every indication of diversity of character amongst humankind is a caution against taking oneself as a reliable guide to the attitudes and actions of others.

he did. Indeed, the agent may have an interest in contributing to the difficulty rather than easing it. But exceptions should be viewed as illuminating what is normal, rather than blinding us to it. Instances in which people wish to conceal their motives, or to mislead others about what they really want or really think, are placed within a general context of straightforward self-presentation. If this were not so, deception would be impossible.

Once this has been seen, a number of other points fall into place. Pettit, for example, has remarked upon the 'soft-edged' character of folk psychology (or 'rational man theory', as he calls it): if expectations derived from attributions of beliefs and desires are disappointed by some agent's conduct we simply revise our views of what the agent thought and wanted. He goes on to draw the interesting conclusion:

> it would be seriously misleading just to say that rational man theory is a second-rate instrument for predicting human behaviour: we must also add that it is a predictive instrument specifically suited to giving those expectations required for interpersonal interaction.[16]

In other words, folk psychology is a system of interpretation fashioned as if to facilitate self-presentation, by allowing an agent a degree of control over the way in which his or her behaviour will be interpreted by others. Moreover, our actual epistemic situation with regard to different sorts of cases of R-explanation is exactly what would be expected if self-presentation were functioning in such a way as to countervail the under-determination of explanatory intentional states. Thus when we attempt to apply R-explanation to non-human animals the intentionalistic attributions we can make are at best shadowy and indeterminate, because those agents have no way of helping us to a further refinement of psychological ascription. A dog cannot pretend because, lacking folk psychology he lacks the power to present himself as anything other than a passive subject of interpretation.

This resolution of our problem seems highly appealing. It accords with the most perceptive recent accounts of folk psychology, and it represents our conception of human nature, not as the apprehension of some inert object or theoretical generalization, but as a subject of

[16] 'Rational Man Theory', in C. Hookway and P. Pettit (edd.) *Action and Interpretation: Studies in the Philosophy of the Social Sciences* (Cambridge, 1978), 43–64, esp. p. 57.

continuing contribution and re-creation. However, there is an apparent paradox in the way that I have presented the resolution. For, how is self-presentation possible at all, if R-explanations are radically under-determined by behaviour? How can anybody act in such a way as to secure a particular interpretation, if any number of rival interpretations are equally available? These are questions which deserve in their turn to be tackled at length. But I think that it is clear that they do not present insuperable difficulties, the answer being that in any community there will be certain acts that carry a conventional interpretation. Such acts are indeed essential to social life, the most common example being the speech act of assertion.

Any further reservation about treating folk psychology as contributing in this way to our conception of human nature is likely to come from doubts about whether folk psychology really is *universal* amongst humankind. Paul Churchland has asserted that 'it has been in active and continuous service in all human cultures for as long as history records'.[17] I think he is right, but one might wish to consider what grounds we have for confidence in this claim. Here I will confine myself to observing that it would be a mistake to suppose that folk psychology requires a possession of exactly those concepts on which it draws in English. For example, it has been argued that there are other cultures in which there is no available term that gives an exact translation for the concept of belief.[18] One might be tempted to conclude that folk psychology, as it has been outlined in the present paper, cannot exist in any culture which lacks the concept of belief. This, however, would not be correct. It is one of the conveniences of English that the concept of belief is available as a sort of cognitive all-rounder. But the word is not indispensable. There is, after all, no ordinary English concept that exactly corresponds to 'pro-attitude'.

It is admitted that in this paper we have investigated just a part of our conception of human nature. But it is an important part, namely that part which contributes to an understanding of the reasons for which individual human actions are performed. The conclusion is that to be human—to be fully, and not just biologically, human—is to be a folk psychologist.

[17] *Scientific Realism and the Plasticity of Mind* (Cambridge, 1979), 115.
[18] In R. Needham, *Belief, Language, and Experience* (Oxford, 1972).

# APPENDIX
## VARIETIES OF MENTAL HOLISM

The variety of ways in which mental states, or the attribution of mental states, can be described as 'holistic' is a topic that deserves separate treatment. Here I will restrict myself to mentioning some of the forms of mental holism that would need to be investigated.

### *'Output Holism'*

An action is not to be taken as the output of an isolated belief-desire pair, but rather as the result of an interplay between a whole complex of intentional states. This, the aspect of holism featured in the quotation from Davidson which was cited above, actually makes the non-sceptical problem all the more complicated. Thus in the example of the man who drinks poison, he may drink *in spite* of a belief that it will kill him and a desire to go on living, should he fear something worse will befall him if he does not drink. Moreover, what might constitute something worse from that agent's point of view will depend upon other attitudes of his that we may or may not share, e.g. a horror of losing face, or a resolve not to disillusion disciples to whom he has often represented death as a transition not to be feared.

### *'Package Holism'*

In interpreting the behaviour of others one must assign a whole package of attitudes, of which the reason made explicit in an R-explanation is but one element. Package holism is sometimes carried to the extreme of contending that, in addition to folk psychology, interpretation of action requires a separate 'theory' about the psychological states of each individual agent. But if that were so, it would pose an insuperable obstacle to mutual intelligibility in any brief encounter.

### *'Intentional-State Holism'*

The holism of the mental is a characteristic of intentional states themselves. They do not exist as discrete, independent states, but rather as areas in an interconnected web of belief or affectivity. That it is inconceivable that a person's state of mind could change as regards just one belief or one desire, and no others whatsoever, is a strong argument for this holistic claim.

### *'Evidential Holism'*

According to this holistic claim a particular action cannot be properly understood in isolation, by concentrating on immediate circumstances and possible purposes, but needs rather to be viewed as a moment in a larger stretch of the agent's behaviour, in which his attitudes and ambitions are more fully revealed.

# 8
# Reason as *Daimōn*

*Stephen R. L. Clark*

### *Scepticism and Unfashionable Truths*

One perennial answer to sceptical doubts about the foundations of morality and ordinary belief is the insistence that 'ordinary moral and practical discourse' cannot be called into question, and that it constitutes the ineliminable framework of all we do and think. It is my conviction that this response is in fact indistinguishable from that made by the ancient sceptics, a willed submission to the quadruple compulsion of nature, sensation, custom, and the rules of such crafts as we elect to practice 'so as not to be wholly inactive'.[1] Those philosophers who offer this supposed solution also, so it seems to me, gravely underestimate the complexity and openness of common discourse. What they propose as the one, unquestionable framework for moral and metaphysical 'knowledge' usually turns out to be their own simplified version of the beliefs and practices taken most seriously by members of their own clique, or club, or college. When they claim that moral and metaphysical 'hypotheses' are 'true' simply if enough of 'us' say they are, they commonly forget what people have said in the past, and what many of them still say. The new conventionalism would never have allowed honest rationalists to question the existence of witches, spirits, and moral pollution, but now forbids us even to consider the existence of such things on no better ground than that the conventionalists' friends and family don't like us to.

> Too many philosophers . . . appeal to our ordinary ways of talking about 'language', 'conventions', 'intentions' and so on as if they could thus browbeat us into believing that we don't talk seriously when we talk in ways they find philosophically distasteful—as if this were obvious![2]

[1] Sextus, *Outlines* I. 11; see D. Hume, *Treatise of Human Nature*, ed. L. A. Selby-Bigge (Oxford, 1888), I. iv. 7, p. 269.

[2] J. King-Farlow, *Self-Knowledge and Social Relations* (New York, 1978), 41.

Even if there were good arguments for the 'real truth' of conventionalism (and if there were, of course, that would be enough to refute conventionalism!), there are, as P. Feyerabend has pointed out,[3] good pragmatic reasons to prefer a non-dogmatic realism. Instead of relying (usually without any empirical evidence) on the conventionalist's personal opinion as to what 'the conventions' actually are, and insisting that 'we' cannot question what millions of people throughout history have in fact questioned, let us seek to draw up presently unconventional answers, to exorcize the idols of the theatre and tribe.[4] Popular answers to our moral and metaphysical problems are, popularly, meant as answers, not as moves in a power-struggle (it is odd that few philosophical conventionalists take much account of the obvious moral of their thesis, that rational and philosophical debate can only be propaganda for their own class-interest . . .). Popular, semi-popular, and unpopular answers may be true or false, even if we sometimes have little hope of settling the question. We have no hope at all if we are not prepared to analyse and develop answers different from the ones we are 'authoritatively' told are popular. 'The commonest sense is the sense of men asleep, which they express by snoring'.[5]

My preamble, however necessary in general, may have been otiose in the setting of the conference where it was first delivered. Those who had gathered to discuss ancient and modern concepts of what it is to be a person must already have admitted the possibility that there is no single approved answer to that question, nor even any steady agreement on what the question is about. It is also true that the conventionalists have not had things all their own way in just this field: a good many philosophers have come to doubt that there is any one distinctive difference between persons and non-persons (any more than there is between weeds and non-weeds, fish and non-fish), though they have not always drawn the right moral for moral or anthropological practice.[6] A good many philosophers no longer have anything to say even for the claim that there is some distinctive thing that it is to be the *same* person from one time to

[3] *Philosophical Papers* (Cambridge, 1981), 17 ff.
[4] Ibid. 142, after J. S. Mill.
[5] H. D. Thoreau, *Walden* (London, 1910), 286.
[6] See S. R. L. Clark, 'Is Humanity a Natural Kind?', in T. Ingold (ed.), *What is an Animal?* (London, 1988), 17–34.

another, any more than the *same* nation or much-rebuilt ship. Post-Humean empiricism has always been ambivalent: either Humeans relapse, like Hume, on the conventional 'opinions' born of beef and backgammon (but without real assent), or they abandon any notion of the one Self that underlies each person's changes, the one nature that distinguishes human beings from the non-human. Post-Humeans, in fact, tend in practice to be as certain as Parmenides that there are Two Ways: the Way of Truth (which amounts, as Parfit and Crook have both, variously, acknowledged,[7] to a secularized—and therefore, in my judgement, *pace* S. Collins,[8] severely distorted—Buddhism), and the Way of Illusion (which is to say the 'opinions' most applauded by the Humean's clique). None the less, philosophers of mind and morals have, of late, been ready to recognize metaphysical questions, and to offer serious answers. There may really be no moral facts, even if popular judgement takes such facts for granted; there may really be no 'natural kind' of 'persons', even if our political and legal systems require us to pretend there is. On the other hand, perhaps there are indeed moral facts, and underlying selves, and even natural kinds (of a kind) even if that offends conventionalists, and even if they have other properties than we had supposed.

The topic I have chosen to address is many-sided. What are we to make of certain moral and metaphysical judgements found in ancient philosophers which moderns tend to ignore, or to dismiss as minor blemishes or as metaphors? What can we learn about presently popular doctrines by directing our attention to presently unpopular or unimagined alternatives? Without such a deliberate refocusing, it seems to me, we may well forget even the real merits of 'our own' synthesis, and the real point even of questions that we have allowed a place in philosophical discourse. One example of this that I have addressed elsewhere is the problem of the Cartesian demon (or its modern avatar, the mad neurological surgeon): no-one who studied this question in an undergraduate course would be likely to have had it drawn to her attention that anyone has ever seriously believed that this life was indeed 'a dream and a delusion' (Aurelius, *Meditations*, 2. 17. 1), and that this made a genuine

[7] D. Parfit, *Reasons and Persons* (Oxford, 1984); J. H. Crook, *Evolution of Human Consciousness* (Oxford, 1980).

[8] 'Buddhism in Recent British Philosophy and Theology', *Religious Studies*, 21 (1985), 475–93.

difference to their life. But of course many people have believed exactly that, and not to realize this is simply not to understand what is at issue.[9]

Similarly—and now at last I approach the central topic of my paper—when we read that what matters more than anything else in us is *Nous*, and that this *Nous* is a *daimōn*, no real part of the psycho-physical organism we call a human animal, there is a tendency to insist, first, that no one goal or value can be so dominant, and second, that to make such a division between *Nous* and the Soul (which is to say, the mental capacities of a certain sort of social animal) is an ill-digested relic of Platonic or Cartesian dualism—and therefore obviously false. Modernist commentators rarely notice that they are rejecting an ancient and world-wide tradition, namely that there is an Unborn and Indestructible which is worth more than anything else, which is an intruder upon the bourgeois certainties of the market-place and assembly but which is also our truest and deepest Self. At the same time commentators hardly seem to notice what the consequence of rejecting this tradition is. According to Sankara:

> Since the Self is the witness of the body, its acts, its states, therefore the Self must be of other nature than the body . . . Of this compound of skin, flesh, fat, bone and water, the man of deluded mind thinks, 'This is I'; but he who is possessed of judgement knows that his true Self is of other character, in nature transcendental.[10]

Plutarch similarly: 'the self of each of us is not anger or fear or desire just as it is not bits of flesh or fluids either, but is that with which we reason and understand' (*De Facie Lunae*, 945a). But the modernist neither agrees that the Self is something other than the physical and emotional being with which we normally identify ourselves, nor that she is no more than a compound of skin, flesh, fat, and bone. The 'human rights' that liberals value are not obviously at home in a godless universe, where human animals are not distinctively different from the beasts that perish, and what are now, conventionally, called 'my' past or future, 'my' achievements and ideas are 'mine' only by current linguistic agreement (and

[9] See S. R. L. Clark, 'Waking-up: A Neglected Model for the Afterlife', *Inquiry*, 26 (1984), 209–30.

[10] *Crest Jewel of Wisdom*, in J. L. Head and S. L. Cranston (edd.), *Reincarnation: The Phoenix Fire Mystery* (New York, 1977), 56 ff.

might as accurately be described as someone else's). Nor can we easily distinguish between a life (which may be more or less rich, worthwhile, and satisfying) and the one who lives that life (whom good liberals do not wish to think less 'intrinsically valuable' than any other) without an anti-empiricist insistence on real identities.[11] It is apparently assumed—without good argument—that no matter what we turn out to be (or assume ourselves to be) we can reasonably maintain exactly the same moral and political code (suitably and quietly amended by class-interest) that once went with quite a different view of what and where we were. Those commentators who notice the problem make some vague gesture towards G. E. Moore's discussion of the 'naturalistic fallacy', as if this excused them from any further examination of the moral and practical implications of modernism. But Gautama was correct:

> There is an Unborn, Unoriginated, Uncreated, Unformed. If there were not this Unborn, this Unoriginated, this Uncreated, this Unformed, escape from the world of the born, the originated, the created, the formed would be impossible.[12]

And in that case we should have no good ground for supposing that human reason was anything but 'a little agitation of the brain',[13] a motion wholly incapable of serving as a model for the world at large. It is because *Nous* is more than an agitation of the brain that we can hope to strip off the soul's tunic of opinion and imagery to enter the Holy of Holies,[14] and begin to understand the world we really inhabit. 'This is what we mean by possession of spirit: to be involved with everything that exists, "to permeate the whole cosmos"'.[15] If that is not possible, or not to be expected, then perhaps the Sceptics have the victory after all—but if they do, then the whole house of cards that modernists have erected against the claims of the perennial philosophy comes tumbling down.

[11] See R. G. Frey, 'Autonomy and the Value of Life', *Monist*, 70 (1987), 50–63.

[12] D. Goddard (ed.), *A Buddhist Bible* (Boston, 1970), 32.

[13] D. Hume, *Natural History of Religion and Dialogues concerning Natural Religion*, edd. A. W. Colver and J. V. Price (Oxford, 1976), 168.

[14] Philo, *Legum Allegoriae*, 2. 56; see E. R. Dodds, *Pagan and Christian in an Age of Anxiety* (Cambridge, 1968), 95.

[15] J. Pieper, *Love and Inspiration*, tr. R. and C. Winston (London, 1965), 75; see R. Niebuhr, *The Self and the Dramas of History* (London, 1956), 38 f., recounting Lindbergh's experience of the 'aspatial nature of the self'.

## Pluralism and the Self

What then do I mean by speaking of 'Reason as *Daimōn*'? One possible interpretation, worth mentioning to convey a warning, is that the rules and techniques of reason be regarded as demonic, such as may at last disrupt a decent and humane existence. Demons, popularly so-called, are intrusive elementals, at war with Heaven and with Humankind's true self. Their powers are real, but must be put at the service of humane endeavour. Ares and Aphrodite, great Olympians, are still readily conceived as powers that can shake the human heart and world. Aphrodite Ouranios, despite Plato's joking transvaluation of values (*Symposium*, 180d6 ff.), is a Titan, an untamed power that owes no duty to the God of Justice and Hospitality: before she becomes Olympian, deserving of her own due honour, she must be born of Zeus and Dione. Metis, who is crafty wisdom, must also be swallowed up by Zeus and reborn as Athene.[16] Reason as cleverness or intellectual technique, and reason as the objectifying eye of far-shooting Apollo, must be put to service lest they destroy humane order. Intellectual curiosity has no more title than any other overmastering passion to our whole devotion. This thought is indeed the truth behind the commentators' casual rejection of the thought that some one thing, like *Nous*, could count for more than anything else. If cleverness or science were such a value then nothing could be wrong that was clever or scientific: but we know very well that only barbarians think that 'science' excuses all, or that a clever piece of work is its own justification.

The techniques and rules of practical and theoretical reason may be intrusive, domineering, and destructive (quite as much as homicidal fury, intoxication, or sexual desire): in brief, they may be considered demonic, even by those who have no serious ontological commitment to the separate existence of demons. 'I define "daimonic" as any natural function in the individual that has the power of taking over the whole person. Sex and *erōs*, anger and rage and the craving for power are examples'.[17] Demons, or the demonic, may be real and powerful elements in human character,

[16] See M. Détienne and J.-P. Vernant, *Cunning Intelligence in Greek Culture and Society* (Brighton, 1978), 108 f.; S. R. L. Clark, *The Mysteries of Religion* (London, 1986).

[17] R. May, 'Psychotherapy and the Demonic'; in J. Campbell (ed.), *Myths, Dreams and Religion* (New York, 1970), 196–210, quotation from p. 196.

and the less we think that there is some one thing, the Self, in each of us, the less we can claim that 'Reason' or the operations of reason have any different status from lust or anger or the rules of etiquette. If there were a real Self, and 'Reason' were another name for it (which was perhaps Descartes's conviction), then 'Reason' names no *daimōn* in the sense of something that might disrupt the whole system of the individual personality or of society. Other moods and modes of human existence might prove disruptive, but 'Reason' named the still centre of the individual soul, the point where all souls might agree. Without that conviction, 'Reason' names only a set of animal capacities as little to be trusted as any other.

This is part of what it might mean to speak of 'Reason as Daimōn', but it is not the central theme of my paper. The *Daimōn* that is *Nous* or Reason is not wholly and straightforwardly to be identified with the Ego-consciousness, but neither is it an intrusive and destructive element that must be made to serve some yet higher value in the personality or in society lest it prove demon. If the life well-lived is *eudaimonia*, 'having a good *daimōn*', and that *daimōn* is *Nous*, as Xenocrates[18] suggested, it is not surprising that to be *eudaimōn* we must identify ourselves with *Nous*, with what is most especially ourselves and yet something more than human (Aristotle, *Nicomachean Ethics* (hereafter *EN*), 10. 7, 1177b26 ff.). *Nous* is (1) the most valuable and god-like element of the human organism, (2) the organ of fundamental intellectual intuition, of those truths that cannot without absurdity be supposed to be demonstrated from yet firmer truths, (3) conscience or consciousness itself (though this last perhaps goes beyond what earlier Hellenic thinkers would have said).

It has been argued in the past that Homeric Greeks—or even Greeks in general—lacked any clear sense of their own single identities.

> We believe that a man advances from an earlier situation by an act of his own will, through his own power . . . [Homer] has no recourse but to say that the responsibility lies with a god . . . Homeric man was not yet awakened to the fact [*sic*] that he possesses in his own soul the source of his powers . . . he receives them as a natural and fitting donation from the gods.[19]

[18] Xenocrates, fr. 81, in *Darstellung der Lehre und Sammlung der Fragmente*, ed. R. Heinze (Leipzig, 1892); see Aristotle, *Topics*, 2. 6, 112a32.

[19] B. Snell, *The Discovery of the Mind*, tr. T. G. Rosenmeyer (New York, 1960), 21.

The evidence for this assertion, and for the even wilder claim made by J. Jaynes[20] that 'at one time human nature was split in two, an executive part called a god, a follower part called a man', is not very strong, though the idea clearly has its attractions for the imaginative psycho-historian. What interests me here is that Snell, and his followers, seem to assume that the belief they attribute to the Greeks is obviously false, that there is instead a single being straightforwardly identifiable with a particular material object such that it is self-evident that all the powers, moods, faculties, and thoughts associated with that object actually 'belong' in some clear sense to that single being. This is supposed to be self-evidently true even though there is no sign that the being thus postulated can actually control its moods, powers, thoughts, and faculties. As E. R. Dodds remarked, before going on to dismiss such failure to admit to one's 'real' ownership of thoughts, 'Often a man is conscious of no observation or reasoning which has led up to the recognition, the insight, the memory, the brilliant or perverse idea—but how then can he call them his?'[21] How indeed, especially when we have no coherent theory to explain just how material events can issue in just these mental happenings?

It is also obvious that the identity and limits of any complex organism or aggregate—which is what the human creature is now supposed to be—must be a matter of 'more or less', not 'all or nothing'—a point which it takes no special insight to recognize, and considerable nerve to apply! Even at a material level, biologists can point out that things which we habitually regard as unitary systems are better conceived as aggregations of smaller units: what looks like (and, in a sense, certainly is) a swarm of fish or flock of birds may not really be managed by any unitary purpose shared among the individuals. Its apparent unanimity is a by-product of the self-serving choices of many individual organisms, as they jostle to get away from predators, or to take advantage of the updraught from the leader's wings. Such reductionism is so popular a stance that it is very puzzling that it should be considered obvious that there are real human individuals who are not thus decomposable. If Homeric man did address his *thumos*, or did experience waves of anger or lust or sudden insight as things 'from outside', it certainly does not follow that he was in any comic or psychotic 'dissociated

[20] *The Origin of Consciousness in the Breakdown of the Bicameral Mind* (New York, 1976), 84.

[21] *The Greeks and the Irrational* (Berkeley, 1951), 11.

state': he simply spoke rather differently about the common human condition. As M. Nilsson acknowledged, 'pluralistic teaching about the soul is founded in the human condition'.[22] As Mary Midgley has remarked, 'some of us have to hold a meeting every time we want to do something only slightly difficult, in order to find the self who is capable of undertaking it'.[23]

Atomistic reductionism offers one challenge, Platonic realism another. When Apuleius defines a good *daimōn* as 'animus virtute perfectus' ('a mind perfect in virtue; *De Deo Socratis*, 15. 150 f.),[24] he is speaking at once of a discarnate intellect, and of what moderns would see only as an abstract universal, not a concrete one. But we can quite intelligibly and helpfully recognize the *same* moods, thoughts, powers, and faculties in association with different material objects. It may be that when we try to explain what is going on we must abandon our implicit belief in effective universals, and rely instead upon the particular local mechanism that gave the misleading impression that one and the same Form was present on many particular occasions: nominalism may be the truth (though I doubt it). But if we take that step, and rule out any appeal to gods, spirits, forms, we must also rule out appeals to a unitary self (ourself) that manifests upon separate particular occasions. If an accurate ontology contains no forms of the kind that 'Homeric man' imagined, but only 'punctiform particulars' that happen to remind us (who?) of each other, neither does it contain individual human selves with obvious boundaries.[25] That the seven-year-old whom my mother remembers by my name was *me* is not, on modern terms, a fact of nature which I would be merely ignorant or deluded in denying: it is as much a socio-legal convention as the claim that this suit is mine.

If all this is so, then it is simply silly to complain or sneer if other peoples have had different rules, especially if our actual rules are a lot more like the ones attributed to them than those which patronizing commentators claim for us. What dogmatists insist is a

[22] 'Letter to Nock on Some Fundamental Concepts in the Science of Religion', *Harvard Theological Review*, 42 (1949), 71–107; cited by Dodds, *Greeks*, p. 134 n. 111.

[23] *Wickedness: A Philosophical Essay* (London, 1984), 123.

[24] J. C. Nitzsche, *Genius Figure in Antiquity and the Middle Ages* (New York, 1975), 31.

[25] S. R. L. Clark, 'Abstraction, Possession, Incarnation', in A. Kee and E. T. Long (edd.), *Being and Truth: Essays in Honour of John Macquarrie* (London, 1986), 293–317.

single, simple entity (though they decline to believe any of the metaphysical doctrines which are implied by such a dogma) can as well be described as a battleground, a complex apparatus, or a chimera. That description of what we actually are fits very well with the popular account of what we should take seriously: if values are many and incommensurable (if polytheism, in effect, is true) then it makes sense to say there is no one thing that is central or essential to our well-being or identity.[26] If, on the other hand, we are indeed single, simple entities, then it must be plausible to suggest that, after all, some one thing matters more to us than others.

Consider the case proposed by Popper:

> In order to save our life, we all would be prepared to have a leg cut off. And we would all, I think, refuse an operation which would prevent us from being responsible for our actions, or which would destroy the consciousness of our numerical identity at different times: an operation that would save the life of the body, but not the integrity of the mind.[27]

If may be true, as Aristotle said, that there are many things we value for themselves, irrespective of any further good they do (*EN* 1. 6, 1096b17 ff). It is also true, as Aristotle also said, that there are some things which, when we have to choose, we should certainly prefer. Those who wish to live a life well-lived will recognize many duties that, as occasions offer, they must fulfil: that is the truth hidden in the claim that most modern commentators make, that *eudaimonia* must be taken to be an 'inclusive' concept, incorporating everything that the person of sound judgement does or should prefer. But it cannot be thought that the fulfilling of those duties is, in the abstract, what the person of sound judgement would choose to be doing. If it were possible we would choose to have no occasion to act bravely, temperately, justly, or the rest. Action in accordance with moral virtue is predicated on needs and misfortunes that we would not wish for. If we seriously thought that the exercise of courage or compassion was the highest good, we should be compelled to create occasions for such exercise if none were forthcoming in the course of nature: good Samaritans need people who have been mugged. Those imaginable or real beings who have escaped such occasions do not live less well than we do, so long as

[26] See J. O. Ogilvy, *Many Dimensional Man* (New York, 1977).
[27] K. R. Popper and J. Eccles, *The Self and its Brain* (Heidelberg, 1977), 115.

they exercise the higher, independent virtues, and are—correspondingly—possessed of the sort of character that would, if it were necessary, be expressed in moral action.

So what is it that each of us would wish to be and see? What would it be that we would never surrender? Aristotle's answer was that it would be the life lived according to the best and highest virtue, even though that life is more than humankind can hope for, in these or any other troubled times. That virtue is one that needs no occasion for its proper exercise, nor any equipment beyond the immediate power of the agent. Contemplative virtue is an excellence that allows us to stand a little apart from our ordinary selves:

> I am conscious of the presence and criticism of a part of me which, as it were, is not a part of me, but a spectator, sharing no experience but taking note of it, and that is no more I than it is you.[28]

Thoreau's account makes clear, what Aristotle unfortunately does not, that the part or non-part of me which is spectator can also stand in judgement over my own moral action. It is because I can see the whole of which this organism here is a part that I can pretend to a more objective, morally critical stance. If I could not thus stand over against myself I should be limited (of course without knowing it) by my immediate desires and prejudices. What contemplates in me is conscience. As Jerome declared, *synterēsis* is a fourth element of the soul, symbolized by the eagle of Ezekiel's vision, 'which is not mixed up with the other three but corrects them when they go wrong, and of which we read in the scriptures as the spirit which intercedes for us with ineffable groaning'.[29] Potts, revealingly enough, does not pick up Jerome's clear statement that the eagle is separate, and not straightforwardly a part of the whole human creature, but relapses into the modern convention that conscience is simply one faculty of the soul.[30]

Conscience, as our predecessors thought, is in essence the voice of a wider and greater spirit than our common self, a critical commentator which was citizen of a greater kingdom. Heraclitus'

[28] Thoreau, *Walden*, p. 119.

[29] *In Ezekiel*, 1. 7, in J.-P. Migne (ed.), *Patrologia Latina* (221 vols.; Paris, 1844–64), xxv. 22; see T. C. Potts, *Conscience in Mediaeval Philosophy* (Cambridge, 1980), 79 f.

[30] Ibid. 6 f.

[31] J.-P. Vernant and P. Vidal-Naquet, *Tragedy and Myth in Ancient Greece*, tr. J. L. Lloyd (Brighton, 1981), 13; see V. J. Verdenius, *Parmenides* (Groningen, 1942), 29.

obscure comment that '*ēthos anthrōpō(i) daimōn*' (22 DK B 119) quite likely makes a similar point: not that it is a person's character which determines his fortune ('the fault, dear Brutus, lies not in our stars, but in ourselves . . .'), but that 'what one calls character in man is in reality a *daimōn*'.[31] Socrates' *daimōn*, as it was understood by later commentators, operates as Philo of Alexandria reckoned conscience did, not 'as a force innate in and the property of the human soul'.[32] W. B. Yeats's description of 'the voice of conscience':

> It is a voice in my head that is sudden and startling. It does not tell me what to do but often reproves me. It will say perhaps 'That is unjust' of some thought; and once when I complained that a prayer had not been heard, it said, 'You have been helped'.[33]

As V. Moore[34] comments: 'Is it not an almost exact description of Socrates' *daimōn*?' Only a minority of later commentators deliberately and openly equated *nous*, conscience and guardian *daimōn*[35], probably because not everyone is actually led by *nous*, but those who did so seem to have caught hold of a significant point. Plato's picture of the whole psychic organism, especially in the *Timaeus*, is of a divinely created *nous*, encapsulated and barnacled (*Republic* (hereafter *R.*), 10, 612a) by other psychic functions with which it is not identical.

> It would be too easy just to say that for Plato, a divine spirit given to man by God was indwelling in man too, and that man's most proper life-task was honouring and cultivating that divine spirit that dwells within himself. Yet it should be noted that this was literally what Plato said.[36]

I would add that this is 'too easy' only in the sense that we run the risk of ignoring genuine puzzles when we compare great metaphysical systems. It does not seem to me to be false to Plato's intention.

The awakening in us of this wider vision of things, and a

[32] R. T. Wallis, 'The Idea of Conscience in Philo', in D. Winston and J. Dillon (edd.), *Two Treatises of Philo* (Chico, Calif., 1983), 207–16, quotation from p. 212.

[33] *Autobiographies* (London, 1955), 13 ff.

[34] *The Unicorn* (London, 1954), 8.

[35] Plutarch, *De Facie Lunae*, 943a; *Genio Socratis*, 591d; *Corpus Hermeticum*, 1. 22, 10. 19 f.

[36] C. J. de Vogel, 'The Sōma–Sēma Formula', in H. J. Blumenthal and R. A. Markus (edd.), *Neoplatonism and Early Christian Thought: Essays in Honour of A. H. Armstrong* (London, 1981), 79–95.

correspondingly critical attitude to the ordinary self, can be prompted by ethical or by aesthetic factors. 'Beauty can prod man out of the realm of comprehensible habituation, out of the "interpreted world"'.[37] Beauty, in the radical sense that we often prefer to ignore, is a reminder that things are not tools or ornaments for our everyday purposes, not even objects of our comfortable aestheticism. True beauty may be 'terrible as an army with banners', a power that makes demands and sets up ever higher standards. The love awakened by such beauty may be contaminated by concupiscence and personal fear, but it points toward its own purification, to the demand that the beautiful simply be, even if the lover, as single, temporal creature never yet enjoy it.[38] 'Love is important only in Plato's sense, in so far as it gives wings to the imagination—whatever in love is personal and not imaginative, matters not at all'.[39] The awakening may also come with the discovery of our own ordinary self's mortality. It is because we can be aware of a wider world in which this self has ceased to be that we can contemplate our death, and in the contemplating of it know ourselves—our higher self—to be immortal. 'That which experiences and knows about the divine and consequently about the universe is identical with his own being . . . the divine is man's own being'.[40]

The objective, critical mind that wakens in us enables us to see before and after our ordinary self's life. 'Memory'—by which is meant the impersonal memory of science and tradition—'is exalted because it is the power that makes it possible for me to escape time and return to the divine state'.[41] 'The effort involved in remembering makes it possible for us to learn who we are and to know our own *psyche*—that *daimōn* which has become incarnate in us'.[42] If the world before 'my' birth and after 'my' death is present to me, the Self to which it is present is something more than the complex of desires and personal memories that moderns now equate with my 'real' or 'true' self. The Self of which the ancients, in Greece, India,

[37] Pieper, *Love*, p. 81.

[38] Id., *Death and Immortality*, tr. R. and C. Winston (London, 1969), 20 ff.

[39] K. Raine, *Collected Poems* (London, 1956), p. xiv; her 'imagination' is what others have called 'spirit' or *nous*; see also, disapprovingly, M. C. Nussbaum, *The Fragility of Goodness: Luck and Ethics in Greek Tragedy and Philosophy* (Cambridge, 1986), 156 f.

[40] Verdenius, *Parmenides*, p. 29.

[41] J.-P. Vernant, *Myth and Thought among the Greeks* (London, 1983), 88.

[42] Ibid. 86.

and elsewhere, were speaking is something of which we catch a glimpse in these various experiences and activities. That Self, which we dignify by the title of Conscience, Consciousness, or Mind, is what no one who has experienced its presence would give up, and which is the condition of moral action in the world where we find ourselves. Those who set themselves to live from that standard make discoveries:

> The more the seeker learns to listen above, to follow the intimations of the Silence (which are not imperious, not noisy, which are almost imperceptible like a breath, hardly thought out, only felt, but terribly rapid), the more numerous, exact, irresistible they become; and gradually he sees that all his acts, the very least, can be sovereignly guided by this silent source above, that all his thoughts come from there, luminous, beyond dispute, that a sort of spontaneous knowledge is born in him.[43]

I add in passing that the strange remark of the Pythagoreans, that myriads of souls can be seen dancing in a sunbeam (Aristotle, *De Anima*, I. 2, 404a17 ff.),[44] is matched by the report from Aurobindo's ashram that supramental illumination is 'like a vivid gold, a warm gold dust . . . a crowd of tiny little points of light, nothing but that'.[45] One frequent conclusion is, unsurprisingly, that this Self whose knowledge reaches out to embrace the whole world and which far transcends our own individualities, is numerically the same in each of us. 'To be possessed of spirit is to be involved with everything that exists, to permeate the whole cosmos.'[46] That awakening centre—or rather, since it is not possible that it should ever be anything but awake—that centre as we awaken to it, is described, after Aurobindo, as follows:

> Not only an impersonal force but a presence, a being in our depths, as though we had a support there, something that gives us a solidity, almost a backbone, and a quiet outlook on the world. With this little vibrating thing within, one is invulnerable and no longer alone. It is there everywhere, it is there always. It is warm, close, strong. And strangely enough when one has discovered it it is the same thing everywhere in all beings, all things . . . not the thin and dry 'I think, therefore I am', but the fundamental reality of our

[43] Satprem, *Sri Aurobindo: The Adventure of Consciousness*, tr. Tehmi (Pondicherry, 1968), 190.

[44] W. Burkert, *Lore and Science in Ancient Pythagoreanism*, tr. E. L. Minar, Jr. (Cambridge, Mass., 1972), 73.

[45] Satprem, *Sri Aurobindo*, p. 280, citing the Mother.

[46] Pieper, *Love*, p. 75.

being, ourself, truly ourself, the active centre, warmth and being, consciousness and force.[47]

## *Plotinian Beginnings*

So far I have, as it were, been expounding the phenomenology of spirit, with occasional reference to ancient and modern descriptions. It is, of course, open to us to agree with the modern psychologist that '(while) an adult person may find himself toying with the idea of having an acute personal difficulty eliminated by magical appeal to some imaginary guardian angel, [it is a mark of hysterical dissociation that it is] devoid of the actor's playful as-if approach to his stage assignments'.[48] Maybe it is really obvious that nothing that is done or experienced in the human world is more than an operation of the psychophysical organisms, the social mammals that we often understand ourselves to be. Certainly the sort of consciousness I have been describing is a capacity of the human organism: we can have those experiences, can engage in those self-critical analyses, can take a wider survey of our situation. We can even go on to try and isolate what it is about our specific animal inheritance that gives us those capacities. Why is that not all there is to it? Why distinguish *nous logizomenos* and *nous logizesthai parekchōn* (Plotinus, *Enneads*, 5. 1 [10]. 10. 13 f.,[49] the former being eternal and transcendent?

It should be obvious that our ability to explain—or at last to make gestures towards explaining—our experience does not imply that what we experience has no objective reality. What we experience here is a consciousness whose objects range far beyond our own mortal identities, which is at once the thing most essential to our futures and puzzlingly non-identical with the appetitive and sensuous mammals that it knows us to be. We experience it also in the thought of what it would be like to be someone else: most ethical systems require us at some point to conceive how we would wish to be treated if we were a child, an immigrant, a neighbour, or an animal. But this psychophysical organism here, the one called

[47] Satprem, *Sri Aurobindo*, p. 61.

[48] D. B. Klein, *Abnormal Psychology* (New York, 1951), 300.

[49] P. Merlan, *Monopsychism, Mysticism, Metaconsciousness* (The Hague, 1963), 6. The square-bracketed numbers in refs. to Plotinus' *Enneads* identify the order in which Plotinus probably wrote the separate essays.

Stephen, simply could not be and never could have been James, Nazreen, Timothy, or Tabitha. In many cases Stephen could not even be supposed to be in the 'same' situation, although it is clearly imaginable that I be so. The I that could be or could have been Nazreen is not identical with Stephen (any more than it would then be identical with Nazreen). The relation between Stephen and I is not one of identity, but participation. Stephen could exist, but not be I; I could exist and not be Stephen. Accordingly 'Stephen' and 'I' do not, for moral purposes, name the same thing.[50] The I, the Self that awakens in Stephen (or rather, that Stephen occasionally wakes up to share) is the very thing that Nazreen may also 'be'.

> What looks forth from another's eyes, what feels itself in the writhing of a worm, what perhaps throbs with felt if dim emotion within an electron is really the very thing which when speaking through my lips, calls itself 'I'.[51]

Just as I and Stephen can be distinguished, so must Stephen's animal capacity to be illumined be distinguished from the undying light. *Nous poiētikos*, as Aristotle told us, albeit elliptically, always thinks, and is unmixed and unaffected (Aristotle, *De Anima*, 3. 5, 430a17 ff.): *nous pathētikos* is the human animal's capacity to be enlightened, to come awake to the world that exists before and after. 'Our metaphysical centre is always conscious, but we, as sensitive-imaginative-dianoetic creatures, are not always conscious'.[52] That our separate visions do not always quite agree is evidence only of our incapacity: there is still one world only which these animal intelligences reach towards, and in the end only one undying intellect (though it is possible that there are many levels of consciousness between 'us' and It).

*Nous* comes from outside the animal (Aristotle, *De Generatione Animalium*, 2. 3, 736b27), and its exercise is not a bodily function even if the bodily being that receives it must have some natural capacity to receive it. Consciousness, despite a host of loyal

[50] See Z. Vendler, *The Matter of Minds* (Oxford, 1985); G. Madell, *The Identity of the Self* (Edinburgh, 1981), 26, 78 ff.

[51] E. Schrodinger, *My View of the World* (Cambridge, 1964), cited by T. L. S. Sprigge, *The Vindication of Absolute Idealism* (Edinburgh, 1983), 274.

[52] E. W. Warren, 'Consciousness in Plotinus', *Phronesis*, 9 (1964), 83–97; it must be obvious by now that I have no sympathy at all with the view, still fashionable among Aristotelian scholars, that one ought not to interpret Aristotle's texts in the light of later, neo-Platonic philosophy even though those interpreters had more texts available to them than we do, and were inheritors of a continuing oral tradition at which we can only guess.

believers, is simply not the sort of thing that can be intelligibly related to particular bodily states.[53] It is imaginable, as far as our present understanding goes, that there be exactly the same physical configurations and neural processes without the real existence of any phenomenal world, let alone mine. To talk of 'emergence', as if this were more than a confession of intellectual failure, leaves the relation between physical state and conscious experience—at whatever level—entirely unintelligible. The point is actually confirmed—if confirmation is necessary—by neurological experiment: 'there is no place in the cerebral cortex where electrical stimulation will cause a patient to believe or to decide . . . To suppose that consciousness or the mind has localization is a failure to understand neurophysiology'.[54] Aristotle was right to say that *nous*, consciousness strictly so called, has no bodily organ (*De Anima*, 3. 4, 429a26 ff.), and that it is not to be explained as the product of brain, heart, or sense-organs.

But this still leaves us with the ontological problem. Granted that there are certain experiences which are recognizably alike all over the world, and in a variety of traditions; granted that there are some good reasons to take the apparent implications of those experiences seriously; granted that we cannot insist upon the unity of the ordinary self, and cannot explain at any theoretical level why creatures like us should have these experiences and capacities: what is the Self that is the invading *Nous*, and what are 'we' if not that Self? To these questions Plotinus attempted answers. My exposition of those answers is very much that of an amateur where Plotinian scholarship is concerned: my only excuse is that I think I partly recognize what he is talking about, and why, although I cannot give a full exposition and justification of his psychological system within the confines of this paper.

*Nous*, it must be obvious by now, is not the ratiocinative or calculative faculty (*Enneads*, 5. 4 [49]. 3. 15 f.):

> One must not suppose that the gods or the exceedingly blessed spectators in the higher world contemplate propositions, but all the Forms we speak about are beautiful images in that world, of the kind which someone imagined to exist in the soul of the wise man, images not painted but real. (*Enneads*, 5. 8 [31]. 5. 20 f.)[55]

[53] S. R. L. Clark, *From Athens to Jerusalem* (Oxford, 1984), 121 ff.
[54] W. Penfield, *The Mystery of the Mind* (Cambridge, Mass., 1975), 77, 109.
[55] See Pieper, *Death*, p. 115, v. Mendelssohn's corruption of Plato's *Phaedo*.

Nor are 'we', straightforwardly, *nous*; rather is *nous* our king (3. 32 f.): but 'we too are kings when we are in accord with it' (4. 1 f.). 'The nobly good man is the man who acts by his better part . . . *Nous* is active in the good man. He is then himself a *daimōn* or on the level of a *daimōn* and his *daimōn* is a god' (3. 4 [15]. 6. 1ff.; see Porphyry, *Vita Plotini*, 10. 15 ff.). In brief, by obeying *Nous*, living in accord with that divinity, we are identified with it—and correspondingly look upward to yet higher beings. 'Every man is double, one of him is a sort of compound being and one of him is himself' (2. 3 [52]. 9. 31 f.).

> He himself is the god who came Thence and his own real nature if he becomes what he was when he came, is There. When he came here he took up his dwelling with someone else whom he will make like himself to the best of the powers of his real nature, so that if possible this someone will be free from disturbance or will do nothing of which his master does not approve. (1. 2 [19]. 6. 7 ff.)

Before coming-to-be we were other men, pure souls, and *nous* joined to all being (4. 4 [2], 12). Now 'we' are in the middle: lying between *nous* and sense and able to rise or sink (5. 3 [49]. 3. 34 f.).

> [The one above] knows himself according to intellect because he has become that intellect; and by that intellect he thinks himself again, not any longer as a man, but having become altogether other and snatching himself up into that higher world. (5. 3 [49]. 4. 8 f)

The real eternal *nous* does not come to itself from outside (5. 8 [31]. 3. 10), because it does not need to be actualized: it is itself the actuality, the presence that is multiply refracted here below. It seems likely that Plotinus intended that each partially awakened soul, binding itself to *nous*, awoke as one distinct being in a community of *noes*, which were in turn united in obedience to a god (very much as Plato's *Phaedrus* myth would have it). The effort to expound these twists and turns often leaves it unclear just what 'we' refers to on any particular occasion, and how many of 'us' there are meant to be. That is perhaps implicit in this whole attempt to isolate what most matters in our identities.

Jung's recollections of his childhood include the thought that he was, as it were, two persons: the ordinary self and its predilections, and 'the other in me was the timeless imperishable stone'.[56] The

[56] C. G. Jung, *Memories, Dreams, Reflections*, ed. A. Jaffe, tr. R. and C. Winston (London, 1967), 59.

thought he recorded or read back into his past is also the shaman's, who meditates on his enduring skeleton, the image of what lies underneath 'the bits of flesh and fluids', anger, fear, desire, and ignorance.[57] Plotinus' worries about the 'boundaries of the self'[58] reflect a similar experience or discovery. The occult self that Empedocles (frs. 9–12) called *daimōn* and Plato identified with the undying intellect,[59] and the personal masks with which we greet our ordinary world can both be spoken of with the aid of personal pronouns. Our fragmentary, empirical selves are what comes to light as the undying light plays over these fragments of existence: as the fragments turn to the light, 'the man driven by his *daimōn* steps beyond the limits of the intermediary stage, enters the untrodden, untreadable regions'.[60]

'Abiding among the senses is a person who consists of understanding, a light within the heart'.[61] 'What [Lindbergh] defines as "spirit" might be regarded as the ultimate freedom of the self over its functions'.[62] That person is both the Self, the true subject, and not what we are in our ordinary inattention. That undying Self is not the mortal person which moderns recognize as the only subject. As Aquinas declared long before Strawson, the human person is both body and soul,[63] and if this person here is to be thought immortal it must be as a bodily being. The fault of moderns is that we have, unaccountably, forgotten the undying Self without ever quite admitting to ourselves what it is really like to live in a world without it. It is perhaps worth drawing this paper to a close by recalling the error of an earlier generation. Fichte's peroration:

> What is called death cannot interrupt my work . . . I have seized hold upon eternity. I lift my head boldly to the threatening precipice, to the raging cataract and to the rumbling clouds swimming in a sea of fire, and say: I am eternal and defy your power. Rend apart the last mote of the body I call mine: my will alone will soar boldly and coldly above the ruins of the universe.[64]

57 M. Eliade, *Myths, Dreams and Mysteries*, tr. P. Mairet (London, 1968), 82 ff.
58 Dodds, *Pagan*, p. 77.
59 Id., *Greeks*, pp. 62 ff.
60 Jung, *Memories*, p. 377.
61 *Brhadaranyaka Upanishad*, cited by M. L. West, *Early Greek Philosophy and the Orient* (Oxford, 1971), 183.
62 Niebuhr, *The Self*, p. 41.
63 *Summa Theologica*, 3. 5. 1, cited by Pieper, *Death*, p. 40.
64 *Werke*, i. 250 f., cited by Pieper, *Death*, p. 111.

But the undying intellect which is the true subject of consciousness and conscience, the thing united in loving contemplation with all objects of all thought, is not Fichte, and does not defy the material universe. This sort of 'idealistic absolutizing of autonomous man', whether couched in Fichte's terms or in the still sillier versions of modern materialists, deserves to be countered by the blunt reminder that Socrates and Plotinus, Fichte and Nietzsche are all dead, even if—while they yet lived—the undying intellect enjoyed their service. The Will that Fichte identified with the undying Self would, to Plotinus—or so I suspect—be that mistaken desire that creates us as uncivil creatures. That is not the immortal one.

# 9
# Presocratic Minds

*M. R. Wright*

According to the mixture at any one time of the body as it travels, so is the structure of men's thinking. (Parmenides)

As a man's constitution changes, so changed thoughts are present to him. (Empedocles)

Our understanding shifts with bodily changes. (Democritus)

Whatever exists is material, and what is taken to be mental and thus immaterial either does not exist or is really identical with something material. (Corman and Lehrer)

We suggest that there are no mental phenomena that will in the end prove recalcitrant to our style of physicalist theory. (Smith and Jones)

To explain the mind, we have to show how minds are built from mindless stuff. (Minsky)[1]

In a volume devoted to the concept of a person, it is appropriate to include a discussion of the first European philosophers, known collectively as the Presocratics. Although the concepts expressed in English by 'self' and 'person' have no exact equivalent in the language of the early Greeks, there was in their time a way of regarding thought processes and the thinking subject which is directly related to this topic. As is shown by the brief sample of quotations given above, the materialist theory of mind and its activities has its origins in the Presocratics and continues through the history of philosophy to contemporary physicalism.

[1] Parmenides, fr. 16, Empedocles fr. 108, Democritus fr. 9; J. W. Corman and K. Lehrer, *Philosophical Problems and Arguments* (London, 1974), 279, on Hobbes; P. Smith and O. R. Jones, *The Philosophy of Mind* (Cambridge, 1986), 236; and M. Minsky, *The Society of Mind* (London, 1987), 18. The source for quotations of the Presocratics throughout is H. Diels, *Die Fragmente der Vorsokratiker*, rev. H. Kranz (10th edn. 2 vols.; Berlin, 1941). The fragment numbers follow the 'B' ordering of this edition; the translations are my own. For text and commentary on these fragments see M. R. Wright, *The Presocratics*, (Bristol, 1985); for translation and discussion, J. Barnes, *Early Greek Philosophy* (Harmondsworth, 1987), and in general W. K. C. Guthrie, *History of Greek Philosophy* (6 vols., Cambridge, 1962–81), i–ii.

From the sixth century BC the soul (*psychē*) came to be regarded as the body's vital principle, and as such was assumed to be present in all forms of life, ensuring nutrition, growth, and reproduction of the species. In higher animals it would be responsible for locomotion and perception and, at its most sophisticated, would also explain the ability to think, endowing human beings with the unique potential to understand the external world and their own relation to it. In the study of this particular aspect of specifically human activity the early philosophers found a means of characterizing the human mind generally, and also of differentiating individuals in the range of possible variations in psychic structure as well as noetic effort and achievement.

The thesis will be tackled first by considering the external objects that are perceived and thought, and which supply the knowledge that is taken in. From there I shall move to the complementary knowing subject, and attempt to pin down what it is in the individual which responds to this knowledge. And thirdly I would like to look at the mutual reaction between object thought and thinking subject, and consider to what extent the reaction can be purposefully controlled. This brings with it the suggestion that each man has an intellectual history particular to himself, and its particularity might be markedly recognized in some instances by the individual's achievement of heroic or quasi-divine status as a consequence of successful control and development of the thinking process.

## *The Object Thought*

First then, what would an 'object of thought' or 'piece of knowledge' mean to a Presocratic? It could only be described in materialistic language since no other was yet available. Aristotle sets this out clearly at the beginning of his short history of philosophy in *Metaphysics* Alpha:

> The majority of the earliest philosophers thought that the only general principles were those of a material kind. They say that the material of which all things consist, and from which they first come and into which they eventually disintegrate—the substance persisting while the attributes change—is the element and principle of all things. (983b6–11)

And he later summarizes this section:

> These philosophers are concerned only with the study of generation, destruction and change, for their research overall concentrates on the principles and explanations of physical substance. (989b21–4)

Aristotle here oversimplifies, and his language is anachronistic, but the core of his analysis can be accepted. The Presocratics did not have the linguistic or philosophical skills to express what there is in other than materialistic terms, but, *pace* Aristotle, this does not imply that they were novices. They deserve respect as planters of trees that still bear fruit.

The early philosophers developed their understanding of the physical world by concentrating on three main issues: (1) the interaction of opposites, (2) the assumption of a basic 'stuff', and (3) the nature and function of an element. It will be useful to examine these themes briefly.

Starting with the Milesians, and with Anaximander in particular, we find that the working of oppositions in the cosmos as a whole is expressed in political and social terms of aggression, justice, and atonement. For Heraclitus similarly the cosmos is a battleground of opposing forces: 'War is common and justice is strife, and all things happen by strife and necessity' (fr. 80). And the same is true on the smaller 'microcosm' scale. Alcmaeon, following Heraclitus and working in both the Milesian and the medical tradition, suggests an indefinite number of opposites functioning in the individual ('most human things are two' as he puts it). He is particularly interested in the medical application, and so explains health in terms of the equilibrium of these opposites, and disease as the *monarchia* or dominance of one of them.

A parallel theme was the identification of a natural 'stuff' that would explain economically the perpetuation of generation and change. Air or fire, for example, could be posited both as an enduring substance in the make-up of the individual and the cosmos, and as a storehouse for the continuing supply of life. Anaximenes went further, and attempted to show how the basic stuff of air could become fiery by a process of 'thinning', and also condense into liquid and solid form, so that a wide variety of phenomena could be explained by a criterion of quantitative discrimination.

The third development, which was grounded in the first two,

related to elements. It came to be realized that, contrary to appearances, a large number of disparate objects might be composed of a limited number of basic ingredients. This is found initially in the second part of Parmenides' work, the *Doxa* or *Way of Opinion*:

Men have distinguished (two forms) as opposites in appearance, and assigned them marks distinct from one another—to one the aetherial flame of fire, gentle and very rare, identical with itself in every direction, but different from the other; the other is its opposite, dark night, a compact and heavy body. (fr. 8. 55–9)

And again:

All is full of light and dark night together, both equal, since nothing is without either. (fr. 9. 3–4)

This key concept of an element having its own specific and inalienable nature, yet being capable of entering into combinations without violating that nature, was developed by Empedocles on this Eleatic foundation. Parmenides had suggested the minimum plurality of two, but Empedocles realised the inadequacy of this, and supposed instead that everything was made of four elements (or 'roots' as he preferred to call them). These (i.e. earth, air, fire, and water) are the only real things, but as they run through each other they become different objects at different times, yet 'they are throughout forever the same' (fr. 17. 35). Anaxagoras, more enigmatically, also had an elemental materialist world, and Leucippus and Democritus brought this way of thinking to its extreme form: 'in reality there exist only atoms and void' (fr. 9).

All that there is then is made up of a variation of some basic stuff or of a combination of basic ingredients. In Presocratic terminology 'these are the only real things', 'all is full of them' and 'nothing is without them'. So when the outside world impinges on the individual, it has to be through some form of physical contact; and this is in fact how the working of the different senses was explained.

Theophrastus, Aristole's pupil and successor, wrote a history of early perception theories, a major section of which survives. There are some fragments extant from the Presocratics themselves, and the fourth book of Lucretius preserves many details of the original atomic version. It is clear from the evidence of these and other sources that the early philosophers agreed that the common and fundamental feature of perception is contact between two bodies.

Touch and taste obviously involve immediate contact, but complex and quite sophisticated explanations were given to show that seeing, hearing, and smelling had a similar basis, in that effluences of various kinds that were emitted from objects actually entered into channels or pores in the relevant organs and affected them. In vision, effluences from objects were assumed to fit into commensurate pores in the eye. In hearing, external sounds, explained as emanations of air particles, enter the channel of the outer ear, and reverberate as in a bell in the inner ear. Odour similarly, in the form of actual particles emitted by the object, stimulates a sense of smell when the particles are symmetrical with the pores of the organ.

Not all the Presocratics would go as far as Anaxagoras who said, according to Theophrastus (*Sens*, 17, 29), that all perception is accompanied by pain. Generally, pain would be assumed to result if the 'effluence' overwhelmed the organ or did not fit well, as is the case with bright lights and glaring colours in vision, loud voices and grating sounds in hearing, or various nasty smells. If however the external object is agreeable and there is a symmetrical fit, then the result is a smooth feeling of pleasure in the sense organ which may spread through the body.

It would not be relevant to elaborate on details, but two general points may be made. (1) In these theories the individual is a passive recipient in the first instance. A panoramic view, a melody, or a fragrance may 'hit' a traveller unexpectedly and there is no control over what happens in the organ as a result. (The metaphor of hitting and striking is still idiomatic in this context.) But (2) there is considerable control over future recurrences—the disagreeable sight or sound or smell can be avoided as far as possible, and the source of the pleasant sensation revisited. And when the traveller goes back to the view or the fragrance or the music because 'he couldn't take it all in the first time' (and again the metaphor is preserved) he refines and extends his perceptive faculties. In listening repeatedly to the same piece of music he hears more in it and 'gets more out of it', and hearing another work of the same kind would be more meaningful to him than the original experience of just listening to an agreeable noise. With practice more subtle and sophisticated nuances in sounds, as well as in sights and smells, can be apprehended. The benefits are in proportion to the effort and attention invested.

Now, although the external world impinges on the senses, it is obviously not the case that *all* that there is is accessible to the senses, or even that what does reach them does so in a reliable form. The Presocratics of course were well aware of this. They were more than ready to denounce the limits of sensory experience, and to set themselves apart, as men of reason, from the run of mortals who are restricted by their immediate perception of the external world. Human achievement in the realization of how things are is generally belittled. So Xenophanes:

Concerning gods and all of which I speak, no one has clearly seen, nor will any man have knowledge. Even if by chance someone should speak the exact truth, still he does not recognise it, but opinion is found over all. (fr. 34)

Heraclitus is also contemptuous:

Those without understanding, even when they hear, are like the deaf; of them does the saying bear witness, that they are absent when present. (fr. 34)

Eyes and ears are bad witnesses to men if they have souls that do not understand the language. (fr. 107)

The many do not heed the things they meet with, nor do they mark them when they are taught, though they think they do; they live as if they had a private understanding of their own. (frs. 17, 2)

Parmenides' goddess talks of men who wander along the wrong path:

knowing nothing, two-headed, deaf and blind, dazed uncritical crowds. (fr. 6. 6–7)

Empedocles is similarly dismissive:

After observing a brief span in their lifetime, subject to swift death, men are borne up and waft away like smoke; as they are driven in all directions, each is convinced only of that of which he has experience, yet boasts that he has found the whole. (fr. 2. 3–6)

Melissus also has a strong argument to support the downgrading of perception as a guide to what there really is. It is worth quoting in full for its strong denial of reliable perception in a world of change:

If there is earth and water and air and fire and iron and gold, and if some are living and others dead, and if things are black and white and all that men say that they really are—if that is so, and if we see and hear aright, each one of these must be as we first decided, and they cannot be changed or altered, but each must be as it is.

So we say that we see and hear and understand aright, and yet we believe that what is warm becomes cold, and what is cold warm; and that what is hard turns soft, and what is soft hard; that what is living dies, and life comes from what is not alive, and that all these things are changed, and that what they were and what they are now are in no way alike . . .

Now these two positions do not agree with one another. We said that there were many things that lasted, and had forms and strength of their own, and yet we fancy that they all suffer alteration, and change from what we see each time. It is clear then that we were not seeing aright after all, nor that those many things obviously exist. (fr. 8. 2–5)

These early philosophers were generally ready to recognize that there is knowledge external to the individual that can be assimilated by means other than the sense-organs. In Parmenides' argument the goddess's very starting-point is that an object is needed for speech and thought to be meaningful; it is peculiarly impossible to think a blank or speak of nothing. Since reasoning and intelligent speech require an object, what can be thought and spoken can exist, whereas what does not exist cannot be thought or said—'for the same thing is for thinking and for being' (frs. 2. 7–8, 3). This is expanded in the summary of the main argument in fragment 8:

What is there to be thought of is the same as what is thought, for you will not find thinking apart from what is, in which the reference lies—for nothing else either is or will be apart from what is, since *Moira* has bound this so as to be whole and immobile. (8. 34–8)

And *Moira* here is Parmenides' metaphor for the logical necessity of the argument which requires the conclusion that an object of thought exists.

Heraclitus had posited a state of super-awakeness, related to our present waking state as that is to sleeping. Empedocles contrasted objects that can be seen and touched with that which it is not possible to bring close within the range of our eyes, or to grasp with the hands, 'by which the broadest path of persuasion leads to the mind' (fr. 133). Anaxagoras also condemned the weakness of the senses, which are unable to judge the truth, and established *nous* as the principle of understanding. The whole tradition was summed up in the famous distinction made by Democritus between a bastard kind of knowing produced by the five senses, and the true knowing, separate from it.

The Presocratics therefore contrasted perceptible objects which impinge on the senses and result in opinions with thought objects, which are accessible to reason and result, when absorbed, in increased understanding. But, as has been shown, the Presocratics cannot but be materialists, and so these thought objects or bits of knowledge have to be actual 'things'.

Furthermore, thought objects could obviously be expressed and transferred in speech, with the result that what is spoken tends to be of similar status to what is thought. This is in a tradition that goes back to Homer of winged words passing the barrier of the teeth and being put into the *thymos*. So for Heraclitus *logos*, in one of its meanings, is 'that which is thought', but, more basically, 'that which is spoken'. Parmenides, as was shown above, argued that an object must exist for intelligible speech as well as for reasoning, and Empedocles in particular regarded as 'things' the thoughts, expressed in solemn epic style, which he exhorted Pausanias to take in and 'push down' within him. Spoken words therefore as well as the thoughts they express have a material representation. The philosopher acts as an intermediary, passing on truth in speech form as a 'bit' of knowledge to be assimilated by those who are awake and alert and ready to learn.

### *The Thinking Subject*

In the external world then there is something to be thought. So what is it within the individual that has access to that which is external to itself, and can reach beyond what is available to the organs of sense to an awareness of the objects of thought and speech?

To start with the Milesians, and in particular with the one surviving fragment of Anaximenes. This states:

As our soul [*psychē*] which is air maintains us, so breath and air surround the whole cosmos.

Now *psychē* in the Homeric poems had not been connected with the living, but referred only to that which leaves the living at death, and continues as a flitting shade in the realm of the dead. Anaximenes, however, transformed it into the principle of life, which holds together, strengthens, and controls the individual. And the *psychē* that is air relates to us in a way comparable to the functioning of air in the world as a whole. The cosmos is like a large animate being, and the individual man a miniature world or 'microcosm'.

Heraclitus continues and develops this theme of macro-microcosm. There is, he says, a world-controlling *logos*, that 'one wise' which is comparable to Zeus not in anthropomorphic attributes but in its eternity, knowledge, and power. Within the individual too *logos* is a principle of control and understanding. The inherent ambiguities of the term are exploited to the full. On the cosmic and the human level *logos* is what speaks and is spoken, what thinks and is thought, rational explanation and the objective truth of what is explained as well as universal law, and its expression in proportion and measure. But it also has a physical instantiation, and this is as fire. The divine principle is then identifiable with the physical structure of the world, in terms of ever-living, intelligent, and all-controlling fire, and takes its place in the cycle of the changes of the world masses while remaining the standard by which these transitions are regulated, as gold is exchanged in trade but sets the standard for the measure of the exchange (cf. frs. 30, 64, 90, 31).

The transitions or 'turnings' of the world masses recur on the microcosmic scale within the individual—from fiery *psychē* through water to earth, and back through water to fiery *psychē*. But, as with the cosmos, the principle of fire guides and controls, with the result that 'dry soul is wisest and best' (fr. 118). It would seem that the more fire predominates, the greater is the soul's wisdom, and then, correspondingly, the greater is its capacity for wisdom. 'There is a *logos* of soul which increases itself' as Heraclitus says in fragment 115, and again in the same context:

> You could not in your going find the limits of *psychē* though you travel the whole way—so deep is its *logos*. (fr. 45)

Parmenides' goddess also emphasizes *logos*, and in opposition to the senses:

> Do not let habit-forming custom cause your heedless eye and echoing ear and your tongue [i.e. the sense of taste] to mislead you, but judge by reasoning the hard-hitting argument I give you. (fr. 7. 3–6)

In the second part of the poem, the *Doxa*, which deals with opinion rather than truth, there is a suggestion of what judgment by *logos* might mean. This section expounds the belief that what there is consists of fire and night and 'there is nothing without either' (fr. 9. 4); thinking therefore would also be a function related to a mixture of these two 'forms'. Fragment 16 preserves the original wording:

According to the mixture at any one time of the body as it travels, so is the structure of men's thinking. For it is the same thing, the *physis* [i.e. the natural physical constitution] of the body, which has understanding in each and every man; and what prevails is thought [*noēma*].

'What prevails' between fire and night determines the character and scope of the thinking—limited if dark predominates, wide-ranging and superior if light does. Such would be the state in which judgement and understanding of the 'hard-hitting argument' would be reached. Yet in Parmenides' case that very argument in the first part of the poem, the *Alētheia*, abrogates the physical light which, according to the *Doxa*, makes understanding possible.

For Empedocles, as we have seen, earth, air, fire, and water are the only things in existence, functioning under powers of attraction and repulsion which he calls 'Love' and 'Strife'. So it is to be expected that the noetic principle will also be expressed in terms of the four elements or 'roots' acting under Love and Strife. What Empedocles actually says is:

In seas of blood coursing to and fro, there above all is what men call thought, [*noēma* again] because for men blood around the heart is thought. (fr. 105)

This enigmatic statement is glossed by Theophrastus:

We think chiefly with the heart-blood, for there the elements are more fully mingled than in any other part of our body. Those who have an equal or almost equal mingling of these elements are the most intelligent [*phronimoi*], and have the keenest sense-perceptions, and others are intelligent in so far as they approach to such a mixture; but those whose condition is the very reverse are the most stupid. (*Sens*, 10–11)

So in Empedocles' theory there is a concentration of blood in the individual sense-organs, which accounts for their relative efficiency. The heart-blood is purest, having the four elements most uniformly mingled, and it is on this mixture that the quality of thought depends.

Democritus uses the old word *phrēn* for 'mind', which may

originally (in singular and plural) have meant 'diaphragm' or 'midriff', but even in Homer refers to little more than the location of a range of psychological activities—feelings, emotions, wishes, and thoughts—that were not clearly distinguished. For Democritus everything is explicable by movements and arrangements of atoms in void, and the soul (the mind or *phrēn*) therefore also has an atomic structure. To account for the speed and mobility of thoughts, however, the atoms of which the *phrēn* is made would be especially small and smooth and round. In the end his theory is close to that of Empedocles, as Theophrastus again reports:

Concerning thought [*to phronein*], Democritus says merely that it arises when the soul's composition is duly proportioned. But, he adds, if someone becomes excessively hot or cold, then that thinking changes . . . So it is clear that Democritus explains thought by the *krāsis* of the body, and the view is perhaps not unreasonable for one who regards the soul itself as corporeal. (*Sens*, 58)[2]

Lastly in this section we come to the Mind or *nous* of Anaxagoras. This too ranges the cosmos, and is also present in the composition of some individuals:

In everything there is a portion of everything except *nous*, and there are some things in which there is *nous* too. (fr. 11)

These must obviously be, or at least include, intelligent humans. In attempting to describe and explain this cosmic and individual intelligence Anaxagoras stretches physical language to its limits. In the long twelfth fragment he describes *nous* as the most rarefied of all things and the purest, and sets it apart from everything else:

Other things have a portion of everything, but Mind is unlimited, self-determining, and mixed with no other thing; it alone has independent existence.

Yet the material basis is still there. The cosmic *nous* knows all things and controls them, but it is by an actual 'push' that it caused the initial rotation in the mixture which resulted in the emergence of this world and its continuing arrangement. *Nous* similarly on a smaller scale physically controls the individual body and 'knows'

[2] *Krāsis* here refers to the proportionate mixture of the ingredients which make up the totality of the thinking subject. It was the word used by Parmenides in his fr. 16, and in Theophrastus' comment on Empedocles, and became almost a technical Presocratic term for the proportionate combinations of physical parts.

by touching. This is why Socrates (in Plato's *Phaedo*) was so disappointed to find in Anaxagoras' book only mechanistic explanations for the working of *nous*.

### *Contact between the Object Thought and the Thinking Subject*

So far then I have tried to show that the Presocratics worked on the assumption that external objects of thought were to be regarded as actual 'things'. They were available for study either after entering directly into the thinking subject, or indirectly via the spoken words which were heard and then assimilated. And the thinking subject contained within himself an intellectual principle which was similarly regarded in physical terms. I turn now to the processes and consequences of the *act* of thinking, when the thinking subject makes contact with the object thought.

I earlier summarized briefly the common Presocratic theory of perception, which assumed that external objects (in the case of touch and taste) or emanations from external objects (in sight, hearing, and smell) impinged on the related sense-organ and affected it; and there was the corollary that the particular resulting sensation could be deliberately developed and refined, or correspondingly rejected. Now one of the main criticisms of the Presocratics by Aristotle and Theophrastus was that they did not distinguish sharply between thinking and perceiving. This has been shown to be misleading in that there are objects of thought different from and contrasted with the objects of perception, and which, as propounded by the teaching philosopher, are immune from the errors and limitations of things perceived. But the Peripatetic criticism does suggest that, although the objects are different, the activities are similar. This would mean that for the Presocratics thinking a thought with the intellectual principle is basically similar to seeing an object with the eye, hearing a sound with the ear, or making immediate contact with the hand. It is this suggestion that I would like to develop.

With perception, as was shown, there is a physical impact between subject and object. We blink in strong light, loud sounds make the ears ring, a foot hurts if it is trodden on. These are extreme cases, but all the time a variety of sights seen, sounds heard, and things touched are affecting us, usually in slight ways, but occasionally significantly. Similarly, within the framework of Presocratic materialism, both the object thought and the thinking subject have the same physical basis. Contact between the two is a kind of touching, and the result is a structural change, generally minor, but sometimes major. A range of reactions is therefore possible between subject and object. At the lowest end of the spectrum is the most basic awareness of the simplest object, then intermediate stages of perception of more detailed objects, and at the highest level sophisticated thinking of very complex thoughts.

For evidence that this is so, let us start with Parmenides. The argument of the *Alētheia* (the *Way of Truth*) showed that thinking required an object, and went on to deduce various characteristics for this—eternity, constancy, wholeness, and self-sufficiency—that were usually associated with divinity. In the second part of the poem, the *Doxa* or *Way of Opinion*, a minimum plurality was established of light and night, and all things were said to be composed exclusively of one or both of them. The whole of the *Doxa* is deliberately said to be deceptive, but even so Parmenides offers a plausible account in physical terms of the process of thinking. If there are only light and night, then it has to be the mixture of these two, the proportion of light and night in the physical structure, that makes up the principle of thought and determines the nature of its thinking. But from fragment 16 it is also possible to understand how contact is made with objects of thought, and the range of such objects that would be available to any individual subject. Here are the lines again:

According to the mixture at any one time of the body as it travels, so is the structure of men's thinking. For it is the same thing, the constitution of the body, which has understanding in each and every man; and what prevails is thought.

Men, like everything else, are made of a combination of the two basic elements, but the proportion differs, and it is in the subtle range of minutely varying proportions that one man is marked off from another and given his individuality. Not only the quality of one's thinking about the outside world but also the quantity of knowledge that one can take in depend on the amount of light in proportion to dark in the thinking subject. A mainly dark subject can only react to a mainly dark object, and a mainly light subject reacts to a mainly light object. This interpretation is supported by

Theophrastus' comment just before he quotes the fragment, that 'according as the hot or the cold predominates, so does the understanding vary, and the better and purer understanding is derived from the hot (and the light)'. Later Theophrastus says that Parmenides 'also attributes perception to the other element in its own right, as is evident from his saying that a dead man—since the fire has now left him—is not aware of light and warmth and sound, but *is* aware of cold and silence and the other contrasting qualities' (*Sens*, 3).

So at one end of the spectrum is the corpse, devoid of life and light, and reacting in a minimal way to what is like itself, dark, silent, cold, wet, and clammy. At the other extreme would be the highest intelligence in a state of total light, reacting in a maximum way to the totality of being. And this presumably would be Parmenides' condition when he has assimilated the goddess's revelation. The intermediate cases are proportionate between the extremes—limited understanding of a limited range if dark prevails in the thinker's mixture, superior and wide-ranging if light does.

Heraclitus probably had been working along much the same lines. For him thought should be concentrated on one object, the 'one wise', which is manifest or instantiated in ever-living fire, and can be apprehended in so far as the soul is fiery. There are 'turnings' in the soul (as in the cosmos) from water to earth, and back from earth through water to *psychē*. The admission of water into the physical structure of the individual soul is in a sense a lessening of wisdom and a beginning of death, and that is why indulgence in *thumos*—the impulse to action motivated and affected by desire and anger—is at the expense of soul. On the other hand an increase of fire gained by intellectual effort rouses the whole from a state of stupor, revitalizes the body, and enlarges the individual's understanding.

One example that Heraclitus offers to support this interpretation is that of the drunkard. The healthy *psychē* performs two main functions—it maintains the physical frame and engages in thought expressed in speech. The imbibing of a quantity of alcoholic liquid impairs both these functions, for the drunkard is unable to guide his bodily movements, and his speech is slurred. The physical act of drinking has had an immediate effect on his mental faculties, almost literally 'making his soul wet'.

At the other extreme, however, Heraclitus set no limit to the possible range of human understanding and control when the *psychē* is in the right condition. The possession of 'dry' soul—that which is 'wisest and best'—is a state achieved by a continuing victory over impulse, reinforced by intellectual dedication; in this state of 'super-awakeness', awareness of the unseen *harmonia* governing the functioning of the cosmos becomes possible. The self-increasing *logos* of the soul makes contact with the 'one wise' which steers all things, and this in turn enlarges the soul's potential for wisdom. The capacity is inexhaustible, as that other enigmatic fragment had explained: 'You could not in your going find the limits of soul though you travelled the whole way, so deep is its *logos*' (fr. 45).

The tenor of Heraclitus' psychology therefore, like that of Parmenides, is best understood in terms of a spectrum. Individual effort can push one higher up the scale, and, by the consequent contact of internal with external *logos*, bring enhanced understanding, which in turn raises the threshold for further contact and consequent knowledge. This is the context in which another obscure fragment is to be understood:

A man's *ēthos* is his *daimōn*. (fr. 119)

What happens to a man, his destiny, can be attributed to his *ēthos*, the individuality resulting from the habit of certain kinds of thoughts and actions which affect the physical composition of the *psychē*. Self-indulgence and intellectual laziness can pull us down, whereas austerity and hard-thinking make us wiser and increase the potential for further wisdom.

A similar spectrum-pattern can be found in Empedocles. According to his theory:

With earth we perceive earth, with water water, with air divine air, with fire destructive fire, with love love, and strife with baneful strife. (fr. 109)

and also:

All things have intelligence and a share of thought. (fr. 110. 10)

How would these fragments relate to such a pattern? I would suggest that at the lowest end of the spectrum a bit of earth is aware of another bit of earth and moves towards it, as we are told that bits of fire are drawn to each other (fr. 110. 9). The simplest forms of life have a basic awareness corresponding to their simple structure, more complex animal life has more complex perceptions, while in human heart-blood all four elements are mixed in proportion. As the elements within us make contact with those outside in simple and compound forms, so we are able to have a range of awareness from simple perceptions to complicated thoughts.

But Empedocles insists in addition that:

> Man's wisdom grows according to what is present. (fr. 106)

and:

> As a man's constitution changes, so changed thoughts are always present to him. (fr. 108)

Empedocles then, like Heraclitus and Parmenides, has the concept of a continual change of ingoing and outgoing thoughts, corresponding to continual fluctuations in the outside world and the inner condition. External circumstances affect the growth of the thinking, and the consequent internal structural change results in a change of thought objects available to it. But, as with the other Presocratics, there is a conviction that, if a determined effort is made, the external effects and the internal consequences can be controlled. Empedocles warns his townspeople of the effort that is needed:

> My friends, I know that there is truth in the words which I speak, but it comes hard to men, and the onrush of conviction to the mind is unwelcome. (fr. 114)

But he also gives encouragement, in particular to his student Pausanias, to take in and foster the true thoughts, and so achieve wisdom. The main evidence for this is a long fragment at the end of the poem *On Nature* (fr. 110), which could be paraphrased as follows: Empedocles' thoughts, expressed in his words, are combinations, like everything else, of the four elements, but, being wise thoughts expressed in wise words, they are well-blended combinations. If Pausanias literally takes them in (and he can do this because of the materialist presuppositions), and, if he then assimilates and studies them, he will find that they increase, in the appropriate way, the related pieces of knowledge which he already has—'they will grow into the character [*ēthos* again] according to the nature of each'; and this increase will make Pausanias more receptive to additional knowledge. If however he is lazy or easily distracted, the thoughts will leave him, and then disintegrate and be lost.

The evidence from Anaxagoras is more limited, but it is clear that he also is working along the same lines. He sets up an all-pervasive mind or *nous*, as we have seen, which is separate from the material structure of the cosmos, but which knows and controls it, both from the beginning and in its continual expansion. *Nous* is itself described in a way which tends to strip it of material qualities, yet it still is a 'stuff' of sorts, and has spatial extension. But as well as having a cosmic function *nous* is also present in the individual man as his intellectual principle. So with Anaxagoras too there is a correspondence between the mind within and the mind outside, and it is an exact correspondence in that they are the same substance. Logically then, since mind knows all things, this should result in each individual mind being omniscient. However, 'individual minds or souls are not sufficiently receptive of this understanding, or they may have their understanding restricted to the particular condition of the individual'.[3]

And finally the atomists follow the same trend. 'In truth we know nothing' says Democritus in fragment 7, 'but each of our opinions is a "reshaping" ' (*epirrhusmiē*, a technical term for a new configuration of atoms). Opinions depend in general on the atomic structure of the whole, and in particular on the position, proportion, and arrangement of the soul atoms. That this is the case is confirmed further in another fragment:

> Our understanding shifts in accordance with the disposition of the body and of the things which enter it and of those which press against it. (fr. 9)

So our ability to be aware of the outside world is dependent on our physical make-up, and this continually changes as a result of fluctuations in both the external objects and the internal structure.

The atomists seem to have been sceptical about the attainment of truth, and lacked the sheer enthusiasm of some of their predecessors. Although they worked in the same tradition, and regarded the thinking subject as having a material structure which continually changes as it makes contact with and is affected by the external world, they did not, as far as the evidence goes, indicate how—or even if—it is possible to have access to 'true-born' knowledge. But the Presocratics in general did accept that complete

[3] Cf. M. Schofield, *An Essay on Anaxagoras* (Cambridge, 1980), 18.

understanding is difficult but not impossible, and some were ready to assign to those few men who reach it a special heroic-type status.

Heraclitus tried to wake people up to a state of awareness that is as superior to our normal mental activity as our present waking is to sleeping. If this is achieved after much 'self-searching', and impulse has been rejected, then, in his view, the soul becomes more fiery and wiser. He then suggests that, like the young and courageous war-dead, those who are wise are free of 'wetness' and have 'better portions', and enjoy a time as 'guardians of living and dead'. Parmenides' goddess urged that her 'hard-hitting argument' be judged by reason, and the prologue of his poem, with the young man's journey in a chariot guided by the daughters of the sun along a route 'far from the paths of men', assigns a special destiny to one who makes the effort to rise above dependence on perception and achieves understanding. Empedocles also envisaged a heroic future for 'the one who knows', since knowledge of the forces of nature may bring with it the ability to control them, and the wisest—the prophets, poets, healers, and leaders—are one step away from the divine.

I would like to finish with two quotations which show how, in psychology and epistemology, as in other areas, the Presocratics were the source of some of the most influential theories in Greek philosophy. The first is a passage from Plato's *Symposium* (207d–208b), from Diotima's speech:

> In the time in which each living thing is said to live and stay the same—as for example a man is spoken of as the same man from when he was a little boy until he becomes an old man—he does not in fact continually have the same things in him although he is called the same, but is always becoming new, and losing some parts—hair and flesh and bones and blood and in fact his whole body. And not only his bodily attributes but those of his soul as well—habits, opinions, desires, pains, fears—none of these is ever constant, but some come and others go. And what is even stranger than this is that not only bits of knowledge come and go, and we don't stay the same in this respect either, but that the same thing happens with each bit of knowledge . . . all that is mortal is preserved not, like the divine, by always staying the same, but by replacing what is going out and becoming past with something new of a similar kind.

The quotation is appropriate because it expresses clearly and in an extreme form the way of regarding knowledge that has its roots in the beginnings of philosophy. It summarizes what was established by the Presocratics—that bits of knowledge are entities as material as physical parts, and, like them, are in a state of continuous change. It takes motivation and practice to contain such knowledge, to improve one's understanding, and so ultimately be assimilated to the divine.

Finally Aristotle, as so often, adapts and refines the Presocratic groundwork. In the following passage he clarifies and promotes these earlier fundamental theories of physical mind and noetic effort. For him, as for the Presocratics, the internal psychic structure, combined with high intention evinced in repeated activity, shapes each man's individuality, and, in allowing him to be most truly his human self, gives him a glimpse of immortality. We should not—as some advise—think just of human things because we are human, and of mortal things because we are mortal—

> Rather we must as far as we can immortalize ourselves, and do everything possible to live in accordance with the best thing in us [i.e. mind or *nous*]. For however small in bulk it may be, in power and value it surpasses everything. Indeed, this would seem actually to *be* each man in that it is the authoritative and best part of him. It would be strange then if a man were to choose not his own best life but that of something else. (*EN* 10. 7, 1177b33–1178a4)[4]

[4] For further reading on thought, mind and matter in the Presocratics see the following authors in the Bibliography: Coxon, Havelock, Hussey, Kahn, Robb, Robinson, Sullivan, Vlastos ('Ethics and Physics in Democritus'), Willard, and Wright (*Empedocles*, 57–75). For materialist accounts of mind in modern philosophy see especially: Armstrong, Davidson ('The Material Mind'), Hopkins, McGinn, Minsky, Quine, Quinton, Ryle, Smart, Strawson ('Self, Mind and Body'), and Wilkes ('Is Consciousness Important?').

# 10

# Philosophy, Love, and Madness

## *Christopher Rowe*

This paper has the strictly limited purpose of trying to get clearer about what Plato has to say in one dialogue—the *Phaedrus*—about what it is to be a human being, and about the nature and importance of love between such beings—which involves, centrally, the question of what inherent value (if any) he attaches to the idea of bonding between individuals as such. My reasons for focusing on the *Phaedrus* are two: first, that while Plato's position on the topics in question in dialogues like the *Phaedo*, *Republic*, and *Symposium* can be fairly readily understood at least in its general outlines, and by and large has caused little disagreement between commentators, the position developed in the *Phaedrus* has now become a matter of serious dispute;[1] and second, that the treatment of these topics in the *Phaedrus* is richer and (so I claim) subtler than any we find elsewhere. My conclusions may or may not have consequences for our understanding of the relationship between the *Phaedrus* and other dialogues, but the argument itself will not depend on any assumption about that relationship.

The question 'what is it to be human?' is posed early on in the *Phaedrus*, by Socrates himself. He explains his rejection of rationalistic interpretations of traditional stories, like the one about Boreas and Oreithuia:

> For myself, in no way do I have leisure for these things, and the reason for it, my friend, is this. I am not yet capable, in accordance with the Delphic inscription, of 'knowing myself'; it therefore seems absurd to me that while I am still ignorant of this subject I should inquire into things which do not belong to me. So then saying goodbye to these things, and believing what is commonly thought about them, I inquire . . . not into these but into myself,

[1] See pp. 229–30 below. This is not to ignore the continuing debate, e.g. over the role implied for interpersonal love in Diotima's account in the *Symposium*: see e.g. the articles by Kosman and Price referred to respectively in nn. 61 and 12 below. But in my view that debate is less than fundamental; nearly all sides agree, for example, that the *Symposium* has little time for the way of thinking of such love which we ourselves might instinctively favour.

to see whether I am actually a wild beast more complex than Typhon, or both a tamer and a simpler creature, sharing some divine and un-Typhonic portion by nature [*Phaedrus* (hereafter *Phdr.*), 229e4–230a6].

It has been suggested that the search to which Socrates commits himself in this passage is for knowledge of himself *as an individual*.[2] In one sense this is true: he wants to know what *he* is—whether a monster, or sharing something in common with the gods. But his own myth, later in the dialogue, shows that the same question, and the same (provisional) answer he wants to propose to it, are applicable to all of us. On his view, all of us contain within us both a monstrous, or bestial, element,[3] and an element of the divine: if we give rein to the first, we become indistinguishable from beasts; if we allow the second to rule, we become capable of assimilating ourselves, if only temporarily,[4] to the state of gods. Unless we are prepared, as interpreters of the dialogue, to deny any connection between two contexts which refer to the same topic, of self-knowledge, in the same or similar terms, it must be in this way that we are to understand the disjunctive form of Socrates' question. Rather than inviting us to join him on the analyst's couch,[5] he is proposing a grand investigation into the human condition. 'Which am I?' implies 'what choice should we make, if we are fully to realize our human nature?' But it may be that the question itself, as posed by Socrates, is in any case only intelligible

[2] Charles Griswold, *Self-Knowledge in Plato's Phaedrus* (New Haven, 1986): 'Socrates wants to know what he in particular—as an individual—is' (p. 2); 'the *Phaedrus* suggests that self-knowledge includes understanding one's character' (p. 3); and *passim*.

[3] i.e. appetite. As it happens the myth represents this as a single-headed beast—the black horse—rather than as a many-headed monster like Typhon (cf. *Republic*, 588c). But that is presumably because the story there is exclusively concerned with one form of it, i.e. sexual appetite. Its many other forms are mentioned, and separated off, in Socrates' first speech (*Phdr.* 238a–b).

[4] It is allowed that the best kind of non-divine soul may *perpetually* escape incarceration in a body (*Phdr.* 248c); but even this soul, unlike its divine counterparts, has to resist disturbance from its horses while feasting, and '*scarcely* catches a sight of the things that are' (*Phdr.* 248a).

[5] I am aware that this is a gross caricature of Griswold's interpretation. To represent it more accurately, however, would mean outlining the larger part of the complex argument of his book, for which there is no space here. (But see my review in *Washington Book Review* (May 1987), 21–2 and 32.) My aim in the present context is merely to resist the suggestion that Socrates' question as such implies any interest on his part in acquiring 'knowledge of himself in particular' (Griswold, *Plato's Phaedrus*, p. 43), i.e. as a unique person. At the same time, I shall myself later argue that the idea of individual differences plays at least some role in other parts of the *Phaedrus*: see below, with nn. 6 and 7.

against the background of a developed Platonic psychology (whether tripartite or bipartite); if so, then it already implies the broader question. Perhaps each of us must discover the answer for himself or herself.[6] Perhaps, too, there are important differences between us.[7] The initial question, however, is about which way we should look, *qua* human, for our self-realization. *Are* we beasts, even worse than the worst imagined in myth, or can we, and should we, aim higher?

This as it stands is no more than a rhetorical question. But apart from warning us of the dangers of allowing it its head (or heads),[8] how exactly does the author of the *Phaedrus* mean us to regard this beast[9] in us, and indeed our irrational aspect as a whole?[10] In the *Republic*, Plato's talk is largely, if not exclusively, about the need to repress our non-rational drives;[11] in the *Symposium*, he proposes their transformation and sublimation.[12] Both dialogues display an irretrievably negative attitude towards the irrational as such. But according to Martha Nussbaum, in her powerful new book *The*

[6] That, at least, seems to be one of the implications of Socrates's later proposition that the truth cannot be properly learned from *books* (*Phdr.* 274b ff.; cf. *Seventh Letter*, 341c–d).

[7] The myth, and the discussion of rhetoric which follows it, both clearly recognize that human beings (or human souls) fall into different *types*; but—as I shall argue later—the passage at the end of the dialogue, which recommends a one-to-one relationship between dialectician and pupil, may also be seen as implying the view that each individual (intellect) is, or can be, different from every other.

[8] See n. 3 above.

[9] It might be said that this is a loaded way of putting the question. But (1) Plato certainly represents appetite as a beast (a horse); and (2) even bad horses can become useful, if properly treated, so that calling this part of our natures beast-like is not necessarily to devalue it. (Calling it 'bestial'—a *wild* beast—is a different matter; but that epithet, I take it, will apply to the black horse only in its unreformed state.)

[10] i.e. as including both of the two lower 'parts' of the soul, as the *Republic* describes them: both the appetitive part, and the 'spirited', which is responsible for our (higher) emotions and feelings. The *Phaedrus* represents the second as well as the first as a horse; it listens to reason, but like other animals is presumably incapable of reasoning for itself. (*Some* animals are evidently rational in this sense, but only potentially. Souls may pass from animal to human bodies, but only on the condition that they have at some time seen the truth, which alone will allow them to exercise that capacity which is a defining feature of humanity, of 'comprehending what is said universally, arising from many sensations and being collected together into one through reasoning': *Phdr.* 249b–c.)

[11] See esp. R. 571b ff., 588b ff. The model suggested by 485d, on the other hand, is more like that offered in the *Symposium*; while 611a ff. seems to hold out the prospect of our being able—in some future existence outside the body—to slough off our lower parts altogether.

[12] See esp. A. W. Price, 'Loving Persons Platonically', *Phronesis*, 26 (1981), 25–34.

*Fragility of Goodness*,[13] there is evidence of a radical rethinking of this attitude in the *Phaedrus*.[14] The major part of what follows will be occupied with a detailed critique of her interpretation; after which I shall turn, more briefly, to a related thesis proposed by Gregory Vlastos. Nussbaum's interpretation deserves such extended treatment because, if correct, it would revolutionize our understanding not only of the *Phaedrus*, but of Plato in general. As well as admiring him for his intellect, *her* Plato we could even like. It is an enticing prospect. If on closer inspection it turns out to have been a mirage, much of a positive kind will, I hope, have been achieved along the way.

Early on in the *Phaedrus*, in the first speech he gives on love, in competition with Lysias', Socrates attacks *erōs*. But then, in his second and main speech, the one which includes the great myth, he proceeds to recant his attack. On Nussbaum's view this recantation is also Plato's: a recantation of his earlier ideas about the value to be placed on the appetites and the emotions.

In the *Republic* and *Phaedo*, the appetites and emotions, particularly sexual feeling and emotion, were held to be unsuitable guides for human action. Only the intellect can reliably guide a human being towards the good and valuable . . . In particular, lasting erotic relationships between individuals are not constituent part of [the best human] life . . . [T]he *Symposium* . . . develops this picture further . . . The life of the philosopher achieves order, stability and insight at the [admitted] price of denying the sight of the body and the value of individual love. In the *Phaedrus*, however, philosophy itself is said to be a form of madness or *mania*, of possessed, not purely intellectual activity, in which intellect is guided to insight by personal love itself and by a complex passion-engendered ferment of the entire personality . . . Erotic relationships of long duration between particular individuals (who see each other as such) are argued to be fundamental to psychological development and an important component of the best human life.[15]

[13] M. C. Nussbaum, *The Fragility of Goodness: Luck and Ethics in Greek Tragedy and Philosophy* (Cambridge, 1986), ch. 7: ' "This story isn't true": Madness, Reason, and Recantation in the *Phaedrus*'. This ch. is a revised version of a paper originally published in J. Moravcsik and P. Temko (edd.), *Plato on Beauty, Wisdom, and the Arts* (Totowa, NJ, 1982), 79–124.

[14] Nussbaum chooses to underplay the undoubted stress in the myth on the necessity for *controlling* the black horse (see above), which she attributes to 'the old Platonic suspiciousness of the body' (*Fragility*, p. 220).

[15] Ibid. 201.

This alleged change is combined with a further one: the rehabilitation of poetry. 'The style of Socratic philosophising now fuses argument with poetry; Socrates presents his deepest philosophical insights in poetic language, in the form of a "likeness" [the "myth" of his second speech]'.[16]

There are already some assumptions here which may be called into question. First, Nussbaum's view of the relationship between Socrates' two speeches is not the one which he himself later explicitly adopts. For him, the first speech is one which *tells the truth* about a certain kind of love—that is, ordinary, left-handed love, in which appetite overcomes reason (265c–266b). What he recants is just his implicit suggestion that *all* love is like that. It is not, he now says: there is also a different kind of love, which is divinely inspired, and brings real benefits both to lover and to beloved (245b–c, 256a–b). That position is in itself entirely compatible with what is said in the *Symposium*. It may still be true that Socrates is recanting his earlier views on *erōs*, but if so the recantation is not reflected in the form of the argument of the *Phaedrus* in the way Nussbaum suggests. A second objection is that Socrates' attitude towards poetry is a good deal more ambivalent that she implies. For example, he *appears* to defend inspired poetry as a gift of the gods (245a); but if we bear the *Ion* in mind, that 'defence' turns out to be two-edged.[17] Again, if he appeals for inspiration from the Muses in making his own first speech, he then proceeds to treat its onset—or its pretended onset—rather as something to be avoided (237a–b, 238d); and he points to the poetic language of his second speech only to say that it was forced on him by Phaedrus.[18] This is hardly the behaviour we would expect from a serious devotee of the poetic Muse. Thirdly, we should entertain at least a certain anxiety about Nussbaum's suggestion that the second speech 'presents [Socrates'] deepest philosophical insights', in view of his later remark that nearly everything in both his speeches—everything, that is, apart from the illustration contained in them of the procedures of collection and division—was 'really playfully done, by way of amusement'

[16] Ibid.

[17] See C. J. Rowe, *Plato: Phaedrus* (Warminster, 1986), 169, and id., 'The Argument and Structure of Plato's *Phaedrus*', *Proceedings of the Cambridge Philological Society*, 212, NS 32 (1986), 106–25, esp. p. 119.

[18] *Phdr.* 257a. On the general implications of this remark, see Rowe, 'Argument and Structure', pp. 116–20.

(265c8–9). He *may* not mean it; but I think he does, and if he doesn't, we need some explanation of why he says it, which Nussbaum does not provide. Fourthly—and this is in a way my most important point of disagreement with Nussbaum—I deny that the *Phaedrus* treats 'philosophy itself . . . [as] a form of madness or *mania*'. But of this more later.

To return to Nussbaum's argument: the Plato of the *Phaedrus*, she says, also recants his earlier view of *mania*. This earlier view, which is again represented in Socrates' first speech (and in the speech of Lysias which is the occasion of the whole dialogue), says that a person is mad when his intellect is controlled by the irrational elements in him.

> The insights of *mania* [are] reached not by the measuring, counting, and reckoning of the *logistikon*, but by non-discursive processes less perfectly transparent to the agent's awareness and possibly more difficult to control. He or she is led to action on the basis of feeling and response, by complex receptivity rather than by pure intellectual activity.[19]

The argument of the two initial speeches—Lysias', and Socrates' first—is that we are better off in life, even—especially—in its sexual aspect, without the dangerous involvement of emotion and passion. 'Coolness of vision' is all: 'having sex in this spirit might be, for some people, a very good way precisely of distancing oneself from its power and gaining intellectual control'.[20] By contrast, Socrates' second speech directly urges its addressee (to be identified, according to Nussbaum, with Phaedrus) to surrender himself to the madness of passion, as Socrates himself does in speaking. Some kinds of madness are, after all, good, and their products better than those of sanity, *sōphrosunē*: so it is, Socrates says, with the seer and the inspired poet—and with the lover, as he now promises to demonstrate. We here reach the core of Nussbaum's reading. She claims that Socrates' demonstration establishes the value of madness by means of a threefold re-evaluation of the non-intellectual elements in us: (1) they are 'necessary sources of emotional energy'; (2) they have 'an important guiding role to play in our aspiration towards understanding'; and (3) 'the passions, and the actions inspired by them, are intrinsically valuable components of the best human life.'[21]

[19] *Fragility*, p. 204.  [20] Ibid. 210.  [21] Ibid. 214, 218–19.

I shall take each of these points in succession. (1) Nussbaum urges, against Guthrie, that we should take seriously the fact that *all* souls, even divine ones, are made irretrievably tripartite, consisting of charioteer plus horses.[22] But a charioteer, as such, cannot move without his horses; just so, Nussbaum takes Plato as saying, 'we require the cooperative engagement of our non-intellectual elements in order to get where our intellect wants us to go'—though she is silent on Guthrie's reasonable question about the appropriateness of this idea in the case of gods.

> The power of the whole is a *sumphutos dunamis*, 'a power naturally grown-together' (246 A). If we starve and suppress emotions and appetites, it may be at the cost of so weakening the entire personality that it will be unable to act decisively; perhaps it will cease to act altogether.[23]

Horses, too, need to be *fed*: divine horses receive ambrosia and nectar, while ours get 'the food of opinion' (247e, 248b5). There is a mistake in Nussbaum's account of the text here: it is the *charioteer*, 'the best [part] of the soul', who gets this form of nourishment, if he fails to gain access to the pasture of truth.[24] Inappropriate though the image may be, of *him* cropping there, that is what Plato says. The 'food of opinion' Nussbaum interprets as emotional experience: 'here Plato seems to grant that the ascetic plan of the *Republic*, which deprives emotion and sense of the nourishment of close ongoing attachments, of the family, of dramatic poetry, may result in crippling the personality even while it purifies it'.[25] Rather, Plato is surely alluding to the simple point (itself central to the *Republic*) that if we cannot have knowledge, we shall have to make do with opinion. The long description of the struggle of the lover with his evil horse shows just what at least part of *that* horse's preferred diet is: sexual intercourse. On the other side, it seems clear that the charioteer's vision of the truth gives no satisfaction to his horses; if it did, divine horses could presumably do without their ambrosia and nectar; and the horses of the fortunate

[22] Ibid. 222.

[23] Ibid. 214.

[24] To be precise, Nussbaum's 'mistake' is to say that 'the food of opinion' belongs to the *horses*. What the text actually says is that *souls trophēi doxastēi chrōntai*. But they do so as a result of 'not achieving a sight of what is'; and since that is then identified as the proper *trophē* of the charioteer, it is reasonable to suppose that the *trophē doxastē* is his substitute for it.

[25] *Fragility*, p. 214.

few among other souls would not disturb their charioteer, as they are said to do, just while he is feasting.[26]

We certainly need to make room for the notion of the 'cooperative engagement of our non-intellectual elements' in the project of the intellect. But at least in the case of non-divine souls, there seems to be a limit to that co-operation: it seems as if the horses will do as their charioteer wants, but only on the understanding that they will then get what *they* want. Divine horses have done it all before, on an infinite number of occasions, and they know that their rations will be waiting for them at home; what the horses of other souls want is on earth, and time aloft is time wasted. The second horse of the lover, again, can be constrained to go along with his charioteer, but continues asking for 'some small recompense for his many troubles',[27] until finally tamed.[28] There seems no room for anything like the picture Nussbaum wants to find, except perhaps, remotely, in the divine case: here the horses will want the same thing as the charioteer, but only because the successful completion of his project will enable them to complete theirs. To be sure, the good horse in human souls seems happy enough to accommodate the charioteer's wishes in any case—at least, he does not actively resist him when on earth; he might under some circumstances, as a lover of honour, but in the erotic situation he is content to join the charioteer in applying standards of ordinary decency, being the good horse he is. (His goodness seems to consist largely in his willingness to obey reason: where the control of reason is weak, as in the case of the second grade of lover described at the end of Socrates' speech—the kind who lives a 'more vulgar, unphilosophical, but honour-loving' life (256b7–c1)—this horse too, or rather the soul of which he is part, will go astray.) But that the second horse should ever positively attach itself to the charioteer's project appears to be ruled out, since the success of that, on earth, is conditional on the horse's not completing his, and in heaven it will prevent him from doing so for at least another ten thousand years (248c, e).

[26] *Phdr.* 248a4: strictly, again, it is the *soul* which is disturbed (*thorubein*) by its horses, while *it* is feasting, or trying to feast. But in any case only the head of the charioteer pokes out 'into the region outside' (248a2–3).

[27] That is, in the course of events on earth (255e6–256a1).

[28] I refer here to *Phdr.* 256a–b, which talks of the 'victory' of 'the better elements of the mind', and the 'enslavement of that through which evil attempted to enter the soul': on the interpretation of this passage, see further below.

Or is it wrong to represent the evil horse as *necessarily* aiming at the full sexual act? Anything short of that—touching, kissing, lying together with the beloved—seems to be consistent with the charioteer's aims (255e); and perhaps the training of the recalcitrant horse means habituating him to be satisfied with that.[29] If so, then once he is trained there will be harmony between all the elements of the soul; and the lover's condition will indeed turn out to be one of full intellectual, emotional, and sensual involvement (though the emotional impact is not restricted, as Nussbaum sometimes suggests, to the irrational elements).[30] But what of the other scenario, in heaven? There is plenty of intellectual excitement to be had there, but nothing, evidently, which could evoke a direct and positive response from the lower parts in us. This raises the old problem, of why the gods need to have irrational parts (if they do). Nussbaum herself appears to give no answer to this. The only plausible way out, to my mind, is to suppose that the picture given of the gods is intended as a model for human aspirations: what we are to aspire to is that complete harmony of desire which the gods enjoy.

The account of the painful progress of non-divine souls through the heavens shows that this is in fact impossible: part, or parts, of us always pull downwards.[31] There is in us an ineradicable drive towards emotional and sensual fulfilment, of the sort that we find in love for another human being.[32] Thus far I agree with Nussbaum; and if this really is what Plato has in mind, it is certainly different from the kinds of things he suggests in the *Phaedo* or the *Symposium*. But at the same time it is surely clear that he regards intellectual attainment as the true and proper end for the soul—just as he always did. What *all* souls want is to fly upwards. Everything else about our nature is brute fact in the literal sense, though it may be made consistent with our pursuit of the real

[29] But see p. 244 below.

[30] So e.g. at *Phdr.* 253e5–254a1 the *charioteer* is 'filled with tickling and pricks of longing'; at 254b7–8, he 'becomes frightened, and falls on his back with sudden reverence'. See pp. 236–7 below.

[31] *Phdr.* 247b3–5; 248a4. (i.e. they *try* to pull us downwards; whether or not they succeed in doing so depends on the charioteer. But even the best of non-divine charioteers still has trouble on his hands.)

[32] Though we may also find it in other ways: the myth, after all, describes only one way in which our feelings and appetites may be engaged (cf. the 'honour-loving' second grade of lover, and the different varieties of appetite referred to in Socrates' first speech).

good, and if our intellect is strong enough, may even be turned to advantage.[33]

I turn next to (2), the second of Nussbaum's claims in relation to the treatment of the non-intellectual elements of the soul: that 'they have an important guiding role to play in our aspiration towards understanding'. The claim in this case is that

> certain sorts of essential and high insights come to us only through the *guidance* of the passions . . . The non-intellectual elements have a keen responsiveness to beauty, especially when beauty is presented through the sense of sight . . . We 'apprehend it through the clearest of our senses as it gleams most clearly' ([250] d1–3); this stirs our emotions and appetites, motivating us to undertake its pursuit . . . Sometimes the sight of beauty arouses only a brutish appetite for intercourse, unconnected with deeper feeling (250 e). But in people of good nature and training, the sensual and appetitive response is linked with, and arouses, complicated emotions of fear, awe, and respect, which themselves develop and educate the personality as a whole, making it both more discriminating and more receptive. The role of emotion and appetite as guides is motivational: they move the whole person towards the good. But it is also cognitive: for they give the whole person *information* as to where goodness and beauty are, searching out and selecting, themselves, the beautiful objects. They have in themselves, well trained, a sense of value.[34]

Little of this, so far as I can see, is justified by the text. What Socrates says is that if someone has not recently been initiated, or has been corrupted, the sight of physical beauty 'does not draw him sharply towards Beauty Itself' (250e2), but arouses in him a brutish desire for intercourse; if his initiation was recent, then he experiences the shuddering and fear which he felt when he saw real beauty, and reveres the beauty before him as if it were a god. Then his wings begin to grow, 'under the whole form of his soul; for once upon a time the whole of it was winged' (251b6–7). There is nothing which remotely implies that the irrational elements have any guiding, let alone cognitive role. The reaction of the lover in the preferred case seems to be determined solely by his memory of the original beauty now mirrored in the example before him; and that memory, according to the careful account we have previously been given, belongs to the intellect alone. Indeed, the emotions referred

[33] i.e. in the strictly limited sense that it contributes to an experience which is *as a whole* beneficial. (If the madness of love is claimed to be a blessing, then so, derivatively, must the factors in that madness be.)

[34] *Fragility*, pp. 214–15.

to themselves seem to belong to the intellect: when the same act in the drama is later rehearsed again, after the reintroduction of the simile of charioteer and horses, they are explicitly attributed to the *charioteer* (254b7–8). At this point, too, the evil horse still requires to be forcibly restrained—*its* sights, though not those of the whole soul, are still set firmly on its own unreformed objectives.

It is this process of the training of the second horse which may give sense to the idea of the sprouting of wings 'over the whole soul', since it is that process which will eventually allow the soul to fly free. As Nussbaum says, 'we advance towards understanding by pursuing and attending to our complex appetitive/emotional responses to the beautiful'[35]—but not in the sense she means. There has as yet been no clear 'selection' of goods of the kind she suggests. The lover's reactions are thoroughly confused; something is happening to him, but he is at loss as to what it is; his intellect is only uncertainly in control—he is mad, and behaves for all the world like any ordinary lover, not wanting to leave his beloved's side, valuing him above mother and brothers and friends, neglecting his property, forgetting all the rules of propriety, ready to serve as the slave of his beloved, and to sleep anywhere, so long as it is as close as possible to him.[36] The beloved, after a period of association with him, is similarly affected (or infected) (255a ff.). But all of this mad behaviour will cease when 'the better elements of their minds get the upper hand by drawing them to a well-ordered way of life, and to philosophy' (as Socrates says at the end of his speech).[37] Philosophy, as I suggested earlier, is not madness; it rather supervenes on it, and cures it. The lover—if he is still such[38]—will continue to neglect ordinary concerns, but now for the right reasons—because he has a clear sight of true value. Seeing his behaviour, Socrates says, the many will call him crazy; but his state is rather one of inspiration, the source of which lies in things once seen.[39] That was also the ultimate cause of his previous insanity:

[35] Ibid. 215.

[36] *Phdr.* 250a5–b1; 251d–252a.

[37] Ibid. 256a7–8. True, that madness ceases is not explicitly said. But could a way of life which included behaviour like *that* be described as 'well-ordered' (or 'ordered', *tetagmenē*)?

[38] See below, pp. 241 ff.

[39] *Phdr.* 249c–d. Strictly speaking, the passage only refers to the *philosopher*; his career as a lover has yet to be introduced. But the description of him as a man who 'uses . . . reminders [i.e. what he perceives through the senses] *rightly*' (c6–7) clearly points forward to it—and precisely to its last stage, since only then is 'right use' (of a certain sort of perceptions) assured.

what aroused his passionate reaction was not, as Nussbaum suggests, this particular boy's beauty, but the memory of Beauty Itself which this boy's beauty awoke in him.[40] They will, however, continue in harmony together, since he also originally selected the boy as being someone like himself, by nature philosophical.[41]

Lastly, (3): Nussbaum's third claim, that 'the passions, and the actions inspired by them, are intrinsically valuable components of the best human life'. This depends on the further claim that the madness of love is 'ongoing'. 'The best human life involves ongoing devotion to another individual. This life involves shared intellectual activity; but it also involves continued madness and shared appetitive and emotional feeling.'[42] I have in effect already countered this: if madness means loss of rational control, then the philosophical life is conditional on being cured of madness. (On the other hand, inspiration, being possessed from outside, is itself a form of madness: so in the case of the seer and the poet.[43] The philosopher will then in some sense still be mad,[44] but not in the sense Nussbaum requires. It is, it must be said, a very peculiar kind of madness and of inspiration, one which instead of reducing or replacing the subject's power of reasoning—which is how Plato chooses to represent mantic and poetic inspiration—actually increases it.) Nussbaum's main evidence for this part of her thesis seems to be the intensity of Plato's description of the passion of lover and beloved, which 'stirs us (and Phaedrus) with its beauty and strongly indicates that he finds their madness beautiful and good'.[45] But Phaedrus' response to the speech is in fact primarily to its *skill as a speech*.[46] Plato's view of the madness of love is described in Nussbaum's own text, but only to be rejected:

> Once intellect has been led by mad passion towards the norms of beauty and justice, we can cease to rely on the ferment of madness and clearly contemplate the truth. To say that the highest goods come to us through

[40] See esp. *Phdr.* 249d5–7; 250a6–b1; 250e1–3; 254b5–6.

[41] Ibid. 256a8–b1; 252e1–3.

[42] *Fragility*, p. 219.

[43] *Phdr.* 244b, 245a.

[44] His 'inspiration' (249d2) is connected with his attachment to true reality (249c5–6); alternatively, he is inspired in a more literal sense by his god (253a3).

[45] *Fragility*, p. 219.

[46] *Phdr.* 257c1 ff.: 'For some time I have been amazed at how much finer you managed to make your speech than the one before . . .'. About the *content* of the speech, he says hardly a word.

madness is . . . not to say that madness, or mad actions, are themselves intrinsically good.[47]

Love offers us a route back to our starting-point, contemplation of true beauty, while simultaneously being an expression of another aspect of our nature. If it could be shown that Plato entertained an unequivocally positive view of that aspect of us, then this would in itself give love at least a degree of intrinsic value. But there is no clear evidence that he does, and some rather clearer evidence that he does not.

In the following part of her account, Nussbaum uses her results as a basis for interpreting the concept of the person which is implied in the *Phaedrus*.[48] She seems to take it that what it is to be a person is the same as what it is to be a human being; and what that is, is to be an entity which does not 'disassociate itself from [its] bodily nature and from the accompanying passions' (the view advocated in the *Phaedo*, and in *Republic*, 10), but whose intellectual, emotional, and appetitive elements all operate together in harmony. This is humanity in its ideal form, the model of which is provided by the philosopher in whose progress the non-intellectual elements play an integral part. Another underlying assumption of Nussbaum's is (I think) that Plato is interested in persons as individuals. Socrates' main speech, for her, is primarily about how the mutual love of individuals for each other as such can lead them to knowledge of themselves, a process which she claims is exemplified in the developing relationship between Socrates and Phaedrus in other parts of the dialogue. 'On both sides we find emotions of wonder and awe, a careful concern for the other's *separate* needs and aspirations. Each discovers more about *his own* aims as he sees them reflected in another soul' (my emphases). The claim is not quite that the members of any pair are unique individuals: the 'selves' they ultimately discover will apparently be the same. On the other hand, as the process begins, and before any development has taken place, they may be different. Each loves the other as he is, peculiarly, *now*.

This latter assumption is unjustified. As I have said, Plato clearly identifies the real object of the lover's passion as Beauty Itself, not this particular boy's beauty. (This boy is therefore, *pace* Nussbaum,

[47] *Fragility*, p. 219. ('So far, we might believe that [this was Plato's view] . . . But the *Phaedrus* gives the passions, and the state of *mania*, much more than a merely instrumental role.')

[48] *Fragility*, pp. 222–3.

at least in principle replaceable by another: the lover might have found someone else to love.) He will admittedly have selected someone with the right kind of soul. But that means finding someone of the right *type*, who possesses in embryo certain general characteristics. Moreover, both his choice of that type of individual, and the benefits he bestows on him, seem to be determined at least primarily by selfish motives: he wants someone he can make as like his patron god as possible—that is, the god whom he followed to the feast—so recreating, as far as is possible on earth, the conditions of his own original bliss.[49] If it is all metaphor, the same problem recurs: the lover will want to create someone like the self he wishes to be, the better to contemplate himself.

Socrates' original question about himself ('whether I am a wild beast, or share some divine portion') Nussbaum claims to be 'implicitly rejected [in the myth] as still too much in the grip of the stark dichotomies of the *Republic* and *Symposium*: you can be complex without being Typho, ordered without being simple . . .'.[50] On the contrary, as I suggested at the beginning of this paper, the question seems to encapsulate the central message of the myth rather precisely. The discovery made by the lover and his beloved is exactly of the rationality which they share with the gods, and of the possibility of using this to tame the irrational elements in them. The difference from the position represented in other dialogues is that it is now firmly recognized that these irrational elements are always with us. But that in its turn entails that our fate is irretrievably tied up with the body, since our emotions and appetites—whatever may be said of the gods'[51]—can only function in a bodily context. One part of us may hanker after a bodiless condition—it may aspire to divinity; but such a condition is incompatible with our humanity, and in that sense with the full realization of our selves (even though what each of us is would

[49] Much more clearly needs to be said, and much more subtly, about the issues raised here (see e.g. Price, 'Loving Persons Platonically'). But I would claim to have given at least the broad sense of Plato's text.

[50] *Fragility*, p. 223.

[51] If, that is, Nussbaum is right in saying that gods have such things at all. The traditional gods obviously do—as they also have chariots, and horses which they feed on ambrosial fodder. Plato plays on both ideas: see *Phdr.* 252c (Ares), 246e (Zeus, himself driving a winged chariot: a chariot within a chariot?), and 247e (divine horses now enjoy the food of the gods themselves—since their charioteers have something better). But if he has any serious use to make of either, he does not dwell on it.

remain the same: our personal identity would be preserved, in whatever tenuous way Plato is interested in that notion—we would still be the same bits of soul-stuff). I agree with Nussbaum, then, in supposing that for the Plato of the *Phaedrus* responding emotionally and sensually is part of what it means to live a human life; I differ from her in thinking that he sees the best human life, still, as depending on the *control* of those responses, rather than their enjoyment.

These, then, are my disagreements with Nussbaum's radical interpretation. Perhaps paradoxically, the role of the horses in Plato's simile is not to carry us anywhere. It is our *wings*, when and if we sprout them, which carry us upwards; and in the encounter with his beloved, the lover could well do without at least one of his pair. That the charioteer cannot move without his horses is true only in the somewhat negative sense that he cannot divest himself of them: the one contributes nothing but trouble, and the other is only useful in helping to keep the other in check. Since it is the sole function of chariot-horses to pull chariots, it looks as if it should be part of the point of the image—as Nussbaum claims—that our souls are driven by emotion and appetite. But the details of the narrative as it unfolds actually allow only two cases where horses clearly operate together as a team to pull their chariot and charioteer in the *right* direction—firstly the divine case, and secondly when the lover's black horse has been tamed into submission. If the gods' horses do represent irrational elements, however, this is conspicuously not said;[52] and right up until the end the central theme in the description of the lover is the necessity for him to *restrain* his sensual impulses. The ideal pair will achieve their goal by becoming *masters of themselves* (*enkrateis*), which means '*enslaving* that part by which evil attempted to enter, and freeing that through which goodness enters' (256b1–3). Appetite, Socrates implies, is something which requires to be kept down, not a driving force towards the good.

But what is the relationship after that—purely intellectual, or more besides? This clearly matters to the argument. If it turns into a marriage of minds, which leaves the body entirely behind, then the account of the *Phaedrus* begins to look fairly close after all to that of the *Symposium*, only with repression substituted for sublimation.

[52] See n. 51 above.

Sensual interplay with the beloved would be merely a first stage, giving way to the higher 'eroticism' represented by interchange of an intellectual sort. But does 'control' over the black horse mean that its urgings are no longer felt? Vlastos suggests not. On his view—if I have understood it correctly—the relationship between the ideal lovers will continue also to be erotic in the ordinary sense. He describes it as

> a peculiar mix of sensuality, sentiment, and intellect—a companionship bonded by erotic attraction no less than by intellectual give-and-take. Body-to-body endearment is one of its normal features, though also subject to the constraint that terminal gratification will be denied.[53]

I argued earlier that the assertion of control by the 'better elements' meant the cessation of madness; and since love has been defined as a kind of madness, it too, strictly speaking, ought to have run its course. Yet the philosopher, as he has become, still remains passionately attached to the real object of his longing (Beauty Itself). Why should he not continue to be similarly attached to his boy? This attachment will, presumably, cease in the end, with the fading of the beauty which first attracted him, just as it does for the second grade of lovers (and for lovers of the common-or-garden sort, those described in Socrates' first speech, and in Lysias'). 'These [second-grade lovers] too', Socrates says, 'spend their lives as *friends*, though not to the same degree as the other pair, both during their love *and when they have passed beyond it*' (256c7–d1). But for a time at least the philosopher would live a life which fulfilled, as far as possible, his irrational as well as his rational desires—for as long, perhaps, as he continued to feel them.

This is different from the interpretation tentatively proposed earlier, according to which 'taming' the black horse meant educating it to accept less than its full demands. If it *accepts* that, I take it that it would not go on making its indecent[54] suggestions—as on Vlastos's view it apparently does. The crucial passage, at the end of the myth, can perhaps be taken in either way; but on balance I believe that it tells against Vlastos. After natural and unavoidable body contact between lover and beloved in the gymnasium (255b7–8), there follows 'looking, touching, kissing, lying down

[53] G. Vlastos, 'The Individual as an Object of Love in Plato', app. II: 'Sex in Platonic Love', in *Platonic Studies* (2nd edn. Princeton, 1981), 40.

[54] Or, better, 'improper': lacking in *kosmiotēs* (cf. *Phdr.* 256b2).

together' (255e3): a clear description of foreplay,[55] which if the black horses in both partners had their way would lead directly to consummation.[56] Socrates next describes what happens in the ideal case:

If then the better elements of their minds get the upper hand by drawing them to a well-ordered way of life, and to philosophy, they pass their life here in blessedness and harmony (*makarion men kai homonoētikon ton enthade bion diagousin*), masters of themselves and orderly in their behaviour, having enslaved that part through which evil attempted to enter the soul, and freed that through which goodness enters . . . [256a7 ff.]

Now he might mean to call the lovers' life in this case 'harmonious' just in the sense that they live harmoniously *together* (as they certainly will); and the 'victory' of the better elements might consist in their being able to rely on keeping the black horse down on every occasion. It would also perhaps be consistent with this reading that (in the continuation of the same sentence) the lovers' souls are only said to have won their Olympic wrestling-match *when they have died* in the same self-mortifying condition—as if it is only then that the count is fully completed. But that will also be true on the other reading, which takes the reference to the defeat of the black horse as indicating that it is no longer heard from: we could only be *sure* of its defeat if it in fact never uttered again (since we can never unharness it from us). More importantly, the whole context suggests that the primary reference of *homonoētikos* ('harmonious') is to *internal* harmony; and we might well want to say that a life in which one element in the soul is repeatedly, and actually, frustrated in its aims will be somewhat less than harmonious in this sense.[57] Again, the combination of tenses in the passage quoted (present,

[55] The full description is appropriately teasing. 'His [i.e. the beloved's] desires are similar to his lover's, but weaker: to see, touch, kiss, lie down with him; and indeed, as one might expect, *poiei to meta touto tachu tauta*.' The expression *to meta touto*, by itself, is ambiguous between 'what follows this' and 'after this': when the reader first reaches it, he is likely to take it in the first sense, which implies that *consummation* (what naturally follows the other things) occurs; only when he goes on to *tauta* ('these things') does it become clear that the only things which occur are actually the things already listed ('he does *these things* soon *after this*'). No English translation that I can think of is capable of reproducing this effect.

[56] *Phdr.* 255e4–256a1, 256a3–5.

[57] Cf. esp. ibid. 256c6–7, where it is said that the second-grade lovers indulge in sex only rarely 'because what they are doing has not been approved by their whole mind'. On Vlastos's interpretation, will not the same be true of the ideal lovers' choice—i.e. that it is not 'approved by their whole mind'?

'they pass their life', surrounded by aorists: 'if [once?] the better elements get the upper hand', 'having enslaved . . .') points to a once-for-all victory on the part of the charioteer and his white horse. If the black horse has been 'defeated' and 'enslaved', that surely ought to be the end of its resistance.

If this is right, however, then perhaps 'body-to-body endearment' will disappear from the relationship altogether. If, as it seems to be the case, looking, touching, and the rest are seen exclusively as *foreplay*, and as leading necessarily to the desire for consummation, then there will be no place even for that. The erotic encounter Socrates describes is a single (though complex) episode in the lovers' life, not a perpetually recurring one: with the victory of philosophy, the black horse has had its day, at least until its next chance, in a new life and a new body. Just so in heaven any soul which is able to resist the disturbance caused it by its horses, and is able to get some view of things outside, will be 'free from sorrow' until the next feast (248c4). If the black horse represents appetite in general, there will be other roles for it in life (and other opportunities for excess).[58] But sexual desire, it seems, will play no role in the existence of the mature philosopher, which the *Phaedrus* recommends to us as the ideal.

Or should we rather regard the ideal as intended to include the whole mad drama of love which the myth portrays as preceding that state? In other words, is coming to terms with our erotic impulses (in the ordinary sense), and giving them at least limited expression, seen as being itself an intrinsic part of the best human life, just in the sense of being a necessary stage in it? That we must somehow reach an accommodation with our irrational selves is clear enough; but Plato nowhere commits himself to the proposition that one must either be or have been in love with someone as a condition of philosophizing with them. It is in any case a wildly implausible idea: how, for instance, could entry to the Academy be organized under that condition? The most that Plato says is that the madness of the best kind of love issues in the gift of philosophy—which is not to deny that fruitful philosophical interchange can also arise in other contexts. Indeed, at the end of the *Phaedrus*, when the myth has been left far behind, we find Socrates himself picturing the dialectician as merely 'taking a fitting soul' into which to sow *logoi*

[58] See n. 3 above.

(276e6–7), without any mention of things erotic (except perhaps on the metaphorical level; but even the metaphor of 'sowing' is here less erotic than agricultural).[59] That could, in principle, just be a partial description of the philosophical process, which needs to be filled out by reference to the myth. But from the philosopher's *logoi* '*others* will grow in *other* minds' (277a1–2): *logoi* themselves, evidently, as well as the sight of beauty, can contribute to the growth of philosophy. The myth, I suggest, is no more than a persuasive description of what love *can* be, and *can* do.

This result is in a way thoroughly disappointing. It would be good to believe that somehow Plato was able to build in the emotions and appetites as a positive aspect of human life. Yet that seems not to be the case, at least so far as concerns the *Phaedrus*. They are what makes us human, but only in that they prevent us, or will normally prevent us, from assimilating ourselves to the gods. (At the same time, they offer us the choice of falling even lower: humanity may merge into bestiality.)[60]

The particular cause for disappointment is that the continuing devaluation of these parts of our nature seems to entail an equally continuing devaluation of love between one individual and another. Here, however, the *Phaedrus* does finally strike a more humane note than that other erotic essay, the *Symposium*. Whereas the *Symposium* appears to envisage interpersonal relationships as a means to an end, and as something to be abandoned when the real goal is reached,[61] the myth in the *Phaedrus* sees love as issuing in a lifelong bond. Again, even if what comes to exist between the ideal pair is, strictly, a meeting of two intellects, still—as I pointed out in passing before—the intellect itself, as the *Phaedrus* describes it, seems to be capable of a full range of what we would class as feelings: joy, awe, and reverence. The language of tripartition breaks down at an early stage. True, the real object of those feelings is represented here too as something beyond the individual. Yet by the end of the dialogue room is perhaps found for at least a kind of individual attachment. The dialectician described in the final pages

[59] See *Phdr.* 276b.

[60] Either in so far as we *imitate* the beasts (250e4–5), or in that our souls may actually pass (as a consequence?) into the shape of one in a future incarnation.

[61] As even Price admits ('Loving Persons Platonically', p. 34); though not L. A. Kosman ('Platonic Love', in W. H. Werkmeister (ed.), *Facets of Plato's Philosophy* (Assen, 1976), 53–69).

presumably sows his seeds out of a concern for his pupil's well-being (as well as his own).[62] As part of the process, he will then have to defend his *logoi* against the pupil's questions[63]—and they will be the *particular pupil's* questions: if they were the same as anyone else's, then in theory the interchange could be written up to save others the trouble of going through the same stage (and so on *ad infinitum*, so that the whole thing could after all be done through books, which is what Socrates has been at pains to deny). The consequence is that the dialectical expert is engaged in the improvement of particular and different minds, and will continue to relate to them *as* particular and different.

Should this perhaps also be read back into the myth? When the lover tries to make his beloved like himself and his god, that perhaps means only making him a philosopher in the true sense, someone who will seek with him—in his own way—for the truth. Even the myth, after all, allows for differences between divine intellects;[64] why not between their human counterparts?

[62] The passage at *Phdr.* 276e–277a perhaps suggests something analogous to the idea put forward in the *Symposium:* the dialectician is *eudaimōn* in his brain-children. But in the context as a whole dialectic is also touted as a method of *teaching* (see esp. 276c–e), which surely implies active benevolence on the part of its practitioners.

[63] *Phdr.* 276e7–277a1, with 275d7–9, 276c8–9, 277e8–9.

[64] That is, if we assume—finally—that Zeus, Hera, and the rest are pure thinking beings, and that they are genuinely distinguishable from one another (though that might be difficult to square with the argument of *R.* 2: see C. J. Rowe, 'One and Many in Greek Religion', *Eranos Jahrbuch*, 45 (1976), 37–67, esp. p. 67).

# 11

# Plato and Freud

*A. W. Price*

## *Introduction*

If one looks for similarities between the thoughts of two distant and disparate thinkers, the danger is not that one will fail, but that one will succeed. What can prove such similarities significant? Indicative, certainly, is a sufficient degree of similarity, one that exceeds what is made likely enough by a shared background either minimal (commonplace aspects, say, of our common humanity), or easily located (as in the case of two admirers of Aristotle). And yet, however many the similarities, we may wonder whether they can signify anything until we can suggest what that might be. Accordingly, my project here is not only to pursue resemblances between the thinking of Plato and of Freud to a point at which they become striking, but also to reflect upon what kind of significance they may possess.

Of course Plato and Freud, and we ourselves, do not stand to one another as aliens: we occupy points in the space-time of a culture. So one easy line of explanation is intellectual influence. Was Freud a reader of Plato? Ernest Jones suggests that he was not. Although in 1880 he actually translated Mill's essay on Grote's Plato, 'Freud remarked many years later (in 1933) that his knowledge of Plato's philosophy was very fragmentary, so perhaps what there was of it had been derived from this essay of Mill's.'[1] Yet that cannot be

I am grateful to Adam Morton and Christopher Gill for general suggestions which I have tried to act upon; also to the latter for prompting, or supplying, all too many improvements in formulation. Soon after posting the final version I received Gerasimos Santas's *Plato and Freud: Two Theories of Love* (Oxford, 1988). From much the same evidence we draw very different conclusions, largely for a simple reason: he thinks that Plato's and Freud's great differences make their points of contact insignificant, I that they make them significant. See my review in *The Times Literary Supplement*, 4–10 Nov. 1988, p. 1220.

[1] *Sigmund Freud: Life and Work* (3 vols.; London, 1953–7), i. 62; but contrast iii. 297.

right: fragmentary is not the same as second-hand. What follows also tells another way: 'He added . . . that he had been greatly impressed by Plato's theory of recollection, one which Mill treats sympathetically, and had at one time given it a great deal of thought.'[2] For in fact Mill's treatment is more cursory than sympathetic, with a few remarks (for instance, 'The whole process of philosophizing was conceived by him as a laborious effort to call former knowledge back to mind')[3] suggestive enough to a Freudian ear, but barely nutritious to a young Freud. It is more likely, especially in view of his late allusion to 'the wide extent' of his 'reading in early years', perhaps even extending to Empedocles (*SE* xxiii. 244–5), that Freud had read parts of Plato himself.[4]

What is the internal evidence? Explicit references or unmistakable allusions to Plato in published texts touch on the following:

(1) Generic eros or libido (*PFL* vii. 43, xii. 119, xv. 269).
(2) Generic eros and sublimation (*PFL* xiv. 470).
(3) Eros as preserver and unifier (*PFL* xi. 323, xii. 356, xv. 380).
(4) Miscellanea in the *Symposium*: 'Uranian' love (*PFL* vi. 119), Aristophanes' myth (*PFL* vii. 46, xi. 331, xv. 380 n. 1), and Alcibiades' ambivalence towards Socrates (*PFL* ix. 119).
(5) The bad dreams of good men (*PFL* iv. 134, 782).
(6) The origin of hysteria (*PFL* xv. 207).

The list is short (and published letters barely add to it), quite refuting Jones's surmise but only proving a good knowledge of the *Symposium*.

Even if Jones is fallible, his testimony that Freud 'had been greatly impressed by Plato's theory of recollection . . . and had at one time given it a great deal of thought' is wholly credible. The practices of Platonic dialectic, and Freudian psychotherapy, have obvious resemblances: within both, knowledge that has in a way been lost is fully restored through verbal interchange with another whose task is to elicit memory, not impart instruction. In Plato,

[2] Ibid.

[3] J. S. Mill, 'Grote's Plato', in *Essays on Philosophy and the Classics*, ed. J. M. Robson, *Collected Works*, xi (Toronto, 1978), 423.

[4] Refs. to Freud are to *The Pelican Freud Library* (hereafter *PFL*) ed. A. Richards (15 vols.; Harmondsworth, 1973–86), when the work concerned is included in that collection; otherwise to *Two Short Accounts of Psycho-Analysis* (*2 SA*), ed. J. Strachey (Harmondsworth, 1962), or to *The Standard Edition of the Complete Psychological Works* (*SE*), ed. J. Strachey (24 vols.; London, 1953–74).

prenatal memories are lost either uniformly at the moment of incarnation (*Phaedo*, 75e2–3), or variably through corrupting associations (*Phaedrus* (hereafter *Phdr.*), 250a3, e1); in Freud, infantile memories are driven underground either initially by primal repression, or subsequently by repression proper (*PFL* xi. 147). In both, the memories are retained, but inaccessibly: 'What is forgotten is not extinguished but only "repressed"' (*PFL* xiii. 339). The lost knowledge can only be recovered through recollection, not indoctrination (*Meno*, 82a1–2, *Theaetetus*, 150c3–d2). Both 'Socrates' and the analyst must deny that they have 'talked' the other into anything (*PFL* i. 505, cf. ix. 286, *Meno*, 82e4).

Here, surely, Plato had a causal impact on Freud. Yet I suggest that this only applies sometimes, and never goes deep. Given Freud's willingness, indeed eagerness, to acknowledge precursors so long as they were antique (contrast his enthusiasm towards Empedocles (*SE* xxiii. 244–5), with his reluctance to read Schopenhauer or Nietzsche (*PFL* xv. 244) ), the paucity of his references to Plato suggests that Plato's influence on the mature Freud must largely have been subliminal (or 'cryptomnesia' (*SE* xxiii. 245) ), and hence generalized. Furthermore, such influence can at most have been suggestive, never persuasive: it could never fully explain any actual belief of Freud's, for the question would always remain why his mind was receptive of this antique idea and not of that.

Another simple line of explanation is this: Plato and Freud came to agreement by converging on the truth. This approach is bolder, and may appeal to convinced Freudians or Platonists. However, even they might agree that, in its bald simplicity, it misleads in suggesting that the findings of speculative psychology lie like boulders upon the ground, waiting to be stumbled over. Bare truth cannot explain agreement unless it is supplemented by an account of what makes the truths in question into objects of discovery. It clearly will not suffice to say that Plato and Freud looked in their hearts and wrote. We need some account of how depth psychology, although deep, is accessible from quite different intellectual starting-points.

In a way, the subject-matter makes it unsurprising that Plato and Freud might have agreed between themselves, while diverging from most of their contemporaries. Depth psychology is never likely to be consensual; both Plato and Freud had, more or less persuasively, to be presenting news. Yet we could expect the news that they were presenting, if at all true, to have a kernel of truth less subject to cultural variation than the mind's more familiar contents. How might such truths emerge? It must help that their field is our own mentality, one to be reached neither by escaping from ourselves, nor from our own appearances to ourselves. How our minds are is not independent of how we picture them: explicit theories may be an individual's mistake, but the way we all implicitly model the mind helps to construct and constitute the form it actually takes. While the physicist has to strip away appearances in order to reveal a non-human reality, the psychologist has rather to set aside conventionalities in order to reveal appearances that underly our thinking in ways independent of shifts in focus and fashion. That is not an easy task: ideally it requires a sensitivity to constant ways of thinking and an independence of transient products of thought; yet it depends upon an introspective viewpoint that tends to confound the constant and the transient. The most that can be achieved is a depiction of the mind that in part captures a structure that is an invention neither of the theorist nor of his age. Although Plato and Freud differ about so much, they both bring out, I suggest, natural ways in which the Greek and modern mind insensibly appears to itself, ways that lie somewhere between the unmistakable surface of the commonplace and the depths disclosable only by a special technique. To the extent that appearance and reality are here mutually determining, Plato and Freud were indeed thereby perceptive of the truth. How that is really possible should become clearer after I have explored parallels (without neglecting divergences) in two areas: the objects of love and desire, and the parts of the soul.[5]

## *Eros and Libido, Ascent and Sublimation*

What Freud himself emphasizes is a coincidence between Platonic 'eros' and his own 'libido'. Both terms signal 'a deliberate extension

[5] I can only hope that one simplification will not be too confusing for those who know, and misleading for those who do not: I have had largely to neglect the fact that the thought of Plato and Freud developed. An attempt to do justice to that would have impossibly complicated this paper, without advancing its argument. Suppose (to take the worst case) that its presentation of Plato were a congeries of incompatibilities: that would not show that Plato did not anticipate Freud out of insight, for a distorting theoretical framework may turn even insights into inconsistencies.

of the popular conception of "sexuality"' (*PFL* xii. 356), such as to capture an 'enlarged sexuality' (*PFL* vii. 43) which yet maintains an 'essential unity throughout all its manifestations' (*PFL* xiv. 470). This agreement is real and substantial, not less so because it bridges a gulf between two sharply contrasted world-views.

Plato inherited one term ('eros'), Freud revived another ('libido'), whose prin...y application was narrowly sexual. Eros could be defined as a desire for sexual pleasure directed towards the beauty of bodies (*Phdr.* 238b8–9), and associated with reproduction (*Republic* (hereafter *R*), 4, 436a10–11). Libido can be glossed as 'sexual energy' (*PFL* xi. 71), or 'the desire for pleasure' (*PFL* i. 175); it is that instinct which we come to know from its 'relation to the sexes and the reproductive function' (*PFL* xi. 334 n. 1, cf. xv. 269). Yet such descriptions run together immediate object and biological role: the same pleasure, which consists in 'a release of the sexual tension and a temporary extinction of the sexual instinct' (*PFL* vii. 61), can also arise within 'the sexual aberrations' (the title of an essay of Freud's (*PFL* vii. 45–87) which covers deviations in respect either of sexual object, as in homosexuality, or of sexual aim, as in sadism or masochism). When in a censorious vein Socrates and Plato find one paradigm of sexual activity in non-reproductive copulation (cf. Xenophon, *Memorabilia*, 1. 2. 29–30, *Phdr.* 250e5–251a1). The resulting conception places sexual desire alongside the bodily appetites of hunger and thirst as instincts whose internal object (their own satisfaction) typically, but not always, serves a biological need. Plato often associates eros with hunger and thirst (e.g. *R.* 4, 439d6–7, *Phdr.* 238a6–c4); FREUD classifies hunger and love as contrasted instincts (e.g. *PFL* xii. 308) with analogous satisfactions (*PFL* vii. 61). So far, eros and libido are the sexual instinct, narrowly conceived.

Central to psychoanalysis, however, is the idea that libido enjoys a variable displaceability or plasticity, that is 'the degree of facility with which the libido is able to change its object and mode of satisfaction';[6] hunger has a more obstinate adhesiveness or viscosity. In consequence libido, but no hunger, has a history. Part of that history is sublimation, a process of 'deflecting the sexual instinctual forces from their sexual aim to higher cutural aims' (*PFL* xii. 45). This development follows repression (*PFL* xii.

[6] J. Laplanche and J.-B. Pontalis, *The Language of Psycho-Analysis*, tr. D. Nicholson-Smith (London, 1973), 319.

141–2), which presents an 'internal obstacle' to the attainment of sexual goals (*PFL* xii. 173). Yet sublimation offers instinct a partial escape: 'Sublimation is a way out, a way by which those demands [sc. of the ego ideal] can be met *without* involving repression' (*PFL* xi. 89, cf. xi. 150, 2 *SA* 85–6). Hence Freud can write rather loosely, at once of sublimation and of repression, 'Love with an inhibited aim was in fact originally fully sensual, and it is so still in man's unconscious' (*PFL* xii. 292). Such love can take the forms of 'on the one hand, self-love, and on the other, love for parents and children, friendship and love for humanity in general, and devotion to concrete objects and to abstract ideas' (*PFL* xii. 119).

Plato's outlook was, in a way, the opposite of that. While Freud was writing after the discovery of evolution, Plato prefers to toy (as at *Phaedo*, 81e5–82b7, *Timaeus*, 90a6–92c3) with the idea of devolution. Man's task becomes to recover spirituality, not to acquire it. F. M. Cornford remains illuminating:

> The self-moving energy of the human soul resides properly in the highest part, the immortal nature. It does not rise from beneath, but rather sinks from above when the spirit is ensnared in the flesh. So, when the energy is withdrawn from the lower channels, it is gathered up into its original source. This is indeed a conversion or transfiguration; but not a sublimation of desire that has hitherto existed only in the lower forms.[7]

As he elsewhere encapsulates the contrast, 'To Platonism . . . man is a fallen spirit, to science he is a risen animal.'[8] As Plato himself put it, man is a heavenly not an earthly plant, whose root is his head suspended from heaven (*Timaeus*, 90a5–b1). It fits this, though it surprises us, that narrowly sexual eros becomes secondary and derivative within Diotima's Socratic account of desire in the *Symposium*. There the primary goal, from which all others are derived, is being happy or *eudaimōn* (204e2–205a3), spelled out not (as by Freud, *PFL* xii. 263) in terms of feelings of pleasure, but of possessing the good for ever (206a11–12). That is a goal abstract enough to form the target equally of physical eros, 'a desire for bodily contact', and of that figurative eros prevalent within the Socratic circle, 'a love of moral and intellectual excellence'.[9]

[7] F. M. Cornford, 'The Doctrine of Eros in Plato's *Symposium*', in *The Unwritten Philosophy and Other Essays*, ed. W. K. C. Guthrie (Cambridge, 1950), 68–80, quotation from pp. 78–9.

[8] F. M. Cornford, 'The Division of the Soul', *Hibbert Journal*, 28 (1930), 206–19, esp. p. 219.

[9] I quote from K. J. Dover, *Greek Homosexuality* (London, 1978), 157.

Immortal longings are even adduced to explain the keenness of animals to copulate, reproduce, and if necessary die for their young (207a6–e1). Though they cannot speak to define such behaviour-transcending goals, we share an animal nature with them, and can draw on universal human desires that are communicable in order to interpret their behaviour by an unconscious teleology. Humans individually suppose that they will achieve a kind of immortality through their descendants (208e3–5); their mutual awareness of this is evidence that all 'mortal nature' (207d1) is motivated by an inherent sense of the divine.

Or is that one-sided? W. K. C. Gutherie has retorted, 'Nevertheless, to borrow an Aristotelian tag, if in the species perfection is prior, the individual has to start from the bottom.'[10] This is an important corrective,[11] but one that itself needs correcting. It is true that, at a first glance, the *Symposium* ascent illustrates Freudian sublimation precisely: there the lover advances from an appreciation of beautiful bodies to one of beautiful souls, thence to one of beautiful practices, thence to one of beautiful sciences, and so finally to one of the science of Beauty itself (211c3–8). However, the starting-point is already partly peculiar: the initial expression to which love lends itself, in this account, is not love-making but love-poetry (the 'beautiful discourse' of 210a8); eros is already, Freud would say, 'aim-inhibited'. From the beginning of 209 Socrates has only been describing lovers who, in contrast to the heterosexuals of 208e, are already (for all we are told, innately) pregnant in soul rather than body. Later, in the *Phaedrus*, after Plato has developed his own theory of desire, we do indeed find a progression from sexual to desexualized longing; but it begins from a sudden recollection, at the sight of physical beauty, of Beauty itself, an experience which is only open to those (perhaps identical to Diotima's 'pregnant in soul') who are fresh and uncorrupted from a prenatal initiation into ideal reality (contrast *Phdr.* 250e1–2). Even for the human being beauty is for Plato a starting-point, for Freud (*PFL* vii. 69) already a concept of sublimation. Of course each one of us has to start at the beginning; but that may be *inter faeces et urinam* (as Freud loved to quote), or within the Platonic heaven.

[10] W. K. C. Guthrie, *A History of Greek Philosophy* (6 vos.; Cambridge, 1962–81), iv. 393; cf. iii. 396.

[11] Though I would prefer him to have written, 'If in *soul* perfection is prior, *man* has to start from the bottom.'

And yet within Plato's mature psychology, which neither aims sexual appetite at the good nor leaves it in pursuit of its own good, sexual sublimation does play a valuable role, not of origination but of reinforcement. Freud gives it both roles (of which for him, no doubt, the first is fundamental). On the one hand he can say, 'If this displaceable energy is desexualized libido, it may also be described as sublimated energy . . . If thought-processes in the wider sense are to be included among these displacements, then the activity of thinking is also supplied from the sublimation of erotic motive forces' (*PFL* xi. 386). On the other hand he can write of Leonardo's craving for knowledge, 'We consider it probable that an instinct like this of excessive strength was already active in the subject's earliest childhood . . . We make the further assumption that it found reinforcement from what were originally sexual instinctual forces, so that later it could take the place of a part of the subject's sexual life' (*PFL* xiv. 167). In the terms of this distinction, it is sublimation as reinforcement that is described with the help of an hydraulic metaphor (itself recurrent in Freud) in a passage of the *Republic* that Cornford clearly had in mind:

> When in a man the desires incline strongly to any one thing, they are weakened for other things. It is as if the stream had been diverted into another channel . . . So when a man's desires have been taught to flow in the channel of learning and all that sort of thing, they will be concerned . . . with the pleasures of the soul in itself, and will be indifferent to those of which the body is the instrument.[12]

Here not all human desires flow in some way towards the divine, but most can be diverted to flow along the right course. Freud uses the same metaphor to apply the same thesis when, for instance, he remarks that many become homosexuals because 'a blocking of the main stream of their libido has caused a widening in the side-channel of homosexuality' (*PFL* xii. 52, cf. xii. 294, i. 351). The upshot is a pair of parallels (confirming, essentially, both Cornford and Guthrie): Plato and Freud come to share a conception of sexual sublimation as reinforcement; but to the original sublimation of the sexual in Freud corresponds the natal debasement of the spiritual in Plato. Thinking in similar ways from opposite premisses, they can never wholly agree.

One notion that Plato and Freud have in common (which

[12] *R.* 6, 485d6–12, tr. P. Shorey (London, 1935), as usually below.

distinguishes them temperamentally from Aristotle and Jung) is that of the regressive nature of happiness. In a letter to Fliess, Freud once defined happiness as 'the subsequent fulfilment of a prehistoric wish';[13] L. A. Kosman rightly finds it typical of Plato to present 'the archaeology of love taken up in its teleology'.[14] Of course contrasted specifications of happiness then derive from contrasted prehistories of the mind. If the intensest pleasure is located by Plato in the vision of Beauty itself (*Symposium*, 211d8–e4), by Freud (as by the vulgar, *Phdr.* 256c3–4, *Laws*, 8, 840b6–7) in something less elevated, that is because both associate it with a restoration of primal bliss (union with the Forms, or with the mother). One and the same stretch of mental development may then be evaluated quite differently. Take any process of desexualization: a Freudian might view it as an escape from one's true nature, a denial of one's original goals, and an assumption of inauthentic ones, a Platonist as a return towards one's true nature, a discarding of inauthentic goals, and a recovery of original (or more nearly original) ones. However, neither Plato nor Freud is simple-minded enough to maximize the contrast: in the *Republic* reason treats the appetites like a farmer who cultivates crops while inhibiting weeds (9, 589b1–3); and though Freud was ambivalent about the utility of civilization, and strongly critical of the sexual morality of his day, he neither dismissed the roles of art and religion in mitigating neurosis, nor preached total sexual liberation. Neither Plato nor Freud was an optimist about the human predicament.

One challenge faces both Plato and Freud. Differently though they conceive of the beginnings of erotic desire, they agree that its aims and objects are displaceable. Yet such metamorphosis seems problematic: why talk of redirection and not replacement? We can find in them similar responses to this query, roughly distinguishable as empirical or theoretical, which give substance to the contrast.

Empirically, there is firstly evidence of the constancy of the flow of desire, a hypothesis which owes its inherent probability to the thesis of displaceability. In the *Republic* passage already quoted (6, 485d6–12), Plato indicates such evidence in general terms. More specifically, Freud cites two observations: that an atrophy in one's sexual life is often accompanied, in childhood or maturity, by an

[13] Jones, *Sigmund Freud*, i. 363.

[14] L. A. Kosman, 'Platonic Love', in W. H. Werkmeister (ed.), *Facets of Plato's Philosophy* (Assen, 1976), 53–69, quotation from p. 65.

intensification of sexual curiosity (*PFL* xiv. 167–8); and that it is chaste homosexuals (so long as their homosexuality has not been barred from sublimation by repression, cf. *PFL* x. 202) 'who are distinguished by taking a particularly active share in the general interests of humanity' (*PFL* ix. 199). Secondly, there is the very ease of the transitions from the sexual to the non-sexual, and back again (*PFL* xii. 173). Thirdly, and most interestingly, there will tend to be traces of the old desire within the new one. Once Freud even defines sublimation as the sexual instinct's exchanging 'its originally sexual aim for another one, which is no longer sexual but which is psychically related to the first aim' (*PFL* xii. 39). Sublimation, he claims, is never total transformation: 'Those instincts which are inhibited in their aims always preserve some few of their original sexual aims; even an affectionate devotee, even a friend or an admirer, desires the physical proximity and the sight of the person who is now loved only in the "Pauline" sense' (*PFL* xii. 172, cf. xii. 119).

Within Plato there are several ways of testing this last thought. One question might be, 'Is contemplation of Forms still like a response to persons?' We meet a positive answer in Walter Pater, to the effect that Forms are (or 'almost' are) persons themselves: 'Abstract ideas themselves become animated, living persons, almost corporeal, as if with hands and eyes. And it is a consequence, but partly also as a secondary reinforcing cause, of this mental condition, that the idea of Beauty becomes for Plato the central idea.'[15] Here Pater, rather like Freud, views ideal beauty as an etherialized version of physical beauty, and so not wholly uncorporeal. He is less close to Plato, whose Form of Beauty is explicitly 'pure, clear, unalloyed, not full of human flesh and hues and much other mortal trash' (*Symposium*, 211e1–2). However, a similar question, 'Is contemplation of Forms still like an erotic response?', has to be answered positively: gazing at the Form of Beauty is a quasi-visual experience yet more intense than looking on the forms of boys (211d3–e4). It is striking that, even as he insists on the immateriality of Beauty itself, Plato describes our cognition of it in visual and indeed coital metaphors (211e4–212a5, cf. *R.* 6, 490b5), as if they were appropriate to a human apprehension even of the highest beauty.[16] And yet Cornford's

[15] W. Pater, *Plato and Platonism* (London, 1893), 170, cf. 139–40.

[16] Cf. M. C. Nussbaum on *Phdr.* 251: *The Fragility of Goodness: Luck and Ethics in Greek Tragedy and Philosophy* (Cambridge, 1986), 214–18.

insight suggests a question perhaps stranger still, 'Is sexual attraction still a response to Forms?' The *Phaedrus* claims that it can be, so long as memory of the Forms is not too distant: there Plato counts love at first sight (which causes sexual temptation, indeed preparatory activity, even in the future philosopher (253e5 ff.) ) as a kind of sighting of Beauty itself (250d3–e1). Thus while Freud expects the sexual to colour the ideal, Plato also expects the ideal to colour the sexual.

By way of theorizing, Freud ascribes to all instances of eros a single general aim. Such constancy might be taken to manifest, or to help constitute, displaceability; in either case, to support the thesis. Eros aims 'to establish ever greater unities and to preserve them thus—in short, to bind together' (*PFL* xv. 379). That threatens to generate a tension 'between the ceaseless trend by Eros towards extension and the general conservative nature of the instincts' (*PFL* xii. 310 n. 1), that is their origin in 'a need to restore an earlier state of things' (*PFL* xi. 331). To dissolve the tension, Freud once ventured to speculate that 'living substance at the time of its coming to life was torn apart into small particles, which have ever since endeavoured to reunite through the sexual instincts' (*PFL* xi. 332). He derived this hypothesis from none other than Plato's Aristophanes, whose Just-So Story of a race of Siamese twins whom Zeus split apart has often been taken too seriously (*PFL* xi. 331). Later he rejected the hypothesis as Platonic, but unsupportable (*PFL* xv. 380). Yet he always conceived eros as unifying, also after sublimation: the ego's 'desexualized energy still shows traces of its origin in its impulsion to bind together and unify' (*PFL* x. 250). He claims that there is a unifying aim both in sexual desire ('Eros desires contact because it strives to make the ego and the loved object one, to abolish all spatial barriers between them' (*PFL* x. 227)), and in being in love ('At the height of being in love the boundary between ego and object threatens to melt away' (*PFL* xii. 253)). Civilized eros has as its aim 'to combine single human individuals, and after that families, then races, peoples and nations, into one great unity, the unity of mankind' (*PFL* xii. 313).

Freud is likely to have detected the same theme of unification running through the speeches of the *Symposium* (cf. 'the Eros of the poets and philosophers which holds all living things together' (*PFL* xi. 323)). Eryximachus assigns to eros the role of reconciling and uniting opposed elements both within the body (186d5–e3), and within the atmosphere (188a1–4). Aristophanes has eros seeking satisfaction in a quasi-fusion between sexual partners (192d5–e9). Agathon makes it responsible for a spirit of kinship within social groups (197d1–3). Unification of a kind becomes central to the Platonic ascent: eros seeks to grasp what is common to the beauties of each level (210a8–b3, c4–5, d7), and to create with another person a life of shared appreciation and realization of that beauty (cf. especially 211b5–6). It is perhaps still more remarkable, within the so-called lesser mysteries (207c9–209e4), that procreation, whether physical or psychical, has the goal of running different lives into one another in ways that mimic the unity of a single life.[17]

I conclude that Freud was right to find in Plato's eros (whether that be explicated Socratically as desire all aimed at the good, or Platonically as desires flowing in connected streams) a precursor of his own extended, though never all-inclusive, libido. The extent to which their conclusions are similar, or not less than analogous, is the more remarkable because of their radically different viewpoints. Across the great Darwinian divide Plato and Freud show up as strangely akin.

## *The Tripartite Mind*

Plato's tripartition of the soul (into reason, spirit, and appetite) has often been disparaged. Cornford expresses a common response: 'The scheme is artificial and false, and not such as a philosopher working independently by direct introspective analysis would be likely to reach.'[18] Comparison with Freud, who twice divided the mind into three (first into conscious, preconscious, and unconscious, later into id, ego, and super-ego) need not win a more favourable opinion. R. M. Hare remarks that Plato 'had much more excuse for his crude partition of the mind than some recent thinkers like Freud'.[19] Surprisingly, Freud is silent about this aspect of Plato, though it features largely not only in the *Republic*, but in the *Phaedrus* and *Timaeus* (as also, briefly, in Mill's article). If there was an influence, I take it to have been subliminal; if there was little or no influence, and tripartition is indeed 'artificial and false' (Cornford), we have a cluster of extraordinary coincidences.

[17] Cf. A. W. Price, 'Loving Persons Platonically', *Phronesis*, 26 (1981), 25–34.

[18] 'Psychology and Social Structure in the *Republic* of Plato', *Classical Quarterly*, 6 (1912), 246–65, quotation from p. 259.

[19] R. M. Hare, *Plato* (Oxford, 1982), 73.

The starting-point is conflict of desire. Plato infers the existence of a division by phoney logic: the same thing cannot be simultaneously affected in opposite ways in a single aspect; but, for instance, when thirsty a man may both desire to drink, and refuse to drink; so he must accept and reject in different aspects of himself (*R*. 4, 439b3–6).[20] Freud's approach is similar: 'We explain the psychical splitting dynamically, from the conflict of opposing mental forces, and recognize it as the outcome of an active struggling on the part of two psychical groupings against each other' (2 *SA* 50–1, about the conscious and unconscious). His last three words ('against each other') correspond to a proposal by Terence Irwin that Plato needs to explain the refusal as 'rejection of the desire for the object'.[21] This refinement is implicit in Plato when he writes of reason and spirit berating and being angry with appetite when it masters them (440b1–2), and of reason rebuking unreasoning anger (441b7–c2). Such language is common in Freud: for instance, 'The super-ego . . . observes, directs and threatens the ego' (*PFL* ii. 93–4). What is essential here? It might just be that one part of the soul as subject takes another part as object (cf. PFL ii. 89). That would rest partition on a simple point of logic (rather as Plato's ostensible argument does). However, in fact it is clear that neither Plato nor Freud has that in mind. If spirit becomes an 'ally' of reason against appetite (which signifies that it accepts reason and rejects appetite, a complex attitude with one subject and two objects), that makes only two factions (440a8–b4); we need to find reason and spirit sometimes at odds to distinguish them as two different parts (cf. 441a4–c2). One part of the ego (in a wide sense) takes another 'as its object' in the relevant way only if it 'sets itself over against the other' and 'judges it critically' (*PFL* xi. 256). Essential, in brief, is that one part *confront* another—a Freudian turn of phrase (e.g. *PFL* xi. 373) in which, as Richard Wollheim nicely observes, 'one word does much work'.[22]

How then are we to understand 'part' (a term only occasional in Plato, first relevantly at *R*. 444b3, and not unequivocal in Freud)? Neither Plato nor Freud seems concerned to clarify the concept

[20] Phoney is the presenting of a refusal to act out a desire as a logical paradox demanding a solution, as if 'desire' had the same force as 'intention'; the resultant division may yet justify itself not logically but psychologically.

[21] T. H Irwin, *Plato's Moral Theory* (Oxford, 1977), 327.

[22] R. Wollheim, *The Thread of Life* (Cambridge, 1984), 201—the book that inspired me to read widely in Freud.

before applying it; if I now characterize it in a loose way that fits both, that may be helpful but proves little in itself. A part of the mind seems to be the home of a family of desires, with accompanying beliefs, which are liable to stand in a relation of confrontation, one-way or two-way, with members of any other family. Plato does not generally present the parts as subjects within a subject: they are rather what *we* do things *with*. We learn with one part, feel anger with another, desire sensual gratification with a third (436a8–b2); alternatively, it is the soul that does such things with them (439d5–8).[23] It is true that, with typical verbal nonchalance, thirst may be predicated, within a few lines, of person, soul, and soul-part (439a9–b5). At the same time, both Plato and Freud are given to anthropomorphic language that can seem to generate a 'homunculi' problem (little men inside each man). In Plato, parts can give commands (439c6–7), or be obedient (441e6); they can agree (442c11–d1), or meddle (443d2–3), with one another. Of course the anthropomorphism can always be paraphrased out, if not to very precise effect;[24] but why is it so prevalent, in Plato as in Freud? At least part of the answer must be that it faithfully captures an aspect of the way the mind pictures itself. J. Laplanche and J.-B. Pontalis comment, 'To this extent then, the scientific theory of the psychical apparatus tends to resemble the way the subject comprehends and perhaps even constructs himself in his phantasy-life.'[25] In so far as the mind is its own construct, it can bestow efficacy even on conceptions that remain only partly intelligible. (I shall return to such thoughts in my conclusion.)

Neither Plato nor Freud defines the topography of mind anatomically; yet both were attracted by physiological analogues. In the *Phaedrus* tripartition precedes incarnation, and so is functional before it can be physical; yet in the *Timaeus* the three parts are apportioned to head, breast, and belly (69d6–70a4, 70d7–e2). Freud wrote in 1900, 'I shall carefully avoid the temptation to

[23] When we read 'The soul of the thirsty, then, in so far as it thirsts, wishes nothing else than to drink' (*R*.439a9–10), the qualification more likely attaches to the predicate than to the subject.

[24] There may be problems: for instance, Plato defines temperance as agreement between the parts about which shall rule (*R*. 432a6–9); can we rewrite that without the anthropomorphism and still distinguish temperance from justice, which he defines as each part's minding its own business (*R*. 433b3–4)?

[25] *The Language of Psycho-Analysis*, p. 452.

determine psychical locality in any anatomical fashion' (*PFL* iv. 684); yet in expository diagrams (*PFL* ii. 111, xi. 363) he places the ego closer than the id to the surface of the mind, as if it were 'an extension of the surface-differentiation' (*PFL* xi. 363), in a way that mirrors the actual peripheral position of the cerebral cortex.[26] It seems that both Plato and Freud bore in mind anatomical correlations that they had no resources to investigate.

So far we have found Plato and Freud dividing the mind into 'parts' in loosely the same sense, involving the same general criterion (psychical conflict, or confrontation), and with the same independence of, but leakage into, anatomy. The analogies have been imprecise—like the positions they relate. More striking, therefore, are particular parallels between Plato's single and Freud's second tripartition, between appetite and the id, spirit and the super-ego, reason and the ego.[27] I shall not attempt to expound each tripartition fully, though nothing less could place the parallels in perspective; but I shall concede a number of evident divergences.

The appetitive part contains the appetites, the id the 'passions' (*PFL* xi. 364, xv. 301). Both are closely linked to somatic influences (*PFL* ii. 106, ix. 213, xi. 108; *R.* 4, 439d1–2). The id is governed by the pleasure principle (*PFL* ii. 106, xi. 364); appetite aims at pleasure (*R.* 436a11, 9. 572a1). Id and appetite know no good or evil (*PFL* ii. 107; *R.* 439a5–6). The id is insensitive to internal contradictions, and knows no negation (*PFL* ix. 319 n. 2, xi. 190, xii. 85): 'It has no organization, produces no collective will' (*PFL* ii. 106, cf. xi. 401); 'It is, as we might say, "all to pieces" ' (*PFL* xv. 296). As it happens, the most explicit parallel comes in Aristotle: 'Appetite is contrary to choice, but not appetite to appetite' (*Nicomachean Ethics*, 3. 2, 1111b15–16); but the same thought is implicit in Plato in the fact that the principle of non-contradiction (*R.* 436b8–9, 439b5–6) is not to be applied within appetite even though its 'diversity in kind' (*R.* 580d11) allows it to be pictured as a many-headed monster (*R.* 588c7–10). The id is 'incomparably greater' than the ego (*PRL* ii. 111); the appetite 'is the mass of the soul is each of us' (*R.* 442a6, cf. 588d4, *Laws*, 3, 689a9–b2). Hence the ego can find itself in a 'traumatic situation' of felt helplessness against the id (*PFL* x. 326); that is also the fate of the tyrant, 729

[26] Ibid. 451, cf. *PFL* xv. 434.

[27] Here I follow, with extra detail, in the steps of A. Kenny, 'Mental Health in Plato's *Republic*', in *The Anatomy of the Soul* (Oxford, 1973), 1–27, sec. III.

times unhappier than the king (*R.* 587d12–e4), and 'full of many and manifold terrors and loves' (*R.* 5791b4–5, cf. e4).

It is of course a great difference that the id, unlike appetite, is inherently unconscious; that is, a person can be aware of the contents of his appetite, but only of what used to be contents of his id. That gives rise to one difference between the ego and reason: the ego, but not reason, becomes the repository of whatever emerges into consciousness out of the id. Yet Plato anticipates the Freudian unconscious in two ways: there is the knowledge retained by reason after incarnation, but inaccessible to the person before recollection; and there are desires that belong to appetite but are ordinarily hidden from the person. Here Freud recollects the *Republic*, citing Plato as thinking 'that the best men are those who only *dream* what other men *do* in their waking life' (*PFL* iv. 134), and even 'that the virtuous man is content to *dream* what a wicked man really *does*' (*PFL* iv. 782). The words 'is content to' suggest an attitude of complicity quite out of place in Plato (it is clear in context why Freud slipped them in), but otherwise the allusions are faithful enough. At the beginning of *Republic*, 9, Plato writes of desires that awaken in sleep, when appetite, released from all shame and reason, pursues its own gratifications (571c3–9, cf. 574d8–e3); these even include the pleasures of Oedipus (making love to one's mother, and killing at will (571c9–d2) ). In fact, 'There is a dangerous, wild, and lawless kind of desire in everyone, even the few of us who appear altogether moderate, which is revealed in our sleep.'[28] Absent here, however, is any suggestion of the dream-work by which Freud describes the unconscious as disguising its thoughts so that they can be admitted into consciousness in sleep; this fits Plato's conception that such desires can become conscious fairly easily and without leaving appetite. Where we do meet the distortion and interpretation of latent contents is in the case of the very different dreams of the *Timaeus*, which are reflections (71b4–5) or depictions (c4) in appetite of rational thoughts; there both the dream-work (c4), and the interpretation (72a1), are the task of reason.

The spirited part is that with which we feel anger (*R.* 439e3); Freud writes of 'the super-ego's wrath' (*PFL* xi. 392). This anger is in Freud solely, in Plato also, self-directed: the super-ego 'abuses the poor ego' and 'reproaches it' (*PFL* ii. 92, cf. xi. 395); it is with

[28] *R.* 572b4–7, adapted from the translation of G. M. A. Grube (London, 1981).

his spirit that a man at time 'reviles himself and is angry with that within which masters him' (*R.* 440b1–2). The super-ego is the source of guilt: 'in its later phases' the sense of guilt 'coincides completely with *fear of the super-ego*' (*PFL* xii. 328). In the *Phaedrus*, once the bad horse of appetite has been broken in, the sight of the sexual object 'dissolves it in fear' (254e8), that is fear of the internal sanctions of the charioteer of reason and the good horse of spirit. There is the disanalogy that the super-ego confronts the ego (*PFL* xi. 373, xiii. 363–4, xv. 324), whereas spirit opposes not reason but appetite (*R.* 440b1–2); hence the ego is afraid of the super-ego, appetite of spirit. This contrast partly arises from the different boundaries of reason and the ego, but it causes the super-ego to take on a sinister aspect (not less when it operates unconsciously) that spirit lacks. Yet in inhibiting the instincts the ego is hugely helped by the super-ego, 'which indeed is partly a reaction-formation against the instinctual processes of the id' (*PFL* xi. 397); so also the lion of spirit can become an 'ally' of the man of reason against the many-headed beast of appetite (*R.* 589b1–4). Indeed, in 'normal, stable states' ego and super-ego 'work together harmoniously' (*PFL* xv. 397, cf. x. 249); 'by nature' spirit is reason's auxiliary (*R.* 441a2–3).

Plato's spirited element has seemed to many unduly Protean. In one form, it is displayed even by newly born children (*R.* 441a7–b1) and animals (*R.* 441b2–3, cf. 2, 375a11–12); in another, it has the function of admiring, honouring, and taking pride in—all evaluative activities (*R.* 8, 553d4–6). Parallels in Freud can help us to make a unity of this. An aspect of the super-ego is the 'ego ideal', on which the ego attempts to model itself (*PFL* ii. 96). The super-ego incorporates three functions, 'of self-observation, of conscience and of the ideal' (*PFL* ii. 98). Freud already had those in mind, even before introducing the term 'super-ego', when he wrote, 'It would not surprise us if we were to find a special psychical agency which performs the task of seeing that narcissistic satisfaction from the ego ideal is ensured and which, with this end in view, constantly watches the actual ego and measures it by that ideal' (*PFL* xi. 89). Correspondingly, we need not be surprised by the variety of emotive attitudes that constitute Plato's spirited soul: it is failure to achieve what it admires that arouses its wrath. At the same time, the self-directed aggression of the super-ego has been borrowed from a primitive source, the death instincts that form a dualism with the life instincts within the id; in this as in other ways (cf. *PFL* xi. 376, 390) the super-ego remains close to the id. Plato does not locate such a dualism within appetite, but his extension of spirit to children and animals is a recognition of its roots in a special kind of instinct. The spirit that we never find 'making common cause with the appetites when reason decides that it must not be opposed' (*R.* 4, 440b4–5) is a pugnacious instinct schooled and recruited by reason. However, it would be clearer in the *Republic* that this is alliance, not fusion, if it were consistently allowed (as at 441b7–c2) that spirit remains potentially, and so occasionally, recalcitrant.[29] It is significant that in the *Phaedrus*, where spirit is most emphatically wholly good (253d3–e1), Plato does accommodate anti-rational anger, but not within spirit: it is the horse of appetite that 'angrily' reviles and abuses the charioteer of reason (254c7). Plato's hesitancy in recognizing and locating such anger evinces a fumbling acknowledgement of spirit's instinctive but not erotic origin, and its nearly but not perfectly rational destination.

Whereas Freud's id is all unconscious, his ego is so only in part; for it also extends through most of the conscious and preconscious. It is the seat of all 'conscious feelings', such as pleasure and unpleasure (*PFL* xi. 279 n. 1), and of all 'affective states', including anxiety (*PFL* x. 297–8), whether conscious or not. Yet Freud also contrasts it with the id in a 'popular' way readily evocative (even possibly reminiscent) of Plato: 'The ego represents what may be called reason and common sense, in contrast to the id, which contains the passions' (*PFL* xi. 364). In their cognitive roles Freud's ego and Plato's reasoning part are analogous: they stand in a similar relation to reality—though within the two theories, of course, the nature of reality is conceived very differently. The ego 'observes the external world with the help of its sense-organ, the system of consciousness' (*PFL* xv. 301); in the *Phaedrus*, it is the charioteer of reason that sees what it can, on earth as in heaven, of the Forms (248a5–6, 254b5–7). The ego seeks to replace the id's pleasure principle by the reality principle (*PFL* ii. 108, xi. 363–4, xv. 301), and to dissolve distorted conceptions of the external world through 'reality-testing' (*PFL* ii. 108); equally, 'The part by which we learn is always wholly straining to know where the truth lies' (*R.* 9, 581b5–6, tr. Grube). Reason and the ego also share a

[29] This is implicit later, at *Timaeus*, 69d3, *Laws*, 9, 863b3–4, 11, 935a3–7.

wider responsibility: just as reason has the task of recognizing what will benefit the whole soul and each of its parts (*R*. 4, 441e4–5, 442c6–8), so the ego has the mediating function of reconciling with one another the demands of the id, of the super-ego, and of reality (*PFL* xv. 377–8). As the ego only comes into existence gradually (*PFL* xv. 434), so reason comes to most children only quite late (*R*. 441a9–b1). At night, the ego and reason tend to go to sleep (*PFL* xi. 355; *R*. 571c3–5); yet the ego can still exercise dream-censorship (*PFL* xi. 355), and if quickened before sleep reason can still grasp reality and keep dreams lawful (*R*. 572a6–b1).

Famously, Plato was the first to make more than a metaphor of the notion of mental health.[30] The *Gorgias* spoke of a good condition of soul as of body (464a2), and called the unjust soul 'unhealthy' (479b8). In the *Republic* this is developed into an analogy between the balancing of elements within the body, and the justice of souls whose elements rule or are ruled according to nature: 'Virtue then, as it seems, would be a kind of health and beauty and good condition of the soul' (4, 444d13–e1). The goal is to achieve internal harmony within the soul, so making oneself 'one man instead of many' (443e1), through 'fostering the best element' (9, 590e4–5). Analogously, the goal of psychoanalysis is the pervasion of the ego (cf. *PFL* xv. 299–305); in the pregnant slogan, 'Where id was, there ego shall be' ('Wo Es war, soll Ich werden', *PFL* ii. 112). We may say (though Plato could not, and Freud—so far as I know—did not) that reason or the ego constitute the *person*, in a restricted and honorific sense: that is implicit in Freud's terminology (as just quoted, the ego is, more literally, the 'I'), and in Plato's emblematic representation of spirit as a lion within us, appetite as a many-headed monster, but reason as a man (*R*. 588d3–589b6). In the symbolism of the *Phaedrus* the charioteer of reason, assisted by the horse of spirit, gradually breaks in the horse of appetite, until he 'meekly executes the wishes of his driver' (254e7). That process can be compared to one described by Freud in these terms: 'The ego develops from perceiving instincts to controlling them, from obeying instincts to inhibiting them. In this achievement a large share is taken by the ego ideal, which indeed is partly a reaction-formation against the instinctual processes of the id' (*PFL* xi. 397). Freud even uses closely similar symbolism: the mental apparatus is a vehicle, the id the driving force, the ego the

[30] Cf. Kenny, 'Mental Health in Plato's *Republic*', p. 1.

steerer (*PFL* xv. 300–1); or the ego is a rider, the id his horse (*PFL* ii. 109, xi. 364). However, he also recognizes the disanalogy that, while a rider can exercise his own strength, the ego's forces are borrowed from the id, so that its only victory may be to save face: 'Often a rider, if he is not to be parted from his horse, is obliged to guide it where it wants to go; so in the same way the ego is in the habit of transforming the id's will into action as if it were its own' (*PFL* xi. 364, cf. ii. 109–10). The ego cannot tame the id by coercion; Freud recommends to it instead the same sympathetic sensitivity in unearthing the id's buried contents that Plato reserves for recovering pieces of innate knowledge. This contrast fits their different views of what has gone wrong: Plato blames faction within the soul on the insubordination of appetite, Freud on the repression of the id by the ego. So Plato urges a strong hand in reining in appetites that are out in the open but 'hardly controllable even with whip and goad' (*Phdr.* 253e4–5), while Freud advises the ego 'to tolerate an approach to what is repressed' (*PFL* xv. 305) so that it will no longer go its own way through being 'isolated, left to itself, inaccessible, but also uninfluenceable' (*PFL* xv. 303). It matters here again that Plato and Freud share a regressive conception of human happiness while offering contrasted pre-histories of the human mind: although (as I noted) it is neither the case that Plato would suppress all appetites, nor that Freud would undo all sublimations, yet the ego can adopt the instincts of the id in a way that reason can never adopt the promptings of appetite. If the ego is to succeed, it must be by way of acceptable, not domination. Reason unites by issuing commands (*R.*442c5–d1), the ego is to succeed, it must be by way of acceptance, not domination. Reason unites by issuing commands (*R.* 442c5–d1), if the ego is in possession of its whole organization and efficiency, if it has access to all parts of the id and can exercise its influence on them. For there is no natural opposition between ego and id; they belong together, and under healthy conditions cannot in practice be distinguished from each other' (*PFL* xv. 301). In that way Freud is more of an optimist than the Plato who, in the *Phaedrus*, envisages an eternal tension between reason and appetite even within souls in heaven that will always escape incarnation (248c3–5). Thus Freud's conception of eventual success is more harmonizing than Plato's: while Freud looks ultimately for a happy merger between the parts of the soul, Plato expects disincarnate reason either to disdain the other parts (as in the *Phaedrus*), or to discard them as accretions of mortality (cf. *Timaeus*, 69c3–d6).

The differences matter, but they arise within a common framework: as regards both diagnosis and therapy, Plato and Freud structure the mind in similar ways separated much less than we might have expected by modern discoveries and disillusionments. It is true that Freud would have viewed even this aspect of Plato's thought as a distorting mirror, yet one whose images, like those of dreamers, have only to be reinterpreted to reveal psychological reality.

## *Conclusion*

I have traced parallels between Plato and Freud under two headings: ascent and sublimation, and the tripartite mind. The resultant detail has, to me, been striking. No doubt a few of the points have been strained (if I could discriminate which I would remove them), but I do not think that their number could plausibly be whittled down to a level of uninteresting coincidence. How are we to interpret their significance? I began by arguing that intellectual influence explains little here even when it may explain something. More promising seemed to be a suggestion that Plato and Freud are perceptive of natural ways in which the mind insensibly appears to itself. How plausible does that seem now?[31]

When I noted Plato's and Freud's shared tendency to speak anthropomorphically of the parts of the mind (the homunculi complaint), I suggested, following Laplanche and Pontalis, that it might be justified as a reflection of ways in which we all tend to picture it, and under the influence of which we even tend to reconstruct it. To an extent, the mind is the creature of its own perceptions and fantasies. Even tripartition must arise from self-creation: though Plato presents it as either imposed through incarnation (*Timaeus*, 69c5–d6), or given from the beginning (*Phdr.* 246a6–b4), it is more helpful of Freud to present the ego as a construct out of the id under the influence of the external world (*PFL* xi. 363, xv. 434), and the super-ego as a construct out of the

[31] The reflections that follow will have to be brief, and general in content or relevance; they would need to be developed to match the specificity of many of my parallels.

ego as a response to paternal prohibitions (*PFL* ii. 93–8). We might try to contrast the ego as an acquired reality with the super-ego as an illusive fantasy—but would that be a real distinction? Patients who suffer from delusion of being observed really are being observed, though internally, not externally (*PFL* ii. 90); external hallucination may be a sign of internal perception. Perhaps it will help to clarify the notion of self-partition if I take the origin of the super-ego as an example. The thought that I observe myself arises out of an experience as of being observed within my own mind; the thought that part of myself observes myself reflects the fact that, in such an experience, I feel myself being scrutinized in a way that brings to bear a determinate subset of my beliefs and desires, typically those subserving compliance with parental demands (actual or imagined). As the experience is one appropriately caused by a person, an object of fear and love, guilt and shame, and internalizes experiences actually so caused, this subset is ascribed a psychic personality that amounts to a miniature and schematic human personality. It thus becomes a quasi-personal agency within the mind that in fantasy inherits the powers of a parent, and in reality takes on the causal powers that the mind bestows on it. The apparent state of being internally observed need amount to no more than that; but I may be drawn, in order to remain the subject of the operations of my own mind, to take the supposed observing upon myself, and so make it at once intelligible and actual (whether it be conscious or unconscious) without thereby extending its powers or point of view.[32] By thus advancing from internalizing a parental figure to identifying with it, I create a new locus of personal activity within myself, but one that remains parasitic: it does not become a directing source of intentional movement, and it could not be extracted to operate independently of the creating mind. It becomes a persona of a kind; it will never be a mental substance. In relation to this history, anthropomorphic language functions in two ways: it may speak of this persona of the subject as if it were a distinct person (it is, after all, intrinsic to a persona that it apes a person); or it may express a relapse (often under mental stress) into the fantasy of an alien agency invading the mind. The first usage may be fully intelligible, the second is not;

[32] It is true that the conversion of the super-ego from a presence into a perspective will also serve to facilitate the gradual extension and modification of its repertory of beliefs and desires; but perhaps never so indefinitely as to merge super-ego and ego.

both convey the mind's workings. The story that I have just told is speculative and specifically Freudian, but it illustrates some general points. Such experiences, thoughts, and inferences may be implicit or explicit, conscious or unconscious. If the human mind naturally operates in such ways, it will tend to divide itself into parts which reflect not so much periodic cultural fashions as less variant factors of a personal or interpersonal kind.

About the unity of desire, implicit in the metaphors of ascent and sublimation, somewhat different things need to be said. The thesis of displaceability may have arisen from various sources (apart from such observations as may lend it substance, or point to its truth). Very likely there was some influence from Plato to Freud (who retained a familiarity with the *Symposium*). Very likely too it attracted them both independently as unifying theorists. Yet here also we may suppose them to be sensitive to the mind's self-mutations. The thesis would seem to play an embattled role within the mind's picture of itself. On the one hand, it suits our self-image as subjects both under social pressure to inhibit our sexuality, and personally glad to discover or invent a unity within the confusing variety of our desires; on the other hand, we may also incline to deny (perhaps as a reaction against recognizing) any kinship between ego-syntonic and ego-dystonic desires that would tarnish a finical self-image. If the thesis has a strange power to attract and to repel (even before one has given it any intelligible content), that may be because it articulates a view of ourselves that already provokes our ambivalence. How far can we make the thesis into a truth through incorporating it into our idea of ourselves? It would appear that, as a consequence of implicitly assuming the thesis of displaceability, the mind may come to operate as if in accordance with it. The objects of desire are always, to some extent, imprecise and malleable; a presumption that desire is displaceable gives one hope of a policy, clearly politic if practicable, of uniting one's desires in pursuit of objects that offer something to them all. Thus ideals may take on a sexual colouring, sexual responses may take on a spirituality, in ways that lend them the support of other desires and attitudes. To the extent that all is interfused, it may become an unanswerable question whether sexuality and spirtuality have formed an alliance, or an actual merger. In this way, acceptance of the thesis promotes a process indistinguishable from that of sublimation as reinforcement. This tendency will be further encouraged if, in pursuit of a still deeper unity, the mind implicitly accepts not only that desires can take on new objects (the thesis of displaceability), but that all desires had a single origin (whether sublimation or debasement be the mode of transition); the full explicit doctrine of the derivation of desire from a single source then turns out—if we are sceptical of its truth—to be an aetiological myth that reflects and reinforces a present possibility, that of the integration of desires.

I have ascribed to the human mind an ancient tendency to construct itself as partitioned, and (though ambivalently) as if all its desires were akin. If Plato and Freud agree more often than is explicable by historical influence or cultural similarity, that appears to be because they were both perceptive of relatively invariant aspects of the mind's implicit picture of itself. As I have remarked, it need not tell against this that they were presenting news: to deep perennial reality need correspond no perennial belief. Of course they exploit their perceptions in different ways; it would be interesting, but not easy, to try to determine to what extent their differences arise from individual theoretical assumptions, or reflect aspects of the mind's self-image that are the product of a culture. Those more dismissive of their views than I will need to explain otherwise what they must see as a recurrence of error; if I can understand their convergences it is as evidence of abiding truth.

# Bibliography

This Bibliography contains the modern philosophical and scholarly works cited in the Introduction and chapters it also includes certain specified editions and translations of ancient authors. For ancient authors cited in the volume, see Index.


ANNAS, J., 'Naturalism in Greek Ethics: Aristotle and After', *Proceedings of the Boston Area Colloquium in Ancient Philosophy*, 4 (1988), 149–71.

—— and BARNES, J. *The Modes of Scepticism: Ancient Texts and Modern Interpretations* (Cambridge, 1985).

ARMSTRONG, A., *A Materialist Theory of the Mind* (London, 1968).

ARNIM, H. v. (ed.), *Stoicorum Veterum Fragmenta* (4 vols.; Leipzig, 1903–5; repr. Stuttgart, 1964).

BARNES, J., *Early Greek Philosophy* (Harmondsworth, 1987).

BARON, C., 'The Concept of Person in the Law', in Shaw and Doudera (edd.), *Defining Human Life*, pp. 121–48.

BOETHIUS, *Liber de persona et duabus naturis*, in Migne (ed.), *Patrologia Latina*, lxiv, 1338–54.

BUDRYS, A., 'The End of Summer', in B. Aldis (ed.), *Penguin Science Fiction* (Harmondsworth, 1961), 197–229.

BURKERT, W., *Lore and Science in Ancient Pythagoreanism*, tr. E. L. Minar, Jr. (Cambridge, Mass., 1972).

BURNYEAT, M. F., 'Aristotle on Learning to be Good', in Rorty (ed.), *Essays on Aristotle's Ethics*, pp. 69–92.

CAPEK, K., *War with the Newts* (Evanston, 1985).

CAPP, D., and MACINTOSH, J. J. (edd.), *New Essays in the Philosophy of Mind* (*Canadian Journal of Philosophy*, supp. vol. 11; 1985).

CARRITHERS, M., COLLINS, S., and LUKES, S. (edd.), *The Category of the Person: Anthropology, Philosophy, History* (Cambridge, 1985).

CASTANEDA, H.-N., ' "He": A Study in the Logic of Self-Consciousness', *Ratio*, 8 (1966), 130–57.

CHURCHLAND, P. M., *Scientific Realism and the Plasticity of Mind* (Cambridge, 1979).

CLARK, S. R. L., *Aristotle's Man* (Oxford, 1975).

—— *From Athens to Jerusalem* (Oxford, 1984).

—— 'Waking up: A Neglected Model for the Afterlife', *Inquiry*, 26 (1984), 209–30.

—— 'Abstraction, Possession, Incarnation', in A. Kee and E. T. Long (edd.), *Being and Truth: Essays in Honour of John Macquarrie* (London, 1986), pp. 293–317.

CLARK, S. R. L., *The Mysteries of Religion* (Oxford, 1986).
—— 'Is Humanity a Natural Kind?', in T. Ingold (ed.), *What is an Animal?* (London, 1988), 17–34.
COLLIN, F., *Theory and Understanding* (Oxford, 1985).
COLLINS, S., 'Buddhism in Recent British Philosophy and Theology', *Religious Studies*, 21 (1985), 475–93.
COOPER, J. M., *Reason and Human Good in Aristotle* (Cambridge, Mass., 1975).
CORMAN, J. W., and LEHRER, K., *Philosophical Problems and Arguments* (London, 1974).
CORNFORD, F. M., 'Psychology and Social Structure in the *Republic* of Plato', *Classical Quarterly*, 6 (1912), 246–65.
—— 'The Division of the Soul', *Hibbert Journal*, 28 (1930), 206–19.
—— 'The Doctrine of Eros in Plato's *Symposium*', in W. K. C. Guthrie (ed.), *The Unwritten Philosophy and Other Essays* (Cambridge, 1950), 68–80.
COXON, A. H., *The Fragments of Parmenides* (*Phronesis*, supp. vol. 3; 1986), 247–52.
CROOK, J. H., *The Evolution of the Human Consciousness* (Oxford, 1980).
DAVIDSON, D., *Essays on Actions and Events* (Oxford, 1980).
—— 'The Material Mind', in *Essays on Actions and Events*, pp. 245–59.
DENNETT, D. C., *Brainstorms: Philosophical Essays on Mind and Psychology* (Hassocks, Sussex, 1979).
—— 'Conditions of Personhood', in Rorty (ed.), *The Identities of Persons*, pp. 175–96; repr. in Dennett, *Brainstorms*, pp. 267–85.
—— 'Where am I?' in Dennett, *Brainstorms*, pp. 310–23.
DÉTIENNE, M., and VERNANT, J.-P., *Cunning Intelligence in Greek Culture and Society* (Brighton, 1978).
DIELS, H., *Die Fragmente der Vorsokratiker*, rev. H. Kranz (10th edn., 2 vols.; Berlin, 1941).
DILLON, J., *The Middle Platonists* (London, 1977).
DODDS, E. R., *The Greeks and the Irrational* (Berkeley, 1951).
—— *Pagan and Christian in an Age of Anxiety* (Cambridge, 1968).
DOVER, K. J., *Greek Homosexuality* (London, 1978).
DURKHEIM, E., *The Rules of Sociological Method*, tr. S. A. Solovay and J. H. Mueller (Chicago, 1938).
ELIADE, M., *Myths, Dreams and Mysteries*, tr. P. Mairet (London, 1968).
ENGBERG-PEDERSEN, T., *Aristotle' s Theory of Moral Insight* (Oxford, 1983).
—— 'Discovering the Good: *oikeiōsis* and *kathekonta* in Stoic Ethics', in Schofield and Striker (edd.), *The Norms of Nature*, pp. 145–83.
FARMER, P. J., 'Sketches among the Ruins of my Mind', in H. Harrison (ed.), *Nova 3* (London, 1973), 150–92.

FEYERABEND, P., *Philosophical Papers* (Cambridge, 1981).

FRANKFURT, H., 'Freedom of the Will and the Concept of a Person', *Journal of Philosophy*, 68 (1971), 5–20; repr. in G. Watson (ed.), *Free Will* (Oxford, 1982), 81–110.

FREUD, S., *The Standard Edition of the Complete Psychological Works*, ed. J. Strachey (24 vols.; London, 1953–74).

—— *Two Short Accounts of Psycho-Analysis*, ed. J. Strachey (Harmondsworth, 1962).

—— *The Pelican Freud Library*, ed. A. Richards (15 vols.; Harmondsworth, 1973–86).

FREY, R. G., 'Autonomy and the Value of Life', *Monist*, 70 (1987), 50–63.

GARDNER, H., *The Shattered Mind* (New York, 1975).

GILL, C. 'Personhood and Personality: The Four-*Personae* Theory in Cicero, *De Officiis* I', *Oxford Studies in Ancient Philosophy*, 6 (1988), 169–99.

GODDARD, D. (ed.), *A Buddhist Bible* (Boston, 1970).

GORDON, R. M., 'Folk Psychology as Simulation', *Mind and Language*, 1 (1986), 158–71.

GRAHAM, K., *The Battle of Democracy* (Brighton, 1986).

GRISWOLD, C., *Self-Knowledge in Plato's Phaedrus* (New Haven, 1986).

GUTHRIE, W. K. C., *A History of Greek Philosophy* (6 vols.; Cambridge, 1962–81).

HARE, R. M., *Plato* (Oxford, 1982).

HAVELOCK, E., 'The Linguistic Task of the Presocratics', in Robb (ed.), *Language and Thought in Early Greek Philosophy*, pp. 7–41.

HEAD, J., and CRANSTON, S. L. (edd.), *Reincarnation: The Phoenix Fire Mystery* (New York, 1977).

HEAL, J., 'Replication and Functionalism', in J. Butterfield (ed.), *Language, Mind and Logic* (Cambridge, 1986), 135–50.

HOPKINS, J., 'Wittgenstein and Physicalism', *Proceedings of the Aristotelian Society*, 75 (1974–5), 121–46.

HUME, D., *Treatise of Human Nature*, ed. L. A. Selby-Bigge (Oxford, 1888).

—— *Natural History of Religion and Dialogues concerning Natural Religion*, ed. A. W. Colyer and J. V. Price (Oxford, 1976).

HUSSEY, E., 'Epistemology and Meaning in Heraclitus', in M. Schofield and M. C. Nussbaum (edd.), *Language and Logos* (Cambridge, 1982), 33–59.

INWOOD, B., *Ethics and Human Action in Early Stoicism* (Oxford, 1985).

IRWIN, T. H., *Plato's Moral Theory* (Oxford, 1977).

—— 'The Metaphysical and Psychological Basis of Aristotle's Ethics', in Rorty (ed.), *Essays on Aristotle's Ethics*, pp. 35–53.

—— 'Reason and Responsibility in Aristotle', in Rorty (ed.), *Essays on Aristotle's Ethics*, pp. 117–55.

IRWIN, T. H., 'Stoic and Aristotelian Conceptions of Happiness', in Schofield and Striker (edd.), *The Norms of Nature*, pp. 205–44.

JAYNES, J., *The Origin of Consciousness in the Breakdown of the Bicameral Mind* (New York, 1976).

JONES, E., *Sigmund Freud: Life and Work* (3 vols.; London, 1953–7).

JUNG, C. G., *Memories, Dreams, Reflections*, ed. A. Jaffe, tr. R. and C. Winston (London, 1967).

KAHN, C., 'Democritus and the Origins of Moral Psychology', *American Journal of Philology*, 106 (1986), 1–31.

KANT, I., *Groundwork of the Metaphysics of Morals* (Berlin, 1785), tr. H. J. Paton (London, 1964).

KENNY, A., 'Mental Health in Plato's *Republic*', in *The Anatomy of the Soul* (Oxford, 1973), 1–27.

KIDD, I. G., 'Stoic Intermediates and the End for Man', in Long (ed.), *Problems in Stoicism*, pp. 150–72.

KING-FARLOW, J., *Self-Knowledge and Social Relations* (New York, 1978).

KIRK, G. S., RAVEN, J. E., and SCHOFIELD, M., *The Presocratic Philosophers* (Cambridge, 1983).

KLEIN, D. B., *Abnormal Psychology* (New York, 1951).

KOHUT, H., *The Restoration of the Self* (New York, 1977).

KOSMAN, L. A., 'Platonic Love', in W. H. Werkmeister (ed.), *Facets of Plato's Philosophy* (Assen, 1976), 53–69.

LAPLANCHE, J., and PONTALIS, J.-B., *The Language of Psycho-Analysis*, tr. D. Nicholson-Smith (London, 1973).

LEAR, J., *Aristotle: The Desire to Understand* (Cambridge, 1988).

LEWIS, D., 'Attitudes *De Dicto* and *De Re*', *Philosophical Review*, 87 (1980), 513–43.

LINDLEY, R., *Autonomy* (London, 1986).

LLOYD, G. E. R., *Science, Folklore and Ideology: Studies in the Life Sciences in Ancient Greece* (Cambridge, 1983).

LOCKE, J., *An Essay Concerning Human Understanding*, ed. P. H. Nidditch (Oxford, 1975).

LONG, A. A., 'The Logical Basis of Stoic Ethics', *Proceedings of the Aristotelian Society*, 71 (1970–1), 85–104.

—— 'Greek Ethics after MacIntyre and the Stoic Community of Reason', *Ancient Philosophy*, 3 (1983), 184–99.

—— (ed.), *Problems in Stoicism* (London, 1971).

—— and SEDLEY, D. N., *The Hellenistic Philosophers* (2 vols.; Cambridge, 1987).

LURIA, A., *The Man with a Shattered World* (London, 1973).

MACDONALD, G., and PETTIT, P., *Semantics and Social Science* (London, 1981).

MCDOWELL, J., 'The Role of *Eudaimonia* in Aristotle's *Ethics*', in Rorty (ed.), *Essays on Aristotle's Ethics*, pp. 359–76.

—— Review of B. Williams, *Ethics and the Limits of Philosophy*, *Mind*, 95 (1986), 377–86.

McGinn, C., *The Character of Mind* (Oxford, 1982).

MacIntyre, A., *After Virtue: A Study in Moral Theory* (London, 2nd edn., 1985).

Mackie, J., *Problems from Locke* (Oxford, 1976).

Madell, G., *The Identity of the Self* (Edinburgh, 1981).

Mauss, M., 'A Category of the Human Mind: The Notion of Person; the Notion of Self', tr. W. D. Halls, in Carrithers, Collins, and Lukes (edd.), *The Category of the Person*, pp. 1–25.

May, R., 'Psychotherapy and the Demonic', in J. Campbell (ed.), *Myths, Dreams and Religion* (New York, 1970), 196–210.

Merlan, P., *Monopsychism, Mysticism, Metaconsciousness* (The Hague, 1963).

Midgley, M., *Beast and Man: The Roots of Human Nature* (Brighton, 1979).

—— *Wickedness: A Philosophical Essay* (London, 1984).

Migne, J.-P. (ed.), *Patrologia Latina* (221 vols.; Paris, 1844–64).

Mill, J. S., 'Grote's Plato', in *Essays on Philosophy and the Classics*, ed. J. M. Robson, *Collected Works*, xi (Toronto, 1978), 377–440.

Millikan, R. G., *Language, Thought and Other Biological Categories* (Cambridge, Mass., 1984).

Moore, B., *The Unicorn* (London, 1954).

Morton, A., *Frames of Mind* (Oxford, 1980).

Nagel, T., *The Possibility of Altruism* (Oxford, 1970).

—— 'What is it Like to be a Bat?', in *Mortal Questions* (Cambridge, 1979), 165–80.

—— 'Aristotle on *Eudaimonia*', in Rorty (ed.), *Essays on Aristotle's Ethics*, pp. 7–14.

—— *The View from Nowhere* (New York, 1986).

Nédoncelle, M., '*Prosōpon* et *Persona* dans l'antiquité classique', *Revue des Sciences Réligieuses*, 22 (1948), 277–99.

Needham, R., *Belief, Language, and Experience* (Oxford, 1972).

Niebuhr, R., *The Self and the Dreams of History* (London, 1956).

Nilsson, M., 'Letter to Nock on Some Fundamental Concepts in the Science of Religion', *Harvard Theological Review*, 42 (1949), 71–107.

Nitzsche, J. C., *The Genius Figure in Antiquity and the Middle Ages* (New York, 1975).

Nussbaum, M. C., *The Fragility Of Goodness: Luck and Ethics in Greek Tragedy and Philosophy* (Cambridge, 1986).

—— ' "This story isn't true": Madness, Reason and Recantation in the *Phaedrus*', in J. Moravcsik and P. Temko (edd.), *Plato on Beauty, Wisdom, and the Arts* (Totowa, NJ, 1982), 79–124, repr. in *The Fragility of Goodness*, pp. 200–33.

NUSSBAUM, M. C., 'Aristotle on Human Nature and the Foundations of Ethics', forthcoming in R. Harrison and J. Altham (edd.), a volume of essays on the work of Bernard Williams (Cambridge, 1989).

OGILVY, J. O., *Many Dimensional Man* (New York, 1977).

ORWELL, G., *The Collected Essays, Journalism and Letters of George Orwell*, edd. S. Orwell and I. Angus (4 vols.; London, 1968).

OSTENFELD, E., *Ancient Greek Psychology and the Modern Mind–Body Debate* (Aarhus, 1987).

PARFIT, D., *Reasons and Persons* (Oxford, 1984).

PATER, W., *Plato and Platonism* (London, 1893).

PEMBROKE, S. G., 'Oikeiōsis', in Long (ed.), *Problems in Stoicism*, 114–49.

PENFIELD, W., *The Mystery of the Mind* (Cambridge, Mass., 1975).

PERRY, J., 'Frege on Demonstratives', *Philosophical Review*, 86 (1977), 474–97.

—— 'The Problem of the Essential Indexical', *Noûs*, 13 (1979), 3–21.

PETTIT, P., 'Rational Man Theory' in C. Hookway and P. Pettit (edd.), *Action and Interpretation: Studies in the Philosophy of the Social Sciences* (Cambridge, 1978), 43–63.

PIEPER, J., *Love and Inspiration*, tr. R. and C. Winston (London, 1965).

—— *Death and Immortality*, tr. R. and C. Winston (London, 1969).

PLATO, *Republic*, tr. G. M. A. Grube (London, 1981).

—— *Republic*, tr. P. Shorey (London, 1935).

POPPER, K. R., *Objective Knowledge: An Evolutionary Approach* (Oxford, 1972).

—— and ECCLES, J., *The Self and its Brain* (Heidelberg, 1977).

POTTS, T. C., *Conscience in Mediaeval Philosophy* (Cambridge, 1980).

PRICE, A. W., 'Loving Persons Platonically', *Phronesis*, 26 (1981), 25–34.

—— Review of G. Santas, *Plato and Freud, The Times Literary Supplement*, 4–10 Nov. 1988, p. 1220.

QUINE, W. V., 'What Is It All About?', *The American Scholar*, 50 (1981), 43–54.

QUINTON, A., 'Mind and Matter', in J. R. Smythies (ed.), *Brain and Mind* (London, 1965), 205–34.

RAHNER, K., *et al.* (edd.), *Sacramentum Mundi: An Encyclopedia of Theology* (6 vols.; London, 1968–70).

RAINE, K., *Collected Poems* (London, 1956).

REICHENBACH, H., *Elements of Symbolic Logic* (New York, 1948).

ROBB, K. (ed.), *Language and Thought in Early Greek Philosophy* (*Monist* Library of Philosophy; La Salle, Ill., 1983).

—— '*Psyche* and *Logos* in the Fragments of Heraclitus', in Capp and MacIntosh (edd.), *New Essays in the Philosophy of Mind*, 315–51.

ROBINSON, T., 'Heraclitus on Soul', in Capp and MacIntosh (edd.), *New Essays in the Philosophy of Mind*, 305–14.

RORTY, A. O., 'Literary Postscript: Characters, Selves, Individuals', in Rorty (ed.), *The Identities of Persons*, pp. 301–23.
—— 'The Place of Contemplation in Aristotle's *Nicomachean Ethics*', in Rorty (ed.), *Essays on Aristotle's Ethics*, 377–94.
—— 'Persons as Rhetorical Categories', *Social Research*, 54 (1987), 55–72.
—— 'Persons and *Personae*', in Rorty, *Mind in Action* (Boston, 1988), 27–46.
—— (ed.), *The Identities of Persons* (Berkeley, 1976).
—— (ed.), *Essays on Aristotle's Ethics* (Berkeley, 1980).
ROWE, C. J., 'One and Many in Greek Religion', *Eranos Jahrbuch*, 45 (1976), 37–67.
—— *Plato: Phaedrus* (Warminster, 1986).
—— 'The Argument and Structure of Plato's *Phaedrus*', *Proceedings of the Cambridge Philological Society*, 212, NS 32 (1986), 106–25.
—— Review of C. Griswold, *Self-Knowledge in Plato's Phaedrus, Washington Book Review* (May 1987), 21–2 and 32.
RYLE, G., 'The Thinking of Thoughts', in *Collected Papers*, vol ii (London, 1971), 480–96.
SACKS, O., *The Man who Mistook his Wife for a Hat* (London, 1985).
SANTHAS, G., *Plato and Freud: Two Theories of Love*, (Oxford, 1988).
SATPREM, *Sri Aurobindo: The Adventure of Consciousness*, tr. Tehmi (Pondicherry, 1968).
SCHOFIELD, M., *An Essay on Anaxagoras* (Cambridge, 1980).
——, and STRIKER, G. (edd.), *The Norms of Nature: Studies in Hellenistic Ethics* (Cambridge, 1986).
SCHRODINGER, E., *My View of the World* (Cambridge, 1964).
SHAW, M. W., and DOUDERA, A. E. (edd.), *Defining Human Life: Medical, Legal, and Ethical Implications* (Ann Arbor, Mich., 1983).
SHELLEY, M., *Frankenstein; or The Modern Prometheus* (London, 1818).
SHOEMAKER, S., *Self Knowledge and Self Identity* (New York, 1963).
——, 'Personal Identity; A Materialist's Account', in Shoemaker and Swinburne, *Personal Identity*, pp. 67–132.
——, and SWINBURNE, R., *Personal Identity* (Oxford, 1984).
SINGER, P., *Animal Liberation* (New York, 1977).
SMART, J. J. C., 'Sensations and Brain Processes', *Philosophical Review*, 68 (1959), 141–56.
SMITH, P., and JONES, O. R., *The Philosophy of Mind* (Cambridge, 1986).
SNELL, B., *The Discovery of the Mind*, tr. T. G. Rosenmeyer (New York, 1960).
SORABJI, R., 'Aristotle on the Role of Intellect in Virtue', in Rorty (ed.), *Essays on Aristotle's Ethics*, pp. 201–19.
SPRIGGE, T. L. S., *The Vindication of Absolute Idealism* (Edinburgh, 1983).

STEAD, C., *Divine Substance* (Oxford, 1977).
STOUGH, C., 'Stoic Determinism and Moral Responsibility', in J. M. Rist, (ed.), *The Stoics* (Los Angeles, 1978), 203–31.
STRAWSON, P. F., *Individuals* (London, 1959).
—— 'Self, Mind and Body', in *Freedom and Resentment* (London, 1974), 169–77.
STRIKER, G., 'The Role of *Oikeiōsis* in Stoic Ethics', *Oxford Studies in Ancient Philosophy*, 1 (1983), 145–67.
—— 'Antipater, or the Art of Living', in Schofield and Striker (edd.), *The Norms of Nature*, pp. 185–204.
SULLIVAN, S. D., '*To sophon* as an Aspect of the Divine in Heraclitus', in D. E. Gerber (ed.), *Greek Poetry and Philosophy* (Berkeley, 1985), 285–302.
—— 'The Nature of *phren* in Empedocles', in M. Capasso, F. de Mantino, and P. Rosati (edd.), *Studi di filosofia preplatonica* (Naples, 1985), 119–36.
THOMAS, L., *The Youngest Science* (Oxford, 1985).
THOREAU, H. D., *Walden* (London, 1910).
TOOLEY, M., *Abortion and Infanticide* (Oxford, 1983).
TUR, R., 'The "Person" in Law', in A. Peacocke and G. Gillett (edd.), *Persons and Personality: A Contemporary Inquiry* (Oxford, 1987), 116–29.
VENDLER, Z., *The Matter of Minds* (Oxford, 1985).
VERDENIUS, V. J., *Parmenides* (Groningen, 1942).
VERNANT, J.-P., *Myth and Thought among the Greeks* (London, 1983).
—— and VIDAL-NAQUET, P., *Tragedy and Myth in Ancient Greece*, tr. J. L. Lloyd (Brighton, 1981).
VLASTOS, G., 'Ethics and Physics in Democritus', in R. E. Allen and D. J. Furley (edd.), *Studies in Presocratic Philosophy*, ii (London, 1975), 381–408.
—— 'The Individual as an Object of Love in Plato', app. 2: 'Sex in Platonic Love', in *Platonic Studies* (2nd edn., Princeton, 1981), 38–42.
VOGEL, C. J. DE, 'The Concept of Personality in Greek and Christian Thought', *Studies in Philosophy and the History of Philosophy*, 2 (1963), 20–60.
—— 'The Sōma–Sēma Formula', in H. J. Blumenthal and R. A. Markus (edd.), *Neoplatonism and Early Christian Thought: Essays in Honour of A. H. Armstrong* (London, 1981), 79–95.
WALLIS, R. T., 'The Idea of Conscience in Philo', in D. Winston and J. Dillon (edd.), *Two Treatises of Philo* (Chico, Calif., 1983), 207–16.
WARREN, E. W., 'Consciousness in Plotinus', *Phronesis*, 9 (1964), 83–97.
WELLS, H. G., *The Island of Doctor Moreau* (London, 1896).
WEST, M. L., *Early Greek Philosophy and the Orient* (Oxford, 1971).

WHITE, N. P., 'The Basis of Stoic Ethics', *Harvard Studies in Classical Philology*, 83 (1979), 143–78.
WIGGINS, D. *Identity and Spatio-Temporal Continuity* (Oxford, 1967).
—— 'Locke, Butler and the Stream of Consciousness: And Men as a Natural Kind', in Rorty (ed.), *The Identities of Persons*, pp. 139–73.
—— 'Truth, Invention, and the Meaning of Life', *Proceedings of the British Academy*, 62 (1976), 331–78.
—— *Sameness and Substance* (Oxford, 1980).
—— 'The Person as Object of Science, as Subject of Experience, and as Locus of Value', in A. Peacocke and G. Gillett (edd.), *Persons and Personality: A Contemporary Inquiry* (Oxford, 1987), 56–74.
WIKLER, D., 'Concepts of Personhood: A Philosophical Perspective', in Shaw and Doudera (edd.), *Defining Human Life*, pp. 12–23.
WILKES, K. V., 'More Brain Lesions', *Philosophy*, 55 (1980), 455–70.
—— 'The Good Man and the Good for Man in Aristotle's *Ethics*', in Rorty (ed.), *Essays on Aristotle's Ethics*, pp. 341–57.
—— 'Is Consciousness Important?', *British Journal for the Philosophy of Science*, 35 (1984), 223–43.
WILLARD, D., 'Concerning the "Knowledge" of the Pre-Platonic Greeks', in Robb (ed.), *Language and Thought*, pp. 244–54.
Williams, B. *Problems of the Self* (Cambridge, 1973).
—— 'Personal Identity and Individuation', in *Problems of the Self*, pp. 1–18.
—— 'The Self and the Future', in *Problems of the Self*, pp. 46–63.
—— *Moral Luck: Philosophical Essays 1973–1980* (Cambridge, 1981).
—— 'Persons, Character and Morality', in *Moral Luck*, pp. 1–19.
—— 'Conflicts of Values', in *Moral Luck*, pp. 71–82.
—— 'Internal and External Reasons', in *Moral Luck*, pp. 101–13.
—— 'The Truth in Relativism', in *Moral Luck*, pp. 132–43.
—— *Ethics and the Limits of Philosophy* (London, 1985).
WITTGENSTEIN, L., *Philosophical Investigations*, tr. E. Anscombe (Oxford, 1963).
WOLLHEIM, R., *The Thread of Life* (Cambridge, 1984).
WRIGHT, M. R., *Empedocles: The Extant Fragments* (New Haven, 1981).
—— *The Presocratics* (Bristol, 1985).
XENOCRATES, *Darstellung der Lehre und Sammlung der Fragmente*, ed. R. Heinze (Leipzig, 1892).
YEATS, W. B., *Autobiographies* (London, 1955).

# Index


Alcmaeon 209
Anaxagoras 210, 211, 213, 217, 223
Anaximander 209
Anaximenes 209, 214–15
animal attribute theory 100–4
Annas, J. 137 n. (and Barnes, J.) 8 n.
*anthrōpos* (man) 7, 110, 137, 158
Apuleius 195
Aquinas, T. 205
argument from analogy 175–6
argument from interpretation 166 n.
Aristotle
  *Nicomachean Ethics* 1.7 (human nature and function) 8 n., 137 n., 138–43, 151, 160–1; 10.7–8 (human and divine happiness) 1–2, 9–10, 160–1, 193, 225
  other refs. 6 n., 8 n., 110–11, 114, 147, 193 n., 196, 200, 202–3, 208–9, 218, 261
  *see also* human nature
Arnim, H. von 130 n.
Aurelius, M. 189

Barnes, J. 207 n.
Baron, C. 24 n.
Boethius, 1, 110–11
Bruner, J. 30 n.
Budrys, A. 51 n.
Burkert, W. 200 n.
Burnyeat, M. F. 141 n.

Capek, K. 28 n.
Castaneda, H. N. 47 n.
Churchland, P. 184
Cicero
  *De Finibus* 3.5.16–7.26 (Stoic theory of human moral development, or *oikeiōsis*) 8 n., 119–23, 137 n., 143–8; 3.5.19–20.68 (Stoic theory of human natural benevolence) 8 n., 126–7, 137 n., 148–51
  *see also* Stoic philosophy, human nature
Clark, S. R. .L. 8 n., 160 n., 161 n., 188 n., 190 n., 192 n., 195 n., 203 n.
Collin, F. 166 n.
Collins, S. 189
conventionalism, 187–8
Cooper, J. M. 160 n.
Corman, J. W. and Lehrer, K. 207
Cornford, F. M. 252, 258
Crook, J. H. 189
*daimōn* ('divine being')
  and demonic forces in the psyche 192–3
  and *ēthos* ('character') 198, 221
reason as *daimōn* 190, 192–3, 198–9, 203–6
  *see also nous*, personal identity
Davidson, D. 168, 176–7, 185
Democritus 207, 210, 213, 216–7, 223
Dennett, D. C. 41 n., 49 n.
Détienne, M. and Vernant, J.-P. 192 n.
Diels, H. 207 n.
Diogenes Laertius 111, 144, 150 n., 151 n.
Dodds, E. R. 191 n., 194, 195 n., 205 n.
Dover, K. J. 252 n.
Durkheim, E. 166–7

Eliade, M. 205 n.
Empedocles 205, 207, 210, 212, 213, 214, 216, 221–2
  Freud's enthusiasm for 249
Engberg-Pedersen, T. 110 n., 113 n., 119 n., 130 n., 145 n., 146, 147 n., 148 n., 150 n., 160 n.
ethical naturalism, *see* human nature, person and human being
*ēthos* (character) 222
  see also *daimōn*

Farmer, P. J. 51 n.
Feyerabend, P. 188
Fichte, J. G. 205–6
folk psychology
  and the explanation of behaviour 167–85
  and human nature 165–7, 177–84
  and mutual interpretation 182–3
  and personhood 78–81
  and simulation strategy 80–1, 182 n.
  universality of 184
Frankfurt, H. 1, 4, 5, 12, 41–3, 49, 64

Freud, S.
direct knowledge of Plato 247–9
and personal identity 265
and Plato 247–70
shares Plato's understanding of depth-psychology 249–50, 267–70
theory of sexual desire as displaceable (*cf.* Plato) 250–8
theory of sublimation (*cf.* Plato) 251–2, 253–4, 256, 257–8
theory of tripartite psyche (*cf.* Plato) 258–67
theory of unconscious desires 262, 264–5
*see also* Plato
freedom of the will 129–33
Frey, R. G. 191 n.

Gardner, H. 50 n.
Gautama 191
Gill, C. 7 n., 154 n.
Gordon, R. 182 n.
Graham, K. 43 n.
Griswold, C. 228 n.
Guthrie, W. K. C. 138 n., 207 n., 253

Hare, R. M. 258
Heal, J. 80 n.
Heraclitus 14–15, 197–8, 209, 212, 213, 214, 215, 220–1, 224
holism of the mental 176–7, 185
Homeric psychology 193–5
*homo* (man) 7
'homunculi' in the psychology of Plato and Freud 260
human being as a biological concept 27–8, 36, 63–4, 165
human nature
defined in relation to bestial and/or divine nature 7–8, 148–51, 159–61, 190–3, 198–9, 203–6, 225, 227–9, 233–6, 240–1, 252–3
and folk psychology 165–7, 177–84
'inside' and 'outside' views of 139–43, 146–8, 150–1, 152–5, 160–1
and moral development 119–23, 144–8, 157–8
a normative concept in ancient philosophy 7–10, 110–11, 133–5, 137–61
a subject of interpretation 183–4
*see also* Aristotle, person and human being, Plato, Stoic philosophy
human person 65
a fortuitous not a natural kind 73–81
Hume, D. 111, 187 n., 191 n.
'Hype' (a super-intelligent rabbit)44–9

individuality
in Plato 228–9, 239–41, 245–6
and subjectivity in Stoic and modern philosophy 111–29, 131–5
*see also* human nature, 'inside' and 'outside' views of, personal identity, person defined by the first-personal perspective, Stoic philosophy
Inwood, B. 130 n.
Irwin, T. H. 10 n., 141 n., 147 n., 259

Jaynes, J. 194
Jerome 197
Jones, E. 247–8, 255 n.
Jung, C. G. 204–5

Kant, I. 43 n. 111, 113–16, 127–8
Kenny, A. 261 n., 265 n.
Kidd, I. G. 154 n.
King-Farlow, J. 187 n.
Klein, D. B. 201
Kohut, H. 29 n.
Kosman, L. A. 245 n., 255

Laplanche, J. and Pontalis, J.-B. 251 n., 260
Lear, J. 10 n., 141 n., 160 n.
Lewis, D. 47 n., 94 n.
Lindley, R. 43 n.
Lloyd, G. E. R. 8 n.
Locke, J. 1, 64, 85, 88, 89–91, 93–4, 101, 103, 105–6
Long, A. A. 146, 148, 154 n. (and Sedley, D. N.) 145 n., 149 n., 151 n.
Lucretius 210
Luria, A. 50 n.

Macdonald, G. and Pettit, P. 166 n.
McDowell, J. 10 n., 139–40, 142–3, 153 n.
MacIntyre, A. 139, 141, 142 n., 147 n., 153–5
Mackie, J. L. 93
Madell, G. 202 n.

Mauss, M. 1
May, R. 192
Melissus 212–13
Merlan, P. 201 n.
Midgley, M. 155 n., 165, 195
Mill, J. S. 247–8, 258
Millikan, R. G. 97 n.
Minsky, M. 207
Moore, V. 198
Morton, A., 79, 80 n.

Nagel, T. 10 n., 33 n., 93, 111–13, 117–18, 123–5, 130, 132–4
Nedoncelle, M. 7 n.
Needham, R. 184 n.
Niebuhr, R. 191 n., 205 n.
Nilsson, M. 195
Nitzsche, J. C. 195 n.
non-sceptical problem of other minds 173–7
*nous* ('mind' or 'reason')
  transcendental, comes into us from outside, 190–3, 198, 202–4
  understood in physical terms by Anaxagoras 217–18, 223
  see also *daimōn*, Presocratics
Nussbaum, M. C. 137 n., 160 n., 199 n., 229–41, 256 n.

Ogilvy, J. O. 196 n.
Origen 130–1
Orwell, G. 179 n.
Ostenfeld, E. 10
*oikeiōsis*, *see* Cicero, Stoic philosophy

Parfit, D. 14 n., 50 n., 94 n., 189
Parmenides 1, 207, 210, 212, 213, 214, 215–16, 219–20, 224
Pater, W. 256
Pembroke, S. G. 144 n., 148 n., 150 n., 151 n.
Penfield, W. 203 n.
Perry, J. 47 n., 94 n.
person
  an ancient concept? 7–10, 16–17, 109–11, 134–5, 155–8
  in Classical and Christian thought 7 n., 109–10
  defined as an autonomous agent 25–8
  defined as a possessor of second-order beliefs and desires 41–3, 110–11, 133–4; *see also* Frankfurt
  defined as a shaper of a life 30–2
  defined by a shared human life 65, 70–3, 77–8
  defined by the first-personal perspective 33–4, 44–9, 53–7, 63–7, 84–5, 89–92, 105, 119–21, 127–9, 132–3, 265
  defined in biological terms 32–3
  defined in interpersonal terms 28–30, 70–3
  defined in legal terms 23–5
  defined in moral terms 22–3
  defined in relational terms 61–3, 70–3
  and folk psychology 78–81
  and human being 5–10, 32–3, 39–41, 44–9, 54–8, 63–5, 73–81, 83–6, 101–2, 109–12, 133–5, 155–8, 169–72, 188–9, 190–1, 239
  'liberal-functionalist' view of 169–72
  a metaphysical concept 188–9
  not a determinate, fully analysable concept 106–7
  not a single concept 21–2, 35–8, 39–41, 58–9
  *see also* individuality, human nature, personal identity
*persona* 7, 109–10
personal identity
  and being a (human) animal 83–107
  and 'brain-transplants' 88–9, 93, 97–100
  Freud's view of 265
  not identical with psycho-physical identity 190–1
  and persistence conditions 86–100
  Plato's view of 240–1, 265
  and the impersonality of our true self 197–206
  and the pluralism of the self 192–5
  *see also* person, human nature
Pettit, P. 183
Philo 191 n., 198
Pieper, J. 191 n., 199, 200 n., 203 n.
Plato
  man-beast relations 8 n., 252–3
  mental health 265–7
  the nature of the human psyche (unitary or complex, human, bestial, or divine) 1, 10 n., 159–60, 198, 227–9
  recollection (*anamnēsis*) 249, 255

Plato–*cont.*
sexual desire and its sublimation 241–6, 250–8
tripartite psyche (reason, spirit, and desire) in *Phaedrus*, *Republic*, *Timaeus* 230–41, 245–6, 258–67
understanding of personal identity 240–1, 265
other refs. 192, 218, 224
*see also* Freud, human nature
Plotinus 201, 203–6
Plutarch 190, 198 n.
Popper, K. 175, 196
Potts, T. C. 197
Presocratics 207–25
and materialism 207–8, 214, 218–19
and perception 210–12
and thought 212–14
and the thinking subject 214–18
and the act of thinking 218–25
Price, A. W. 160 n., 229 n., 240 n., 245 n., 258 n.
*prosōpon* 7
psyche
in the Presocratics 208, 214–15, 220–1
as *daimon* 199
*see also* Plato
psychological animalism 103–4

Rahner, K. 7 n.
Raine, K. 199
Reichenbach, H. 48 n.
Rorty, A. O. 38 n., 63, 73 n., 160 n.
Rowe, C. 160 n., 231 n., 246 n.

Sacks, O. 50 n.
Sankara 190
Santas, G. 247 n.
Satprem, 200–1
Schofield, M. 223 n.
Schrodinger, E. 202
Sextus, 187 n.
Shoemaker, S. 84 n., 85, 88, 92–3 (and Swinburne R.) 50 n.
Singer, P. 28 n.
Smith, P. 156 n. (and Jones, O. R.) 207
Snell, B. 193–4
Snowdon, P. F. 74 n., 156 n.
Sorabji, R. 147 n.
Stead, C. 7 n.
stoic philosophy
and freedom of the will 129–33
and human moral development (*oikeiōsis*) 119–23, 143–8
and human natural benevolence 126–7, 148–51
and individuality and subjectivity 111–12, 118–29, 131–5
and moral value 123–4, 125–6, 143–5
and rationality 111–12, 133–5, 144–5
*see also* Cicero, person, human nature
Stough, C. 130 n.
Strawson, P. F. 64, 74
Striker, G. 144 n., 145 n., 146, 147 n.
subjectivity
*see* individuality, person defined by the first-personal perspective

Theophrastus 210, 211, 216, 217, 218, 219–20
Thomas, L. 57
Thoreau, H. D. 188 n., 197
Tooley, M. 6–7, 43 n.
Tur, R. 24 n.

Vendler, Z. 202 n.
Verdenius, V. J. 197 n., 199
Vernant, J.-P. 199 n. (and Vidal-Naquet, P.) 197 n.
Vlastos, G. 242–3
Vogel, C. J. de 7 n., 198 n.

Warren, E. W. 202 n.
we: a relation-based or property-based concept? 65–70
*see also* person defined by the first-personal perspective, person defined in relational terms
White, N. P. 144 n., 145 n., 151 n.
Wiggins, D. 1, 5–6, 13 n., 74–6, 84, 86 n., 93 n., 97 n., 100–6, 139, 141 n., 155–8, 170 n.
Wikler, D. 7 n., 155 n.
Wilkes, K. V. 10 n., 141 n.
Williams, B. 7 n., 11, 84 n., 91–2, 98–9, 111–18, 123–5, 127–9, 133–4, 139–41, 152–3, 161
Wittgenstein, L. 170 n.
Wollheim, R. 43 n., 53 n., 259
Wright, M. R. 149 n., 207 n.

Xenocrates 193 n.
Xenophanes 212

Yeats, W. B. 198